Human Biology of Afro-Caribbean Populations

Lorena Madrigal provides a microevolutionary study of Caribbean populations of African descent, reviewing the conditions endured by the slaves during their passage and in the plantations and how these may have affected their own health and that of their descendents. The book provides an evolutionary framework for understanding the epidemiology of common modern-day diseases such as obesity, hypertension, and diabetes, and in addition looks at infectious diseases and their effect on the genetic make-up of Afro-Caribbean populations. It also reviews population genetics studies that have been used to understand the microevolutionary pathways for various populations and investigates their demographic characteristics, including the relationships between migration, family type, and fertility. Ending with a case study of the Afro-Caribbean population of Limón, Costa Rica, this will be a fascinating resource for researchers working in biological anthropology, demography, and epidemiology, and for those interested in the African diaspora in the New World.

LORENA MADRIGAL is Professor in the Department of Anthropology at the University of South Florida and has worked on historical demography, population genetics, disease and modernization, and the genetics of longevity. She has also published *Statistics for Anthropology* (Cambridge, 1998).

## Cambridge Studies in Biological and Evolutionary Anthropology

*Series editors*

HUMAN ECOLOGY
C. G. Nicholas Mascie-Taylor, University of Cambridge
Michael A. Little, State University of New York, Binghamton
GENETICS
Kenneth M. Weiss, Pennsylvania State University
HUMAN EVOLUTION
Robert A. Foley, University of Cambridge
Nina G. Jablonski, California Academy of Science
PRIMATOLOGY
Karen B. Strier, University of Wisconsin, Madison

*Also available in the series*

# Human Biology of Afro-Caribbean Populations

LORENA MADRIGAL
*University of South Florida*

CAMBRIDGE
UNIVERSITY PRESS

CAMBRIDGE UNIVERSITY PRESS
Cambridge, New York, Melbourne, Madrid, Cape Town, Singapore,
São Paulo

CAMBRIDGE UNIVERSITY PRESS
The Edinburgh Building, Cambridge CB2 2RU, UK

Published in the United States of America by Cambridge University Press,
New York

www.cambridge.org
Information on this title: www.cambridge.org/9780521819312

© Cambridge University Press 2006

First published 2006

Printed in the United Kingdom at the University Press, Cambridge

*A catalog record for this publication is available from the British Library*

ISBN-13 978-0-521-81931-2 hardback
ISBN-10 0-521-81931-8 hardback

*Para mis tres amores: Guido, Sofía y Nadia.*

*To the people of Limón: may they achieve what they deserve, without losing their beautiful culture.*

# Contents

# Foreword

MICHAEL H. CRAWFORD, *University of Kansas*

In the mid nineteenth century an American adventurer, diplomat, archae-
ologist, and newspaper editor (E.G. Squier, who wrote under the pseudo-
nym of S.A. Bard), while exploring the Miskito coast of Honduras,
described the Black Caribs living in the region as: "Most are pure Indians,
not large, but muscular, with a ruddy skin, and long straight hair" (Bard,
1855, p.317). Similarly, British administrator, Thomas Young (1847,
p.123), observed extensive variability among the Black Caribs: "some
being coal black, others nearly as yellow as Saffron."

In the 1970s, having read these graphic descriptions about the Black
Caribs (also known as the Garifuna), I expected to see a Native American
group similar to one I had observed earlier in Mexico. The Black Caribs
originated on St. Vincent Island during the seventeenth century and, after
a rebellion, were deported by the British to Roatan of the Bay Islands in
1798. In the following year, the Spanish transported the majority of the
newly relocated Black Caribs from the Bay Islands to the coast of Central
America. Almost 135 years later, when I arrived in Livingston, Guatemala (a sleepy Black Carib coastal village, nestled against the edge of a
tropical forest), I was shocked to see a scene that could only have been
"staged" in West Africa. The Garifuna were extremely dark with few
morphological characteristics suggestive of Native American origins.
They were trading in a market that could have been located anywhere
along the Gold Coast of Africa. This did not make much sense! What
happened to the Carib Indians who had been deported 177 years earlier
from St. Vincent? If the dissidents of St. Vincent Island had been deported
selectively to Roatan on the basis of their African features, then Young
and Squier should have observed, in the 1850s a predominantly African
population in Central America. This was not the case. The most probable
answer to this puzzle lies in the history of the Garifuna.

### The Rise of the Garifuna

The Caribbean Islands were settled originally by Arawak Indians who had expanded demically from South America in approximately AD 100. This initial settlement was followed approximately 1000 years later by the diffusion of Carib Indians from South America into the Lesser Antilles. Following Contact with Europeans, the native populations of the Caribbean islands experienced a dramatic numerical decline. At Contact, the total aboriginal population of the Caribbean islands was estimated by Cook and Borah (1971) to be approximately 6 million persons. Within 100 years of Contact, as a result of epidemics, warfare, and slavery, many of the islands were totally devoid of Amerindians. A few Amerindian enclaves persisted into the seventeenth and eighteenth centuries on Dominica and St. Vincent, while most of islands saw the tragic disappearance of their Native American residents. With the importation of slaves into centers such as Barbados, the African component was added to the St. Vincent gene pool in the seventeenth century as a result of the sinking of a slaver from Benin and some escapees from the adjoining island of Barbados. Due to a revolt against the British by the inhabitants of St. Vincent Island (possibly inspired by the French), all but a few Black Carib families were deported by the British Navy to the Island of Roatan, off the coast of Honduras in Central America. The Spanish Crown, notified of the presence of a hostile army on their colonial possessions, immediately deployed their military to investigate. On arrival, they learned that the Black Caribs were peaceful and preferred passage to the coast of Central America, which was gladly provided.

Upon arrival in Honduras, the Black Caribs rapidly spread out geographically from a single village to the present 54 communities, distributed over 1000 km of Central American coastline from Dangriga, Belize to La Fe, Nicaragua. Numerically, they have expanded in Central America from fewer than 2000 persons in 1800 to more than 70,0000 persons by 1980 (Crawford, 1983). The success of the Black Caribs in colonizing the Central American coast is not only impressive due to their sheer numbers, but because they were able to survive in an inhospitable region plagued by malaria, brought earlier by infected Africans. In this evolutionary success story, the Carib/Arawak genes from St. Vincent were preserved in Central America, "packaged" with African phenotypes. The numerical success of the Black Caribs can be explained not only by the presence of a large African genetic component but also by the extractive efficiency of Arawak/Carib Indian culture. Because of their African and Native American ancestry, the Black Caribs possess exceptionally high genetic variation and a number of genetic adaptations to malaria. These adaptations were the result of their residence in malarial environments in Africa for thousands of years before coming to St. Vincent Island and the malaria-infested Central American coast (Crawford, 1998).

What does this history have to do with the conflicting reports from the mid nineteenth century of the Amerindian appearance of the Garifuna in Central America in contrast to my observations of an African population, approximately 125 years later? There are two possible explanations. (1) Since the 1850s the Black Caribs could have intermixed with a variety of populations of predominantly African ancestry, brought earlier to Central America to labor on the fruit and sugar plantations. As a result of this gene flow, the Garifuna of 1975 resembled African populations more closely and indeed exhibited African admixture estimates of 70% to 80% (Schanfield *et al.*, 1984). (2) The transplanted, admixed population of Carib/Arawak and African may have experienced the effects of natural selection on the coast of Central America. Did selection favor those individuals with hemoglobinopathies (AS and AC), G-6-PD deficiency, and the absence of the Duffy chemokine receptor ($FY^*0$), or specific gamma globulin markers brought from Africa? These regions of the genome, protective against malaria and bearing the molecular signature of natural selection, would more likely be found in individuals of African ancestry who would survive their encounters with *Plasmodium falciparum*, and their genes would be present disproportionately in subsequent generations. In her dissertation, Lorena Madrigal-Diaz (1988) explored differential fertility as a mechanism of selection in a cohort of Afro-American women residing in Limón, Costa Rica. She concluded that differential fertility of women with hemoglobinopathies (Hb AS) in a malarial environment cannot maintain the balanced polymorphism but that differential mortality better explains the evidence for selection.

This volume by Lorena Madrigal examines the complexities of health, population genetics, and demography of the descendants of the African slaves imported into the Caribbean Islands and into some regions of Central America. In the initial phases of slavery in the Americas, African slaves came primarily from West and Central Africa. In the later phases of slavery the southeastern and the western regions of Africa were also raided for slaves. Thus, the slave populations in the Caribbean were highly heterogeneous, both culturally and genetically, and contained enormous biodiversity – a reflection of the antiquity of human habitation in Africa. In addition to the rich genetic variation brought from Africa, the descendants of the slave populations also interbred with Native Americans, and Europeans. There is considerable variation in the degree of African, Native American, and European admixture seen on various islands of the Caribbean and along the Atlantic coast of Central America. Varying degrees of African, Native American, and European admixture in these Caribbean populations complicate any analyses of risk factors for chronic diseases associated with specific ethnicity.

Lorena Madrigal has been conducting research on the genetics and demography of the descendants of African populations of Central America since her graduate school days at the University of Kansas. Her dissertation focused on the community of Limón, Costa Rica and she has continued working in Central America for almost two decades. Her background and training have qualified her uniquely to write this highly complex history, demography, and genetics of the descendants of the African slaves of the Caribbean. The examination of the genetic and disease patterns of African populations against a backdrop of history and demography allows Professor Madrigal to weave a rich biocultural tapestry, highlighting the unique patterns of human evolution in the Caribbean and Central America.

## References

Bard, S.A. 1855. *Waikna: Adventures on the Mosquito Shore*. New York: Blackwood.

Cook, S.F. and Borah, W. 1971. *Essays in Population History: Mexico and the Caribbean*. Berkeley: University of California Press.

Crawford, M.H. 1983. The anthropological genetics of the Black Caribs (Garifuna) of Central America and the Caribbean. *Yearbook of Physical Anthropology*, **25**: 155–186.

1998. *The Origins of Native Americans*. Cambridge: Cambridge University Press.

Madrigal-Diaz, L. 1988. Hemoglobin genotype and fertility in a malarial environment: Limón, Costa Rica. Ph.D. dissertation, University of Kansas, Lawrence, KS.

Schanfield, M.S., Brown, R., and Crawford, M.H. 1984. Immunoglobulin allotypes in the Black Caribs and Creoles of Belize and St. Vincent. In *Current Developments in Anthropological Genetics. Volume 3. Black Caribs. A Case Study in Biocultural Adaptation*, ed. M.H. Crawford. New York: Plenum Press, pp. 345–363.

Young, T. 1847. *Narrative of a Residence on the Mosquito Shore*. London: Smith, Elder and Co.

# Acknowledgments

I would like to acknowledge the support of Drs. M. Crawford, G. Barbujani, W. Dressler, G. Armelagos, K. Yelvington, and T. Sanderson. In addition, I wish to thank the people of Limón and Westfalia for their hospitality and willingness to teach us. Lastly, to my parents and to my daughters. If anything, working with the people of Limón has helped me see the endless continuity of families.

# 1 The African slave trade and the Caribbean

## 1.1 The Caribbean

The question of what geographical region is actually to be included in a book about the Caribbean is not as easy a question as it sounds. However, since this book deals with the biology of human populations of African ancestry, it will cover those regions in the Caribbean, broadly defined, occupied by people whose ancestors were brought from Africa by the European slave traders. A broadly defined Caribbean includes the Antilles – the Greater Antilles and the Lesser Antilles – the Grenadines, the Windward Islands, the West Indies, the northern coast (the "shoulder") of South America, the Atlantic coast of Central America (Belize had true plantation economies with slave populations, whereas most of Central America did not), and Bermuda (though the latter is situated well into the Atlantic Ocean; Figure 1.1). Excluded here are the coast of the Gulf of Mexico and Florida. The Internet provides excellent cartographic resources on the Caribbean. For example, see http://palmm.fcla.edu/map.

## 1.2 The European invasion of the Caribbean and the early import of African slaves

For an overview on the origin and evolution of Native American populations, the reader is referred to Crawford (1998). For recent work on ancient DNA of Caribbean native groups the reader is referred to Lalueza-Fox et al. (2001, 2003). Also recommended is Cook's *Born to Die* (1998), a book which details the earliest stages of the European–Amerindian contact in the Caribbean. The sad conclusion to Cook's account is that after a quarter century of contact the Taino and their circum-Caribbean neighbors were approaching extinction. When the native populations of the Caribbean essentially died off (Cook, 2002; Kiple and Ornelas, 1996), the Europeans turned to African sources of labor (Klein, 1978).

1

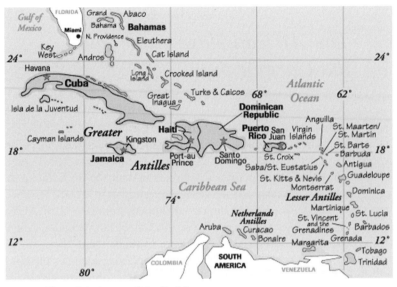

Figure 1.1. A map of the Caribbean.

That Europeans (Franco, 1978; Klein, 1978; Knight, 1991; Thomas, 1997) and Africans (Klein, 1986; Rawley, 1981) were immersed in a culture of slave trading by 1492 was helpful to the establishment of the trans-Atlantic slave trade. Indeed, by the time of the collapse of the Caribbean Indian population, the Portuguese in particular (though not exclusively) had extensive trade routes in Africa, and were ready to engage in a trans-Atlantic trade (Bah, 1993; Rawley, 1981). Indeed, the Portuguese had successfully integrated themselves into the ample slave-trading networks of Arab and African traders (Klein, 1986). According to Bah (1993), most of the African slaves traded in this network were from the eastern and central areas of northern Africa. Curtin (1969) discusses a number of sources, and concludes that for the second half of the 1400s as many as 500 African slaves were brought to Europe. It is interesting to note that within the slave culture of Africa, female slaves were highly valued as producers of children and as agricultural workers who could also perform many other tasks in the household (Moitt, 2001; Morrissey, 1989). Within the Caribbean plantation system, however, they lacked any sort of status, as will be discussed below.

It should be noted that African slaves participated in the earliest stages of the European invasion of the New World, as members of the various conquistador teams (Klein, 1978; Yelvington, 2004). Indeed, African slaves began arriving in the Americas as soon as the European conquest started (Conniff, 1995; Morrissey, 1989). In Costa Rica for example, African slaves were initially brought during the early 1500s as members of exploration teams, who focused their efforts in the north–central Pacific areas of the country, specifically Guanacaste and Puntarenas (Blutstein, 1970). Just like in Costa Rica, there are several African-derived populations in the Caribbean and in Latin America that descend from these early African slaves, quite apart from those that descend from the slaves brought in by trans-Atlantic trade. The former slaves, called *ladinos* by the Spanish and Portuguese, were Christian and actual members of the invading parties. The latter, called *bozales* by the Spanish and Portuguese, were non-Christian, non-Portuguese or -Spanish speakers, and were taken directly from Africa (Klein, 1986).

## 1.3   The establishment of the slave trade: 1492–1650

Due to the Papal demarcation of 1494, Spain owned no land in Africa, the source of slaves (Rawley, 1981). At that time, Portugal had a solid grip on the African supply of slaves, established during the previous century (da Veiga and Carreira, 1979; Knight, 1991). During the 1500s, Spain attempted to counteract Portugal's supremacy in the African trade by assigning licenses (*asientos*) to private Spanish enterprisers and to foreign traders (mostly Dutch and Flemish, according to Klein, 1978) to trade the slaves (Bah, 1993; Franco, 1978). Based on these licenses, Curtin (1969) estimates that approximately 2882 slaves were imported during 1595–1640, and 3880 during 1641–1773. However these figures have been challenged (Bah, 1993). According to Bah (1993), most of these slaves were taken to Peru and Mexico, from where the Spanish were deriving tremendous wealth from mining. In these regions, groups derived from African and Amerindian founders grew dramatically, sometimes becoming part of the ruling, slaving elite (Klein, 1978). Klein (1986) estimates that by 1650 between 250 000 and 300 000 slaves had been brought to these two areas by the Spaniards. Yelvington (2004) notes that most estimates on how many slaves were brought to the New World do not account for the exceedingly large number of Africans who were killed in the raiding wars in Africa, wars often caused by the Europeans themselves.

Portugal, as opposed to the other European powers, did not place as much emphasis on the importation of slaves to Brazil as part of its economic strategy before the 1600s, until French and British merchants started cruising the South American coast. But by the late 1500s, both the

Portuguese crown and the Brazilian colonizers had established the sugar-plantation regime, which demanded a large number of slaves (Klein, 1978). Although the Amerindian population had been enslaved to work in these plantations, it proved to be too elusive and too sickly for the Portuguese, who eventually started mass importations of African slaves (da Veiga and Carreira, 1979). Moreover, the joining of the Portuguese and Spanish crowns (1580–1640) resulted in a push to de-emphasize Amerindian slavery (Klein, 1986). According to Klein (1986), the producers of Brazil (with the help of Dutch merchants) became the prime suppliers of sugar to Europe, and Antwerp and Amsterdam their primary importing centers (Klein, 1978). Supporting this supremacy were the African slaves.

### 1.4   The loss of Iberia's supremacy: the 1600s

Although the French and the British expanded their African slave raids and purchases in Africa, as well as their slave sales in the New World (Thomas, 1997), the supremacy of the Iberian powers lasted until the 1600s (Curtin, 1969; Emmer, 1998). By the 1600s, however, the Dutch, having just gained their independence from Spain, made their entrance into the slave market, eventually turning against their former Brazilian partners, and even occupying Brazilian territory (Rawley, 1981). During the seventeenth century, Amsterdam had become the financial capital of the world, and it supported a large army and a larger fleet of commercial ships involved in trade between Africa, the New World, and Europe (Rawley, 1981). The Dutch started slaving in earnest by 1621, when the Dutch West India Company was founded (Emmer, 1998; van den Boogaart, 1998). Indeed, much of the 1600s saw a constant struggle for African and New World ports and markets between the Dutch and the Iberian powers (da Veiga and Carreira, 1979; Emmer, 1998; Franco, 1978; Klein, 1986; Rawley, 1981; Shepherd, 2002). According to Thomas (1997), most African slaves taken to the New World by the Dutch had been captured at sea from the Portuguese. Interestingly, van den Boogaart (1998) has proposed that the importance of the Dutch in the early Atlantic slave trade has been over-emphasized.

Because of the struggle and eventual loss to Portugal of Brazilian territory, Dutch planters and their slaves migrated in the mid 1600s to Martinique, Barbados, and Guadeloupe to establish sugar plantations. Some also migrated to Dutch Guiana (Emmer, 1998). Opinions vary on the extent to which the rise of these islands in the world economy was aided by Dutch credit and Dutch importation of slaves (Klein, 1986; Morrissey, 1989; Rawley, 1981; Thomas, 1997), since the Dutch West Indian Company had been left bankrupt after the loss of Brazil (Emmer, 1998; Solow, 1998; van den Boogaart, 1998). The rise of other European powers was only helped by the collapse of the joint Portuguese–Spanish Empire, which resulted in a temporary stop to the Spanish slave trade. The Dutch in particular aligned themselves with African suppliers, and nearly achieved supremacy in the Caribbean with Curaçao, a strategically placed port (Thomas, 1997) from which they sold African slaves to the Spaniards (Rawley, 1981).

In the case of the French, the development of the tobacco plantations in colonies such as Guadeloupe, Martinique, St. Lucia, St. Vincent, Grenada, and the Grenadines provided the initial market for the importation of slaves. But this market was amplified with the adoption of sugar as the main crop.

Concurrently, the British had declared the Leeward Islands to be theirs in the early 1600s, and started importing slaves (Klein, 1978). Although cotton, tobacco, and indigo had been planted, sugar eventually became the dominant crop, transforming the Caribbean (Klein, 1986; Thomas, 1997). These changes towards the adoption of a monoculture throughout the Caribbean were accompanied by a change in the composition of the population. In the French colonies, by the end of the 1680s the population of African slaves had increased as dramatically as that of the European indentured servants had fallen (Klein, 1986). In the French colonies after the 1670s the number of farms and property-owning Europeans declined, and the number of African slaves increased dramatically. For example, by the end of the 1600s Barbados had a population of African slaves of 50 000, controlled by fewer than 200 White planters (Klein, 1986). Indeed, during the 1700s the percentage of African slaves in the total population was probably close to 80%. Even in the Caribbean regions with larger European settlements, such as Cuba and Puerto Rico, with the adoption of sugar as a monoculture the number of African slaves increased dramatically and the number of European indentured servants decreased equally, so that the Caribbean became truly Africanized (Morrissey, 1989).

The French and the British attacked, conquered, or occupied former Spanish holdings (Emmer, 1998). In this manner the British gained Jamaica and the French the western part of Santo Domingo. Spain only had Cuba, Puerto Rico, and the eastern region of Santo Domingo left. With the occupation of Jamaica, the British started actively participating in the slave trade (Franco, 1978). Therefore, by the end of the 1600s the

Spanish colonies became the third largest importer of African slaves, with the French and British Caribbean islands being the second, and Brazil being the first (Rawley, 1981; Shepherd, 2002). For a discussion of the participation of other European powers (Sweden, Denmark, etc.) in the African slave trade see Rawley (1981). During this century, slavers in the Caribbean favored the importation of male slaves, whom they conceived to be better workers (Morrissey, 1989).

## 1.5    The establishment of the sugar plantation economy: the 1700s

According to Thomas (1997), the establishment of the sugar plantation economy, dominant during the 1700s, was undertaken by the British and French colonists, but it rested upon the knowledge gained by the Dutch in Brazil, and their capital, trade networks, and African slaves. Such Dutch prominence, however, is challenged by van den Boogaart (1998), who argues that British and French planters were responsible for the creation of the sugar plantation economy, and that the role of the Dutch was marginal.

In the early 1700s the political alliances were changed, as the French and Spanish crowns became aligned with one another, and the Portuguese and British did the same. Thomas (1997) argues that the British clearly had the upper hand against their competitors, and in 1713 were able to take over Spain's *asiento* from the French. The British started importing the African slaves firstly to Jamaica and Barbados, where they would be "refreshed" for further shipping to the Iberian ports, such as Panamá, Buenos Aires, and Cartagena.

According to Klein (1978), by the mid 1700s the Jamaican trade was the largest within the British empire. The sources of the slaves changed from the entire Western coast to the Bight of Biafra and the Congo–Angola region after the 1790s. The majority of slaves were adult males (Klein, 1978; Shepherd, 2002). A large number of ports besides London were involved in the trade. In fact, Bristol overtook London in the 1730s as the most prominent port, only to be overtaken 20 years later by Liverpool. Rawley (1981) discusses the role of other British ports in the slave trade. He notes that the presumed unimportance of London during the 1700s has been overstated, and that the city did remain a vital port. London was apparently very important in the importation of Jamaican-produced sugar (Rawley, 1981). Indeed, it was during this time as well that Jamaica became the largest producer of sugar, surpassing Barbados.

The estimates of how many slaves were transported by the British vary according to historical sources and authors. For the 1700s, the estimates run from 2.5 to 3.7 million slaves from 1701 to 1807, with an annual shipment rising from 12 000 to 14 000 before 1720 to about 42 000 during the 1790s (Richardson, 1987). Curtin (1969) presents a decade-by-decade analysis of the number of slaves imported by the British. He also discusses the place of origin in Africa of these slaves. An important point made by Curtin (1969) is that the place in Africa from which the slaves were taken depended in great part on the choices made by the buyers in the New World, who had specific preferences. During this century as well, the preference for male slaves started to change, and more and more females were being sold as slaves, thus changing the sex ratio of the plantations. This change was probably a result of the slaver's understanding that the female slaves provided them with the possibility of slaves reproducing (although the slavers rarely treated them in a manner compatible with successful pregnancies) and the slavers' wishes to have easy access to sex, but also the slavers' understanding that the male slaves wished for females (Moitt, 2001; Morrissey, 1989).

That British overseas trade grew healthily during the 1700s is not disputed. What has caused more debate among historians is the role of the slave trade and the slave-based plantation economy in the tremendous growth of the British trade and in fostering British industrialization. Whereas some historians (particularly Eric Williams) have seen slavery as the backbone of British industrialization, others see it as an important part of an expanding economy, an expansion in great part dictated by consumer demand for sugar within Britain. Yelvington (2004) states that the slave trade and the plantation system were central to the industrial revolution and that they enabled European colonial expansion. Whatever its cause, the growth of the British slave trade was such that the cost of acquiring slaves in West Africa increased after 1750, simply because the demand was higher than the supply. Moreover, the slaves had such high mortality and low fertility that they were unable to maintain their own numbers. To these rising costs the slave traders responded sometimes by instituting new payment mechanisms which allowed the buyer to afford a higher price. In any case, the slavers had a very high income, and many would be able to pay for the slaves even without credit from the mainland.

The French, on the other hand, after losing Spain's *asiento*, started trading more on an individual basis. In the French Caribbean, St. Domingue was the main port and the main producer of sugar. In France, the main port for the slave trade was Nantes, which obtained its slaves from the coast around Loango Bay (Curtin, 1969; Thomas, 1997). Although the French shipped fewer slaves than did the British and the Portuguese, they were still responsible for sending as many as 100 000 during the 1730s. More detailed numbers are discussed by Curtin (1969).

The importance of the Portuguese in the slave trade changed during the 1700s, it being the largest trader before the 1730s, but then losing supremacy to the British. The slaves brought by the Portuguese came mostly from Angola and Guinea, and were sent directly to Rio de Janeiro. A difference between the Portuguese traders on the one hand and the British and French on the other is that the former never had a prominent port, as did the latter with Liverpool or Nantes (Curtin, 1969).

Dutch traders (both independent and those with the West Indian Company) were still active in the 1700s, bringing slaves to the Netherland–South American holdings as well as to Curaçao and St. Eustatius. Thomas (1997) discusses the participation of the Danes in the slave trade, and Curtin (1969) the participation of the Danes and other European nations. All in all, the African slave trade during the 1700s clearly rested on a mercantilist ideology. Backed with this ideology, the European governments allowed great individuality in the slave enterprise (Rawley, 1981).

The world appetite for sugar did not diminish; indeed, demand for sugar increased even in the 1800s, after the abolition of the slave trade (1807–24, depending on the European government) and the declaration of emancipation (1834–8). During the 1800s there were some technical developments in sugar production and cane juice processing, such as the steam and then the mechanized mill, which increased production (Morrissey, 1989).

### 1.6    Conditions for the slaves during the trans-Atlantic journey

Although this review will concentrate on the conditions for the slaves in the slaver ship, it should be noted that before many slaves were taken to sea they had already endured a long and arduous journey from their place of origin (Miller, 1981). Rawley (1981) emphasizes that the condition of the slaves before they boarded was probably an important factor affecting the slave mortality of a specific ship. The crossing took approximately 2–3 months, with the length of time being cut towards the 1700s compared with earlier centuries.

Klein (1986) mentions that although the Portuguese were and have been noted for being more humane with their African slaves, in fact they were not too different from the other European traders. Just how bad the conditions were during the middle passage is not universally agreed upon (Miller, 1981). Rawley (1981) notes that our current attempts to recon-struct the middle-passage conditions are influenced by the very subjective accounts made by both abolitionists and anti-abolitionists. There seems to be increasing agreement that as abhorrent as the slaves' conditions might seem to an observer of the twenty-first century, the conditions were not significantly worse than those found in European immigrant ships headed for the New World (Bean, 1975; Thomas, 1997). Certainly, from a clearly financial viewpoint, it was not to the captain's advantage to lose a large proportion of the slaves. Rawley (1981) sees the presence of doctors on board slave ships as evidence for concern about the health of the cargo. Bean (1975) proposes that many of what he calls the "horror stories" of the middle passage derived from abolitionist propaganda rather than from actual objective observation. Rawley (1981) notes that the mortal-ity of the European crews in the slave ships was exceedingly high. For Curtin (1968), the mortality of the crew during the eighteenth century was actually higher than that of the slaves.

Although it might be true that European migrants and crew endured great hardship crossing the Atlantic, there are some obvious differences in the manner in which they ended up in a ship, as well as in the manner in which they were transported. Certainly, European migrants did not have to be chained to prevent them from jumping off the ship to try to swim back to their homeland, and nor did they have to be force-fed to avoid suicide by starvation (Thomas, 1997). These behaviors exhibited by the slaves and not by the European migrants speak loudly as to the emotional and psychological state of the slaves. The combination of removal from home, the separation from family and friends, the ill treatment on board, the dismal conditions in the ship, the uncertainty of the future, the fear of being cannibalized by the Europeans, and untold morbid psychological and physical conditions must have affected the slaves' immune system and general health. A number of contemporary ac-counts by British doctors attest that melancholy was responsible for numerous slave deaths and suicides when crossing the Atlantic (Bah, 1993; McGowan, 2002; Rawley, 1981).

There is general agreement that the male slaves tended to be chained more frequently than did the female slaves, who had more freedom of movement. At the same time, the female slaves were in danger of being raped and had to deal with childbirth and its aftermath in a most difficult situation (McGowan, 2002; Thomas, 1997). Some captains kept male slaves in shackles through most of the voyage but some gave them greater freedom after the African homeland was no longer visible (Rawley, 1981).

How crowded the conditions of the slaves were probably depended on the size of the ship, the number of slaves that initially were put in it, and the mortality rate of the trip. Several accounts do indicate that slaves frequently did not have enough room to turn themselves around (Thomas, 1997). Such overcrowding evidently caused extreme heat and thirst, promoted disease transmission, and interfered with breathing (McGowan, 2002). However, a positive linear relation between over-crowding and mortality has been challenged (Rawley, 1981), particularly by Klein (1978). Apparently the conditions of overcrowding were not constant, but were particularly difficult during the early part of the trip, when the coast could still be observed. It was during this time that the crew feared slaves would jump off the boat. But after land was out of sight, the slaves would frequently be released and organized into cleaning parties.

There is also widespread disagreement about how inadequate the food on the slaver ships was. It is obvious that there was competition for space between food and slaves carried, and it is well established that the food taken was not always sufficient (Klein, 1986). Emmer (1998) notes that the food transported on board would easily spoil. This of course would be particularly the case during the longer trips, resulting in a higher incidence of dysentery (Klein, 1978). Thomas (1997) and Rawley (1981) mention that care was sometimes taken to provision the boat with food known to be to the liking of the Africans, as well as to provide vinegar or lime to avoid scurvy. A serious problem was that of water supply. Not only was it difficult to carry enough water for hundreds of people, but the choice of an adequate container was not always obvious. Rawley (1981) notes that frequently it was the surgeon or doctor contracted to work on a ship that oversaw the food and water supply taken on board.

Under the conditions prevalent in a slave ship, it is not surprising that there was a high prevalence of disease, including ailments such as dehydration, dysentery, measles, ophthalmia, yaws, intestinal worms, small-pox, and numerous unrecognized conditions (Curtin, 1968, 1969; Emmer, 1998; Klein, 1986; Rawley, 1981). Some captains tried to control the spread of infectious disease in an attempt to save the other slaves and to maintain a healthy crew by simply throwing overboard the ill slave. Captains knew that the probability of an uprising was higher if the slaves noted that the crew themselves were ill, so they did their best to control disease spread (McGowan, 2002). A relatively common cause of death was violence, usually following rebellion attempts, though of course such situations varied greatly between different ships (Bah, 1993). Rawley (1981) notes that violence and brutality were also endured by the crew, not only by the slaves.

Most rebellions took place when the boat was still anchored in Africa, as the slaves would have a higher probability of sailing the boat to a place where they could disembark and flee. Afterwards, the highest frequency of rebellions occurred within 10 days of sailing, when there was still hope of turning the boat around and going back to Africa. Otherwise, there were frequent rebellions when land was sighted in the Caribbean, as many slaves believed that they were destined to be eaten by their cannibal captors upon arrival. Uprisings on board were also more likely to take place if there was a sizeable number of slaves from the same ethnic group who spoke the same language. As a result, captains tried on purpose to carry slaves of different ethnic groups, thus contributing to the slaves' sense of loss. It also seems that if among the slaves there was a person who had been a leader, whether political, religious, or even a former slave-trader, this person would be better able to convince the slaves to rise and to coordinate the uprising. Women and children, who were not shackled and had freedom of movement, served as sources of intelligence about the crew's ability to keep watch, its health, and even respect for the captain. They supplied guns and the means to unshackle the men, and were thus active participants in the uprisings (McGowan, 2002). Some rebellions were successful, but the fate of a number of ships overtaken by slaves is unknown (Thomas, 1997). Some captains were cognizant of the relation-ship between poor conditions and treatment of slaves in the ship and the probability of an uprising, and tried to ameliorate the situation with variable results. Their purpose was, of course, not to lose the cargo they were carrying and endanger their enterprise (McGowan, 2002).

Slave ships crossing the Atlantic had to deal with difficult situations inherent to the ocean, such as storms, long periods without winds (so-called calms), and pirates (Thomas, 1997). A few shipwrecks resulted in hundreds of deaths (Rawley, 1981).

Not surprisingly, estimates of mortality vary tremendously (Bah, 1993; Klein, 1978; Miller, 1981). Mortality appears to have differed by the century, perhaps by the nationality of the slavers, and obviously by a combination of the issues discussed above. Rawley (1981) notes that if pre-embarkation and post-embarkation mortality are considered, then mortality rates are much higher than usually reported. Bean (1975) pro-poses a 12% death rate for African slaves in British ships. Thomas (1997) cites losses of 15–20% on Portugal–Brazil trips, 10–15% in British and 23–25% in French ships, and an average of 9% mortality during the 1700s, with the Dutch having the lowest mortality rates of all slavers. Rawley (1981) estimates losses of 10–25% for the Danish. Emmer (1998) stresses the tremendous mortality variation across different journeys and centuries, but states that a mortality of 20–30% was not the norm but rather the exception. Klein (1978) agrees, and notes that most ships had a lower mortality rate than the average for a given period, but that a few boats with exceedingly high mortality drove the period mean up. Klein (1978) proposes that these mortality peaks usually resulted from epidemic diseases such as smallpox, not from water- and food-borne diseases such as dysentery. Eltis (1984) disagrees and proposes that epidemics were not major killers, but that endemic disease was. Rawley (1981) and Klein (1978) emphasize the importance of the port from which the slaves departed, and of length of voyage, as predictors of mortality. The former comprised a number of health indicators, such as length of travel from capture to shipment, disease load, food availability, etc. It is generally agreed that mortality decreased in the latter part of the slave trade. However, the causes of such decline are not clear (Klein, 1978, 1986; Rawley, 1981).

This chapter has purposely stayed away from the question of how many slaves were taken out of Africa by the Europeans. This question is so controversial that many pages would have been necessary to discuss it. However, the reader is directed to Curtin (1969), Yelvington (2004), and Bah (1993) for a review of this issue.

### 1.7    Life conditions of the slaves in the Caribbean

This section centers on the issue of health status of slaves in the Caribbean, including information about slave living conditions and culture. In reality, it is not possible to disassociate the lives of slaves from those of their slavers: the Caribbean slave society included a hierarchical set of groups, ranging from the European elite to the urban free Black, to the Creole or Colored (the offspring of a slave and a European or a free Black), to the field slave. Craton (1996) proposes that a better way of looking at these segments of slave society is to see them as going through a process of creolization, which affected not only the African slaves and their descendants but the Europeans as well. In contrast, Beckles (2002) prefers to examine slave Caribbean history by emphasizing the transfer of traditional African cultures to the New World, thus looking at the Caribbean experience as a challenge to the African slaves, who remained culturally dynamic. Yelvington (2004) presents racial taxonomies used in French colonies, taxonomies which used elaborate nomenclatures and endeavored to classify the offspring of all possible matings. The crucial issue was the degree of "Blackness" in the individual.

There are a number of resources for reconstructing slave life in the Caribbean. There are numerous historical records which have resulted in reconstructions of life in the plantation. Of this type of study, particularly noteworthy are the work by Craton (1978), who analyzed life in Worthy Park, and Dunn (1987), who did the same for Mesopotamia, both Jamaican plantations. Hall (1996) has reconstructed life in Jamaican plantations from the viewpoint of a member of the slaver elite, based on Thomas Thistlemore's diaries. Church records can also be used to reconstruct life under slavery; according to Stinchcombe (1995) church records of baptisms, marriages, and deaths were better in the Catholic colonies than in the Protestant ones.

There are also archaeological studies, including osteological analysis of the remains of slaves to determine their health status (Blakey, 2001). Particularly noteworthy is the work of Corruccini, Handler, and colleagues with the skeletal collection of Newton plantation in Barbados. Here will be mentioned their main conclusions about slave health, but a comprehensive summary of their work will not be attempted (Corruccini *et al.*, 1982, 1985, 1987, 1989; Handler and Corruccini, 1983, 1986; Handler *et al.*, 1982, 1988; Jacobi *et al.*, 1992). In Guadeloupe there have been a number of archaeological and osteological studies of cemeteries, which might be slave cemeteries. However, this has not been shown to be the case definitely (Courtaud *et al.*, 1999).

It is obvious that there was not one single life condition for slaves in the Caribbean (Yelvington, 2004). Some were employed in an urban setting as domestic servants, and some still as domestic servants but in a rural environment. Most were employed in the plantations. But even the plantations were not all the same. Although the majority of African slaves labored in large sugar plantations under hot and humid conditions, some worked in coffee plantations in the highlands, under cooler conditions. These different settings implied different epidemiological conditions and diets. The next two sections discuss the living conditions of plantation and house slaves separately, these two categories encompassing the living situations of most slaves.

### 1.7.1   The African slave in the rural setting

In *Slave Society in the Danish West Indies*, Hall and Higman (1992) present a comprehensive overview of life in the Danish colonies; that is, St. Thomas, St. John, and St. Croix. Most of the African slaves in these islands were employed in sugar plantations, where the work was exceedingly demanding and the hours long. Gaspar (1993) notes that in Antigua the amount of work was inversely correlated with the number of slaves in the plantation, so that in properties with few slaves the workload was extreme. Morrissey (1989) is of the opinion that nowhere were the work regimes longer and more brutal than in Cuba during the harvest season, when the slaves were forced to work for up to 20 hours a day. Friedman (1982) concludes that in Trinidad the slaves were short as a result of both undernourishment and overwork. Moitt (2001) notes that, in the French Antilles, African slaves worked like beasts of burden in terms of the hours and the work itself: for example, when the soil was to be prepared for planting, no animal, only human, force was used. The number of hours worked in most of the Caribbean was highest in the 1600s and 1700s, and then decreased in the early 1800s, as a result of new legislature during a period sometimes called the "amelioration period" (Higman, 1984).

In general, slaves were arranged by age group, the youngest of which included children under 6 years of age (Moitt, 2001; O'Neal, 2001; Sheridan, 1996). The field gang apparently had the hardest physical labor, including digging the holes for planting sugar cane, and cutting the cane stalks at harvest time. The difference in life conditions between the field slave and the house slave is obvious when looking at the life expectancy of these two groups in Mesopotamia plantation: the house slave worked an average of 24.1 years (3.7 years more than the field slave average), and died at an average age of 44.8 years (2.6 years later than the field slave; Richardson, 1987). The great majority of workers were destined to be in the field gang, assuming they had the health for it. But working in the fields was very deleterious for the workers. For example, in Mesopotamia plantation, only five males out of the hundreds of field slaves who worked there for several decades were able to keep their position for as long as 30 years. Interestingly, there were three females who worked in the field for 40 years, a record unmatched by the males. This was certainly not due to any preferential treatment of women in terms of labor or food but to their own fortitude (Morrissey, 1989). As Richardson (1987) notes, these women appeared to be simply tougher. When field slaves became infirm, they were switched to other positions. The field gang slave who could withstand exceedingly heavy labor was the one most sought-after, and for whom very high prices were paid.

Other slaves had specific crafts which required considerable job training, such as the boilers and distillers who knew how to produce sugar and rum. In addition there were carpenters, masons, and smiths, and even stock-keepers and transportation workers.

The offspring of slave women and European, Creole or free Black males, whether classified as Colored or Creole, were usually exempt from fieldwork. Thus, lighter-skinned individuals tended to have a better situation than did those who were darker. Still, they inherited their mother's slave status, and had to be either manumitted or bought and granted freedom by their fathers. The improvement in one's life conditions depending upon one's skin color led to what Thompson (2002) calls a neurosis on the part of the victims of the racist slave system, manifested in self-hatred and hatred for dark individuals. In other words, the slaves themselves engaged in an ideology in which dark skin was shunned, and became victims of the slavery system twice.

In most plantations, slaves lived in small "villages" or hamlets of small houses, arranged in a circular fashion or in rows. This arrangement was not universal in the Caribbean, for in Cuba the slaves lived in large buildings called *barracones* in which a family was assigned a room (Morrissey, 1989). Most of our information on the slaves' quarters comes from Handler (2002), who has done exhaustive work on Barbadian plantations. Plantations had a fairly consistent layout, with a central area known as the plantation yard, which had stables, a curing house, a mill and buildings for the processing of sugar and rum, and workshops for the smiths, etc. The manager's or the owner's house (the "Great House") was on one side, and the slave settlement was usually on its western side, contiguous to the plantation yard. It seems that the European elite preferred to have the slave settlement, also called the Negro yard, within close proximity for security reasons.

The arrangement of the village itself, the location of the huts, etc., was mostly up to the slaves themselves, the slavers simply designating the area where the village was to be built. Although sometimes the houses were arranged in a circular pattern, the arrangement was described by European visitors as "chaotic," and dissimilar to European peasant villages. For this reason, Handler (2002) is of the opinion that the slave villages were built in a manner more similar to African than to European settlements. Some of the larger plantations included a sick house and even a school and a chapel, particularly during the final years of slavery. In Berbice, British Guiana, few children benefited from the schools, and there is evidence that the children who were most educated were the offspring of a free father who paid for their private instruction (Thompson, 2002). Nearby was also the slave cemetery, although the slavers complained of the slaves burying their dead under their huts instead of in the cemeteries. These cemeteries were not clearly marked with fences and nor are they shown in any surviving plantation maps.

The construction of the huts was up to the slaves themselves, using whatever material was available in the plantation, such as wooden posts, palm leaves, mud, etc. The earthen floors were a likely source of infectious disease, particularly intestinal parasites, which can be absorbed through the feet. All accounts indicate that the household furnishings were simple and minimal at best (Morrissey, 1989).

A problem faced by the slaves as early as the mid 1600s was the disappearance of the forests, which supplied not only building material but also wood for cooking and warmth. Cooking fuel became an important commodity for both slaves and slavers.

In some of the larger plantations, the slaver dedicated enough land to the slave village so that most huts also had a small plot of land in which food crops were raised and small animals were kept. The amount of time slaves were able to devote to these plots depended on the colony, the slaver, and even the time period. In general, however, if the slaves were expected to provide for their own sustenance partly or wholly, they were allowed more time to work on their garden. Sometimes young children who were not working in the agricultural gangs were in charge of the family plot. Or, if a plot was tended by a couple, the female would be in charge of it while the male would frequently hire himself out, a practice which became frequent in the late 1700s and which is discussed below (Morrissey, 1989).

Another feature of the slave village, either within it or in close proximity to it, was a pond for water collection. Thus, as opposed to the slavers or managers, who collected their water in cisterns and had access to well water, the slaves collected it in ponds for washing, cooking, and drinking. Since these ponds were shared with cattle, and since all the washing took place there, they tended to become contaminated and to be a source of gastrointestinal pathogens, as will be discussed in Chapter 3. Another problem with the ponds, of course, was that in years of drought they would dry up and leave the slaves scrambling for water (Gaspar, 1993; Hall and Higman, 1992; Higman, 1984).

That the slave village was so small, the community so tight, and the resources so few undoubtedly led to interpersonal conflict, often expressed in the form of witchcraft accusations. At the same time, cooperative behavior in the care of the young, the sick, and the elderly was part of communal life (Handler, 2002).

O'Neal (2001) discusses the daily housekeeping chores that female slaves had to do, in addition to the work imposed by the slaver. By all accounts, the female slaves had as much work to do in the fields as the males, besides being in charge of the daily household chores such as cooking and cleaning, plus the more time-consuming chores such as mending or sewing of clothes. If the slaves lived in more communal settings such as the above-mentioned *barracones,* the chores would be shared, but shared by the women (Morrissey, 1989).

The African slaves, having been uprooted from their communities and families, tried as best as possible to establish a widespread kinship network in the plantations, a principle which became the nucleus of the new family. Several writers speak of the importance of matrilineal kinship, as opposed to a strong male–female tie. For example, in Jamaica and in the Danish colonies, family structure appears to have been of an extended-family type along the females' lines, in which much of the support for children came from the mother's kin, whether biological or fictitious (Dunn, 1993; Morrissey, 1989; Olwig, 1981).

Several factors contributed to the low frequency of European-recognized marriage among the slaves. For one thing, mortality was so high that a male–female partnership could end any time (Hall and Higman, 1992). In the same manner, the sale of one of the partners could put an end to a committed relationship between a man and a woman overnight (Morrissey, 1989). In addition, the very high ratio of male to female slaves did not contribute to the establishment of the nuclear families preached by some of the Europeans. Moreover, for slaves born and raised in a plantation, there would be few non-related possible partners, so that they would need to find one in another plantation, without being able to establish a permanent relation (Beckles, 2002; Olwig, 1981). Even in the presence of very difficult situations, including the separation of partners or the lack of a private living quarter, many couples did develop and maintained a strong relation. Apparently, slavers in the French colonies were more willing to contribute to the stability of couples than were those in the British colonies. Fortunately for the slaves, the sale of individual members of a family decreased towards emancipation time or during the amelioration period throughout the entire region (Morrissey, 1989). It is ironic that whereas the Europeans complained of the lack of mores in the slaves, who did not marry in a European-accepted way, they did not try to improve the slaves' conditions. There is abundant documentation that the slaves did not want to marry because their situation was so hopeless that they saw no benefit at all in a marriage. And when they did, they usually did it in late life, past reproductive age (Moitt, 2001).

There were also cases of polygyny and polyandry, the former being associated with high-ranking slaves, the latter being documented in a few cases. It is not clear if the members of a polygynous or polyandrous family were from the same region in Africa, although that is a likely possibility.

Evidently, establishing families, kinship, and community with individuals from different backgrounds, with different languages, and from different ethnic groups would have been very difficult (Beckles, 2002). It is also likely that in many cases a nuclear family was the first step towards the formation of a polygynous family (Morrissey, 1989). In the French colony of St. Domingue, an important factor affecting the formation of slave families was whether the slaves worked in the highland coffee plantations or in the lowland sugar plantations, the former having a lower slave density than the latter (Geggus, 1993). It seems that whatever family type was established (nuclear, female-headed, polygynous, polyandrous), it was usually of no more than two generations, as mortality was high and exogamy out of the plantation likely (Morrissey, 1989).

In short, there is evidence of strong family bonds within the slave communities throughout the Caribbean, despite the separations of spouses and other family members imposed by the slavers and despite the differences in ethnicity and language among many slaves (Beckles, 2002; Higman, 1984; O'Neal, 2001). There are even cases of entire families, headed by a female or by a couple, who were able to buy their freedom together (Moitt, 2001).

An important part of the slave cultural survival and resistance was the so-called crop-over festival, which took place after the sugar cane was cut. The festival included dancing, singing, and drumming – which was forbidden in most other cases – and general merriment. The music or the festival itself was sometimes referred to as Gombay on different islands, and it was always denounced and feared by the European elite. Other occasions for these types of festival were the Christian holy day seasons, during which the slaves had a slight reprieve from their work schedule. Neither festival was devoid of political implications, as the slaves took the opportunity to plan their future, including possible insurrections (Beckles, 2002).

For most of the duration of the slave trade, more males than females were imported, resulting in a very unbalanced sex ratio in many plantations. For example, Geggus (1985/6) notes that on several plantations in St. Domingue the sex ratio was very high. Interestingly, however, in other plantations, because females had lower mortality, the sex ratio was fairly equal, though not concerning the same age groups (Geggus, 1993). As women tended to live longer, there were more women in the aging and infirm slave category. Thus, the more equal sex ratio, which eventually was achieved in the Caribbean in the mid to late 1700s, did not necessarily contribute to higher fertility, as many of the women were old (Morrissey, 1989). In Jamaican plantations of the 1700s the sex ratio was actually reversed, and a majority of the field workers were females (Dunn, 1993). Moitt (2001) sees the evening-out of the sex ratio in the plantations as a result of the creolization process: once fertility increased as a result of the ameliorization laws preceding emancipation, the demography of at least some of the slave populations became less aberrant than it was in the past, because it was affected by the birth and survival of infants.

In his study of the records of a Jamaican sugar plantation, Dunn (1987, 1993) concludes that women slaves did much of the hardest sugar labor, which injured them, impaired their health and fertility, and resulted in a low life expectancy, a proposition also voiced by Geggus (1985/6) about the French female slaves. At the same time, females were excluded from the more valued crafts and skilled jobs, such as being "drivers" of the field workers. This was also the case in St. Domingue (Geggus, 1993), Antigua (Gaspar, 1993), and most of the British colonies (Higman, 1984), where the best positions were reserved for males and for New World-born slaves. Geggus (1985/6) also concurs that in the French sugar plantations most of the drivers (*commandeurs*) were New World-born slaves, and that female slaves had the worst jobs. A job that was open for infirm women who had lost a hand or an arm was that of a water carrier: apparently these women carried the water containers on their heads (Dunn, 1987). In contrast, and because of the small size of the territories, in the Virgin Islands female slaves could be drivers (O'Neal, 2001). One position of high status that was reserved for female slaves was that of midwife. This position was particularly important for slavers who could not afford new slaves or when the slave trade was temporarily interrupted (O'Neal, 2001). However it is fair to conclude that in all of the Caribbean during most of the slavery period, the best jobs were saved for slave males, and that females had little hope of ever acquiring a privileged position in the plantation. For most of the skilled positions (mason, smith, carpenter, etc.) there was an apprenticeship system that was open only to young male slaves. Perhaps the only way left for field female slaves to better their position was by obtaining some economic benefit out of the sexual abuse to which they were subjected, and of this the diaries of Thistlewood, referred to below, give plenty of evidence (Moitt, 2001; Morrissey, 1989; Shepherd, 2002). The specialized craft jobs described above, as well as the domestic positions, were preferentially awarded to the offspring of the European elite and female slaves. This seems to have been the cause of resentment among the slaves and of some fights, with deadly results, between slaves and the so-called mulattoes or Creoles (Dunn, 1987). That the specialized jobs had obvious economic benefits was seen in the better housing afforded by theses slaves, their better clothing, their several wives, and even in their ability to host lavish dances and parties, where the food and drink was abundant, and the clothes were fine even in the eyes of the Europeans. It is possible that the higher status of these skilled slaves was the result not only of their job, but also of the larger plot of land they frequently had adjacent to their hut, which allowed them to have extra produce for selling and bartering (Morrissey, 1989).

Both male and female slaves attempted to escape the plantations, and those who fled were overwhelmingly African-born (Dunn, 1993; O'Neal, 2001). Although it has been suggested that more males than females fled because women had more family duties such as taking care of the elderly and the young, Shepherd (2002) notes that many women slaves did escape. However, those that fled were overwhelmingly childless, confirming that mothers were unlikely to abandon their children in the plantation. Women slaves in the French Antilles usually fled with other females, rather than with a male partner (Moitt, 2001). If they were successful in their escape, they would join Maroon bands, where they were essential to the agricultural activities of the group. There is also evidence of an unusual Obeah Maroon woman named Nanny, who took a leadership position in her band. Although there were even fewer females per male in the Maroon bands, it seems that these groups practiced polygyny with some frequency, probably as a result of greater intragroup stratification (Moitt, 2001; Morrissey, 1989). In Jamaica, run-away slaves had reason to fear the bands of vigilantes or robbers, who could respectively turn them over to the slavers or rob and murder them. Upon return to the plantation, the most inhumane punishments would be inflicted upon the slaves (Hall, 1996).

There is general agreement that throughout the Caribbean the slave diet was poor (Thompson, 2002; see Higman, 1984 for a discussion of Kiples' discordant opinion). According to Hall and Higman (1992) the slave diet in the Dutch colonies was generally low in animal protein, but might have increased in quality by the 1700s, when slaves were provisioning their own food and received some supplementation by the owner. Higman (1984) emphasizes that the slave diet had a number of key deficiencies, specifically of calcium, vitamin A, and thiamine. Corruccini *et al.* (1987) suggest that the diet of the slaves in the Newton plantation in Barbados had vitamin and mineral deficiencies, being seasonally alleviated in not-so-lean times. In the small island of Antigua, slaves were not able to grow as much of their own food, so most of their diet was provisioned by the owners with imported food items. As a result, Antigua slaves faced hunger during the hurricane season, when ships stayed away from the Caribbean, and whenever trade was disrupted. In the Leeward

Islands as well, most food was imported, leading to a very precarious situation for the slaves (Morrissey, 1989). In Barbados, some slaves had a less reliable food supply if their slavers relied on imported food (Gaspar, 1993), although some large-plantation owners did allow their slaves to work on their own food supply on Sundays (Sheridan, 1996). Specifically in Barbados some slaves had their own plots next to their huts, whereas others had communal plots destined for their own use (Handler, 2002). By the end of the seventeenth century the slaves in some Barbados plantations were largely self-sufficient in their food provision (Morrissey, 1989). In Jamaica, the slave diet appears to have been very low in protein and animal fat. Indeed, Dunn (1993) proposes that such inadequacies account for the low fertility of the Jamaican slave women. Gaspar (1993) notes that during the harvest slaves had more access to sugar cane and its juice. Throughout the French Antilles most slaves had access to their own plots of land in close proximity to their huts, and it was the women who were involved in cultivating them, usually on their free day. Moitt (2001) opines that by successfully producing food female slaves inadvertently sustained the slavery system and prevented its decline. In other colonies, food for consumption by slaves was raised by the gangs that worked on the plantation crop (Higman, 1984). Higman (1984) criticizes previous attempts to estimate the average caloric intakes and needs of the African slave in a Caribbean plantation, and discusses variation among plantations and among different colonies. Clearly, some slaves were better off than others, with some having been able to hunt and fish, and raise chickens and pigs (Olwig, 1981), and some having been dependent on rations distributed by the owners. The fact that colonial governments frequently urged slavers to supplement the diet of slaves indicates how poor their diet was (Morrissey, 1989).

O'Neal (2001) notes that in plantations in which slaves raised their own food, the female slaves were usually in charge of bartering or selling surplus produce for their families. In this manner, many of them achieved a distinguished status not unlike the one they would have held in Africa. These transactions would usually take place in weekend town markets, which were very active through the Caribbean, even supplying the European elite with goods. Interestingly, Christian churches tried to dissuade the slaves from engaging in such economic activities on Sunday, supposedly out of concern for the slaves' souls but actually in fear of their increasing economic independence (Morrissey, 1989).

It is undeniable that African slaves in the Caribbean (excepting Barbados) had an exceedingly low fertility (Moitt, 2001). Induced abortions have been proposed to have been very frequent among the slaves, this seen as an act of active rebellion against the slavers (Shepherd, 2002). However, this position has been contested because it is much in contrast with the prevailing pro-natalist philosophy of the slaves and because there is little substantial evidence of effective abortifacients. Indeed, most of the reports we have on abortifacients were written by European observers who feared the unknown magical and healing powers of their slaves (Hall and Higman, 1992; Morrissey, 1989; Thompson, 2002). Thus, although it is likely that slave women some-times controlled their fertility as an act of resistance against their en-slaved state, it is perhaps more likely that the low fertility of slaves was a result of low fecundity due to undernutrition, overwork, disease load (particularly uterine and vaginal infections), amenorrhea, depression, and lack of exposure to coitus rather than due to effective contraceptive measures (Dunn, 1993; Geggus, 1985/6, 1993; Moitt, 2001). Corruccini *et al.* (1989) infer an exceedingly low fertility from their work with the skeletal collection in Newton, Barbados. Moreover, Dunn (1993) reports that both mortality and fertility were seasonally distributed, attesting to the tremendous burden on women. However, in a study in Berbice, British Guiana, several African-born slaves are noted for having had large families. It seems that a few slave women made a disproportionate contribution to the fertility of the slave population (Moitt, 2001; Thompson, 2002). In general, it seems that New World-born female slaves had higher fertility than African-born slaves. This difference was probably a result of greater disease resistance and a greater psychological willingness to establish emotional and sexual ties (Morrissey, 1989).

Another important stress on the women slaves was the threat and reality of rapes and other forms of bodily abuse (Dunn, 1993; O'Neal, 2001). In British Guiana, for example, there is ample evidence of violence towards pregnant slaves (causing miscarriages), their babies, and children. Paradoxically, women slaves were still expected to produce offspring, and they and their midwives risked punishment when babies died (Moitt, 2001). Indeed, Thompson (2002) concludes that children were treated as poorly as older slaves and were spared no brutality. Certainly, the low slave fertility as a result of frequent miscarriages and infant death speak of a population on the limit of survival. However, towards the end of the enslavement period, during the amelioration period, proposals to unbur-den pregnant women were presented and practiced in various areas such as Barbados (Morrissey, 1989; Sheridan, 1996), the Jamaican plantation Mesopotamia under the ownership of Mr. Joseph Barham II, several areas in the French Antilles (Moitt, 2001), and British Guiana (Thompson,

2002). The general conclusion gained from most of the sources is that although some managers might have been interested in promoting maternal and infant health (certainly with the purpose of increasing slave numbers), their efforts failed because they saw the mother first and foremost as a slave. Any attempts to improve breastfeeding and child-rearing would ultimately interfere with productivity, so at the end, most pregnant slaves were overworked, undernourished, and sick, and slave babies were "raised" in nurseries attended by older females and young girls, away from mother's milk and love.

The case of Mr. Barham in Jamaica is interesting, in that he had been to the plantation as a young man, and although an absentee owner, he tried to alleviate the terrible conditions of his slaves from England. In particular, he tried to reduce the workload of pregnant slave women. In the 1790s Mr. Barham voted for the abolition of the slave trade. This compassionate attitude was later changed, as despite what he interpreted to be serious attempts to better the situation of the slaves, the number of Mr. Barham's slaves kept dwindling. In the end, he accused the slaves of being dissolute and ultimately responsible for their poor health, and advocated that emancipation should only occur after the slaves became morally transformed.

Interestingly, on an occasion in which the Mesopotamia plantation slaves were left alone because the plantation managers and overseers were out on patrol during a slave uprising, the slaves did not rise against the slavers and damage their property. Instead, they continued to work in the field and in the production of sugar and rum. Dunn (1987) finds it ironic that the Mesopotamia slaves felt privileged and well taken care of, whereas a careful analysis of the plantation documents indicates that the plantation condemned them to a life of terrible morbidity and early mortality.

There is ample evidence of a heavy disease load throughout the Caribbean, a load including malaria, yellow fever, dropsy, typhoid, cholera, smallpox, elephantiasis, leprosy, yaws, and various venereal diseases (Curtin, 1968; O'Neal, 2001). Particularly noteworthy is the effect of treponematosis on the slaves of Barbados and Suriname, which has been researched osteologically. Both Khudabux (1999) and Corruccini *et al.* (1982) indicate that in whatever its manifestations (yaws, pinta, betel, venereal, non-venereal, and congenital syphilis), treponematosis added a very heavy disease load on the slave population. Khudabux (1999) suspects that in addition to yaws, venereal syphilis was probably endemic in the population, and probably related to the sexual abuse that the female slaves endured during the trans-Atlantic crossing and afterwards in the plantation. In areas of the French Antilles, venereal disease was so problematic that a Monsieur Foache ordered that the plantation nurse and doctor paid surprise visits to the slaves in their huts, to check if they were affected by venereal disease. If a slave was found to be knowingly infecting someone, s/he was severely punished, whereas if a slave asked for medical attention for a venereal disease, s/he promptly received it (Moitt, 2001). Corruccini *et al.* (1982) propose that the presence or absence of syphilis in slave populations might explain the variability in slave health observed in different plantations and in different colonies. Jacobi *et al.* (1992) focus on the frequency of congenital syphilis in the Newton plantation in Barbados, concluding that the slave population had a heavy disease load.

Whether geophagy was the cause or the cure of stomach problems is discussed by Higman (1984). Sheridan (1996) notes that in Barbados, the interpretation of the European elite of this behavior was that if children suffered from intestinal worms, they engaged in "dirt-eating." Dental problems, specifically hypercementosis, were a major issue in the slaves' health at the Newton plantation (Corruccini *et al.*, 1987). Interestingly, the location in the teeth of caries is different between the Newton plantation in Barbados (a sugar producer) and the Waterloo plantation in Suriname (a cotton producer; Khudabux, 1999). According to Khudabux (1999), the slaves in Newton were eating more sugar cane, and thus had more sugary fibers between the teeth, resulting in twice the rate of interproximal caries than was seen in Waterloo. A significant dietary-introduced morbidity was lead poisoning, which resulted in "dry belly-ache", and was probably acquired from rum, which was distilled in lead-rich machineries (Handler *et al.*, 1988).

There is ample evidence that slave clothing and footwear in the British colonies were inadequate to protect slaves from the sun and disease vectors (Higman, 1984). Indeed, Dunn (1993) speaks of numerous skin diseases and of a heavy disability toll. Gaspar (1993) notes that disease itself was distributed in a seasonal manner, as a result of the rain cycle, but also as a result of the seasonal nature of the workload (Higman, 1984).

Accidents frequently caused loss of limbs, particularly in the sugar mill and boiler (Gaspar, 1993). Geggus (1993) notes a high frequency of hernia among the males, who did the heaviest lifting in St. Domingue plantations, and confirms a high frequency of maiming and loss of eyes. A not-uncommon source of injury would have been the slavers' violence towards the slaves, equally handed-down to male and female slaves (Higman, 1984; O'Neal, 2001).

Most British colonies' plantations employed a White "doctor" or apothecary, whose qualifications varied tremendously. But most plantations relied on slave "doctors" or "doctress(es)," sick nurses, or *hospitalieres* in the French Antilles. Still, in most of the Caribbean their presence was tied to plantation size. In Barbados as opposed to other islands slaves had ample access to doctors (Moitt, 2001; Morrissey, 1989; Sheridan, 1996). When a plantation employed a European "doctor" and had a slave nurse, she usually worked under his command, administering medicines, curing wounds, etc. This gave her the unusual benefit of having African and European medical knowledge, which afforded her a much broader knowledge base of medicines and treatments than his (Moitt, 2001). Towards the later part of the slavery period, sick houses were established in the large Barbadian plantations. Ironically, these places were distrusted and avoided by the slaves, who saw them as a place to die. The slaves were probably not too mistaken, given the poor sanitary conditions of the places. The sick houses were usually under the supervision of the African slave nurse, who cared for the patients, fetched their food, cleaned the place, cut the fabric for bandaging wounds, and even prepared the medicines.

Besides the nurse, there were other slave health and spiritual practitioners, such as midwives and the Obeah man or woman. Although midwives were respected by and necessary to the slavers, they were the recipients of suspicion of infanticide and thus could receive severe punishment if the slaver thought that they were actively sabotaging his enterprise by killing newborn babies (Moitt, 2001). The Obeah man or woman had a doubly medical and spiritual role in the community, and helped with ailments of all sorts, witchcraft included (Handler, 2002; Morrissey, 1989; O'Neal, 2001). All spiritual or religious practices of the African slaves, whether obeah, voodoo (in Haiti), or myal/mial (in Jamaica), were based on a belief in the power of mind or spirit over body, and the use of spiritual power to influence one's future (Beckles, 2002).

Higman (1984) shows that African-born slaves tended to be shorter than New World-born slaves, although there was much variation among different ethnic groups. Although it has been suggested that New World-born slaves were healthier than African slaves, Geggus (1985/86) suggests that the place of work rather than that of origin was the most important factor influencing slaves' health.

Hall (1996) has uncovered and analyzed the diaries of a British-born plantation manager and eventually plantation owner named Thomas Thistlewood, which provide a unique male, European view into life on a Jamaican plantation. An often-occurring theme is that of sexual abuse on the part of Thistlewood of the female slaves. Shepherd (2002) describes Thistlewood as a rapist who abused practically every female slave under his management. Thistlewood did develop a long-term and apparently loving relationship with an African slave (Phibbah), with whom he had a son. Phibbah was evidently able to achieve a high economic status, as she even lent Thistlewood money on occasions. A common theme of the diaries of Thistlewood is the occurrence of venereal disease in both slavers and slaves. Thistlewood's behavior towards his slaves, and his eventual long-term emotional attachment to Phibbah, do not appear to have been unique.

A rather brutal account of sexual violence against women and female children is provided by Thompson (2002), who relates the behavior of the European overseers in Berbice, British Guiana. In this colony, the murder of a slave became a capital offence as late as 1811, but even afterwards it was rarely prosecuted. Thompson's account is full of cases of overseers who asked parents or relations to send their female children or teenagers for their own sexual gratification, and who, if refused, brutally punished the girl or a member of the family. A general theme which emerges from the literature is the European male's view of female African slaves as promiscuous, and of an absolute entitlement to these "available" sexual objects. Indeed, many young European males wished to work in the Caribbean knowing that they would be rewarded with frequent and exotic sex.

Less frequently considered is the European female, who in the plantations would be isolated from social interaction and who would be forced to accept her husband's desires for sexual relations with the slaves. It seems that in numerous cases the European wives were so jealous and upset about their situation that they themselves engaged in or ordered brutal torture or even murder of the female slaves and their offspring (Morrissey, 1989). Moitt (2001) also notes that female family members of the European males who were sexually exploiting the African slaves would blame the defenseless female slaves for tempting their male relations into a life of abandon. Other less frequently noted perpetrators of sexual abuse against African slave women were the high-ranking African slave males, such as the slave drivers, who had the authority and opportunity to abuse the slaves they were overseeing. Indeed, if a female slave was punished for whatever reason, it was usually the driver, or another high-ranking African male slave, who carried at the punishment itself. This and the sexual abuse perpetrated by the African male slave against the African female slave pitted the two groups of victims against each other, instead of against their slaver (Moitt, 2001).

Without any doubt, the life conditions of most slaves were terribly poor. During the 1700s, and even in the face of higher prices for slaves, slavers were purchasing them in high numbers. The slaves had such high mortality and low fertility that their numbers kept diminishing (Curtin, 1968; Richardson, 1987). In his analysis of Mesopotamia, Dunn (1987) notes that the number of deaths was roughly twice as high as the number of births recorded, a result also indicated in work by Craton (1978) on Worthy Park. The inability of the slave population to sustain itself was by no means unique to these two plantations, but was a generalized fact that testifies to the horrifying conditions of the slaves. Higman (1984) presents a careful study of the demographic pyramids of slave populations throughout the British colonies. For the most part, these pyramids are truly unique, and not comparable to that of most human groups under normal conditions.

The situation in the Barbados plantations has been and was at the time described as "less intolerable" for the slaves compared with that of the rest of the Caribbean. Indeed, the Barbadian slave population evolved from one of decline, as described above, to one of increase by the time of emancipation. Barbados was unique in several manners: the slaver elite included a large number of European females, and hence a more equal sex ratio, and more stable and non-absentee families. Part of the reason this elite was resident instead of absent was the more agreeable climate of the island. Such elite endeavored to recreate in Barbados a civil and proper British society, which eventually resulted in more legal rights for the free Blacks and Creoles. Moreover, not all European Barbadians were of the elite, as there was a fairly large group of poor Europeans who had to struggle to survive as did the free Blacks and Creoles. Several of these groups, whether the free Blacks, the Creoles, or the poor or rich Europeans, developed a sense of being "Barbadian" over that of being British or African, which resulted in a strong allegiance to the island itself. Indeed, the creolization process was probably more rapid and all-encompassing in Barbados than in other islands (Craton, 1996). In this manner, much was done to better the living conditions of all Barbadians, slaves included. Thus, the Barbadian slaves appear to have had a shorter workday and more holidays than other slaves (Sheridan, 1996).

As will be seen below, the hiring out of slaves became a very common economic arrangement with urban slaves in the 1800s. However, in terms of the number of slaves involved, it was much more important in the rural plantations, where it became more and more frequent from the later part of the 1700s. This is the time, of course, in which slaves became more expensive, so plantation owners or managers preferred to rent the labor of slaves instead of buying them. Since the rented slaves would not include children, the ill, or elderly, the arrangement became increasingly attractive as the prices of slaves increased. Hiring slaves would sometimes be necessary when the crop was unexpectedly large and the plantation slaves were not able to harvest it all, or when all plantation slaves were occupied in the harvest, and more slaves were needed for other plantation tasks such as processing of the crop, building, etc. (Morrissey, 1989). From the viewpoint of the hired slaves, there are different accounts as to whether they were employed in the worst jobs, or if they actually had fewer working hours than did the plantation slaves. After all, the manager who hired the slaves was responsible for restituting the slave owner if the slave died or was maimed. The one slave who was probably in a better position was the skilled slave such as the carpenter, smith, roofer, etc. These slaves had much more independence and would get a percentage of the fee from their slavers (Cateau, 2002).

### 1.7.2    The house slave

Here we include the house rural slave as well as the house urban slave. In the plantations, the need for house slaves depended partly on the composition of the slaver's family. If the household consisted of more than one or two single males but included a European wife or mother, then the desire to emulate a house such as that of the homeland would drive the elite towards having a large number of house slaves. In the French Antilles, some wealthy European slavers had what appeared to be a lavish lifestyle attended by a very high number of house slaves. But not all plantations had such a large set of house slaves, and even in those who did, the number of house slaves was a small proportion to the total number of slaves in the plantation.

Surely, the house slaves received better clothing, as numerous observers attest to their impressive clothing, particularly in the more lavish "Great Houses" (Moitt, 2001). Unfortunately for the female slaves, who usually served as house slaves, tending the house was not considered a skilled position; the economic rewards noted above were associated with the skilled positions of mason, carpenter, smith, etc. Of all the household jobs, the one with the lowest status was that of washerwoman, whose job was very demanding, given that she usually had no cleaning agent to use, and frequently had to walk a long way to the river to do her wash. Pressing the laundry must have been a time-consuming and arduous job, which was accomplished by using flowers and other natural scents so that the pressed laundry had a pleasant fragrance. At the same time, there is evidence that some washerwomen retaliated at some of the White managers by damaging their laundry. The only jobs in the slavers' home that had high status were those of the cook and the seamstress, but the former was reserved for males. Sewing could bring a fair amount of extra income to both the slaver and the slave, as there always seemed to be demand for her labor. For this reason, slavers frequently put their young female slaves into sewing apprenticeship, even sending them to Europe for a proper training. Much of the demand for sewing came from the slaves themselves, who were reported by European observers to go to great lengths to obtain fancy clothing for dances, and even for Sunday market (Moitt, 2001). Another fairly common occupation for the rural house slave was to sell or trade the slaver's extra produce, bringing some additional income to the slaver. Unfortunately for the female rural house slave, her children were not automatically given the same job as the mother, so they could very well be sent to the field gangs from a young age, whereas their mother kept working in the house (Morrissey, 1989). Indeed, the instability of their position must have been a constant worry of the plantation house slave, as they could easily lose their positions if the plantation was sold, the slaver returned to Europe, or a new manager took charge. The threat of sending the slave back to the field was a frequently used psychological weapon, which the slavers used to keep their house slave in place (Moitt, 2001).

There is general agreement that the work of the house slave was less physically stressful than that of the field slave in the plantations (Gaspar, 1993; Geggus, 1993; Higman, 1984). At the same time, because house-work did not produce as much income as fieldwork, it was commonly reserved for partially handicapped slaves or for mistresses of the White elite (Dunn, 1993; Stinchcombe, 1995). Gaspar (1993) indicates that although household-associated work might have been less physically demanding, it might have been more psychologically stressful because the slave was under the constant supervision and whims of the slavers. Such close surveillance might be the reason for the generally lower fertility of house slaves, since they would have been unable to establish relations such as those of plantation slaves. In the French Antilles, there is actually evidence of slavers refusing requests from their house slave to contract marriage so that she stayed in the slavers' house 24 hours a day (Moitt, 2001). Of course, if the house slave had steady sexual relations with the owner, her fertility was not impaired (Higman, 1984). Another negative aspect of serving in the slaver's house was that the house slave was "on call" constantly, including Sundays, whereas the field slave could count on at least Sunday as a day of rest (Moitt, 2001).

Although some slaves in the urban setting had other occupations besides that of house servant, their main occupation was to serve in the house of the owner (Higman, 1984). Slaves in an urban center had more freedom than did those in a plantation, since they were engaged in purchasing food in the market, and other economic activities. Also, they were likely to have a better diet, even if they only ate their masters' leftovers, and to have better clothing. Stinchcombe (1994) notes that the urban slave was much more likely to achieve manumission than was the plantation slave. Higman (1984) indicates that, all in all, morbidity of house slaves, whether urban or rural, was lower than that of the field slaves.

Higman (1984) notes that in British colony towns the sex ratio of slaves was closer to 1:1, as females were more sought-after for housework. He also mentions that a greater proportion of babies were born of European fathers to female slaves. Thus, the slave population in town had a greater proportion of New World-born slaves than did that of the plantations. This was in part a result of the fact that sometimes the house slaves were actually employed as prostitutes in their owners' inns for the latter's profit (Higman, 1984; Shepherd, 2002). Also, since many of the house servants were engaged in sexual relations with their masters, and thus produced Colored or Creole offspring who were frequently manumitted by their father, a large group of freed New World-born slaves or Colored individuals emerged in the towns (Hyam, 1990; Morrissey, 1989; Stinchcombe, 1994). Indeed, most African slaves who were manumitted had been engaged in long-term relations with their slavers, and most New World-born slaves who were manumitted were the offspring of these unions (Morrissey, 1989). As O'Neal (2001) notes, although most sexual liaisons between White men and slave women were probably not consensual, at least some were, and allowed the female and her offspring to become free and to accumulate some wealth. But these were not the only close affectionate relations between slaver and slave. Moitt (2001) tells of the tender regard of a slave woman for the woman of whom she was the wet nurse and minder. When this woman moved to France, her mother, the slaver, wrote that the slave asked about the daughter, and even sent her presents made by the slave.

By the early 1800s and until emancipation, a new economic arrangement became very common among urban house slaves and their slavers; namely, that the slave would hire himself/herself out and pay the slaver a monthly or weekly fee. These slaves had much freedom of movement and independence from their slavers, being in charge of supplying their own food, housing, clothing, etc. If males, these slaves tended to have particular skills such as masonry, carpentry, etc., which made them useful to many urban households. If females, the job for which they could compete was most likely prostitution, which of course put them in danger of disease and brutal physical abuse (Moitt, 2001; Shepherd, 2002).

The advantage of hiring out for the slaver was of course that s/he would maintain ownership of the slave, with the possibility of selling him/her, while being relieved of his/her day-to-day care. It seems that whereas in most of the British colonies the practice of self-hiring was a feature of the later period of slavery, in the Bahamas it was established much earlier. But in all areas of the urban Caribbean towards the time of abolition, many slaves had achieved much independence from their slavers, and had become their own managers. For some, their profits were large enough to be able to buy their own freedom (Cateau, 2002).

### 1.8    Manumission, slave uprisings, and abolition

It is noteworthy that manumissions in the plantations were not so rare during hard economic times for the slaver, who actually saw manumission as an effective way of getting himself rid of the burden of slaves. Similarly, during prosperous economic times, slaves who were able to hire themselves out to other slavers could accumulate enough wealth to purchase their freedom (Morrissey, 1989). A discussion of the abolition legal process is certainly outside the scope of this book. Suffice it to say that the abolition movements within the European centers and in the colonies were complex and not even connected with each other. For example, after a bloody rebellion in Barbados, in which 144 slaves were executed and more than 100 deported to Honduras, Mr. William Wilberforce, a well-known abolitionist, denied that he ever advocated immediate emancipation, but rather abolition of the slave trade followed by amelioration of the working conditions in the colonies, with ultimate emancipation (Craton, 1993). Curtin (1969) discusses the slow process of abolition, started in Denmark in 1805; Bah (1993) discusses the economic reasons behind the abolitionist movement. Rawley (1981) focuses his discussion on the abolition and counter-abolition movements as they coexisted in London, particularly among the merchants beginning at the latter part of the 1700s. Scott (1985) discusses abolition in Cuba. Drescher (1985) looks at abolition within the evolution of capitalism and the growth of British industrialism. A review of the post-1800s slave trade centered in Brazil is also outside of the scope of this book (Klein, 1978).

Most books on the history of the Caribbean slavery include sections on the uprising of slaves (McGowan, 2002), and the reader is directed to the many sources listed in this chapter for information on them. In the opinion of Shepherd (2002), much of the attention on the slave rebellions has been centered upon the male slaves, who took up the arms. But women slaves had an active role in everyday resistance to their situation, in their manner of speech and in their sabotaging of work as well as in the armed struggles (Morrissey, 1989). In reality, given that women slaves had basically the same jobs as male slaves in the field, it is not surprising that both genders took rather similar roles in the resistance movement. Indeed, women were actively involved in the armed struggle throughout the French Caribbean, having demonstrated unusual strength of character in the face of torture and death. Women also supported – in a less radical manner – armed confrontations, as is evident in the old "lame" woman who tried to fool a White patrol into eating poisoned food. This example is not so unique, as poisoning, being difficult to detect, appears to have been directed to the European slavers, to slaves who were favored by the slavers, and even to farm animals (Moitt, 2001). Women continued to have a very active role and voice in the post-emancipation period, up until today, when they continue to work towards the improvement of their lives and those of their families (Shepherd, 2002).

In the end, as Craton (1993) notes so well, abolition together with the processes of creolization and Christianization produced a hard-working, thrifty, long-suffering, and only nominally free working class made up of the former slaves and their descendants. This was much to the taste of the Europeans in the colonies and in the European centers.

### 1.9    Conclusion

This chapter establishes the framework upon which the rest of the book is constructed. We started by defining the geographical area to be covered, and discussed the trans-Atlantic trade of slaves. The health and disease loads of the slaves during the crossing and in the Caribbean under slavery were discussed.

By the time of the abolition of slavery, the genetic make-up of the Caribbean had been transformed dramatically from what it was at the beginning of the European invasion. A great number of Africans had been brought to the Caribbean, and radically transformed the region.

Anybody who is cognizant of the literature on African slavery in the Caribbean will have noticed that in this chapter we have not included a section on the methods of torture and execution of African slaves, which is usually included in books about African slaves. Instead, in this chapter we have focused on the dismal nutritional and health status of the slaves, which resulted in an abnormal demographic structure, not seen under any normal human conditions. It is almost unbearable to think that besides the terrible nutrition and living conditions of the slaves, they were still tortured and executed in most sadistic manners. The literature cited in this chapter is full of descriptions of these acts, and it was not necessary to repeat them here. The rest of this book concerns itself with the health, population genetics, and demography of the descendents of these slaves.

# 2 Obesity, hypertension, and non-insulin-dependent diabetes in Afro-Caribbean populations: an evolutionary overview

The focus of this chapter is on hypertension, obesity, and type-II diabetes and not on broader cardiovascular disease, which includes heart disease and stroke. Given that these three conditions are the major contributors to cardiovascular disease, and given that they have been researched separately by numerous authors, they seem a better target for this chapter than the more broadly defined entity of cardiovascular disease.

Although it might seem that three clinical entities (hypertension, obesity, and non-insulin-dependent diabetes) do not merit an entire chapter, these three clinical entities do. Indeed, the literature on them is so large that the chapter will focus more on theoretical discussions rather than on research communications on frequencies of these conditions. By necessity, the material reviewed here will include Afro-USA, Afro-Brazilian, and Afro-UK populations, since the literature on them is large. Afro-USA populations will be referred to in this manner, because the more usual term in the United States, "African-Americans," is misleading, as it could well refer to African-derived groups in the entire American continent, with the Caribbean, broadly defined, included.

## 2.1 A brief description of the conditions

In this section, we will acquaint the reader with clinical definitions of obesity, hypertension, and type-II diabetes. The review will not consider clinical recommendations on the treatment of these conditions.

### 2.1.1 Hypertension

Hypertension, or high blood pressure, is a condition of complex etiology which results in high pressure being applied to the inside wall of arteries with many deleterious consequences. Under normal situations, the heart beats to push blood out into the arteries and relaxes to fill with blood again. When the heart beats, the blood pressure is called systolic, and when the heart relaxes, it is called diastolic. Thus, measures of blood pressure are provided in two numbers, the first one being the systolic pressure and the second one the diastolic pressure. These measures are reported as, for example, 120/80 mmHg (millimeters of mercury). Blood pressure is divided into the following categories: normal is less than 120/80 mmHg, pre-hypertension is 120–9/80–9 mmHg, stage 1 hypertension is 140–59/90–9 mmHg, and stage 2 hypertension is 160–79/100–9 mmHg (Groer, 2001; Rizzo and Odle, 2003).

If the blood flows with high pressure, the arterial walls thicken and harden, becoming less flexible and causing the arterial space to narrow. As a result of the loss of flexibility of the arteries, fats and cholesterol accumulate on the inside walls, contributing to an even narrower space. When the arteries become narrower, many problems follow: blood clots might get trapped because they are unable to pass and block the flow of blood. In general, if blood flow is restricted, any number of organs can be affected by the lack of oxygen resulting from reduced blood flow. In particular, if this happens in the brain, a stroke can result. If this happens in the arteries leading to the kidneys, the latter will be unable to remove ever-accumulating waste from the body and will eventually fail. Particularly damaging for hypertension is the rise in salt and water which occurs as a result of poor kidney function. Indeed, about a quarter of all dialysis patients deteriorate to that condition because of hypertension. The heart itself is strongly affected by hypertension, as it needs to pump harder to get the blood through the ever-narrowing arterial passages. Due to this extra workload, the heart muscle stretches and thickens, not allowing it to pump enough blood, and possibly resulting in heart failure (Hall, 2003; Rizzo and Odle, 2003).

The hardening of the arteries as described above is properly called arteriosclerosis, and just like hypertension it has a complex etiology. Although arteriosclerosis is a clinical problem in its own right, its contribution to high blood pressure is such that the latter cannot be understood without the former. Blood pressure associated with arteriosclerosis and without other clear causes is called primary or essential hypertension, and it is the pathology found in about 90% of all hypertensive patients (Groer, 2001). Secondary hypertension results from other clearly established pathological situations, such as kidney disorders, Cushing's syndrome, and tumors of the pituitary. Hall (2003) provides an excellent review of hypertension secondary to kidney malfunction.

The genetic bases of essential hypertension have been researched, and continue to be an important line of work in the understanding of the condition (Gloer, 2001; Lifton, 1996, 1997). For example, among the Pima Indians, a particular allele has been shown to be associated with hypertension, although the effect of the gene is modified by environmental influences (Franks *et al.*, 2004).

Hypertension is known to have several risk factors, namely obesity, inactivity, age over 60, use of oral contraceptives, heavy alcohol use, cigarette smoking, low birth weight, stress, and salt sensitivity. Also frequently cited in several health advisories is "race" or "ethnic background." Evolutionary reasons for the higher hypertension rates found in some (though not all) African and African-derived groups will be discussed later in the chapter. Given that all human populations are experiencing increased longevity, it is to be expected that the proportion affected by hypertension in any human group is only likely to increase.

There is no cure for hypertension, but there are effective treatments, which improve life quality even in the very elderly patient (Kaplan, 2001). However, given that many of the risk factors of hypertension are associated with a specific lifestyle, the usual first attempts towards ameliorating hypertension involve changes in diet, stress levels, alcohol and nicotine consumption, and weight control (Rizzo and Odle, 2003). Prevention itself is being emphasized by many practitioners, particularly in patients with close hypertensive relatives. A risk factor that could be easily addressed is low birth weight, which is clearly associated with hypertension, diabetes, obesity, and coronary disease later in life (Ala *et al.*, 2004). Given that most cases of low birth weight are due to low socioeconomic status of the mother and maternal behaviors such as smoking and drinking alcohol during pregnancy, low birth weight can be addressed by effective prenatal care and education. A not so easy-to-address preventive measure is control of obesity, which has become rampant throughout the world and is closely tied to hypertension (Kaplan, 2001). However, it should be obvious that limiting the consumption of foods that are high in fat and sodium (such as much of the so-called fast foods, and potato chips) will address both obesity and hypertension concerns. Equally effective towards the amelioration of both conditions is an increase in physical activity.

### 2.1.2  *Obesity*

Obesity is best defined as excess stored body fat to the extent that it becomes a morbid condition. It has been well established that obesity is associated with degenerative joint disease, respiratory disorders, certain cancers, and obstetric complications, and also with hypertension, diabetes, and cardiovascular disease. Thus obesity is a condition which may impair a person's health on many levels (Anderson and Akanji, 1994).

The most commonly used tool to measure obesity is the body mass index (BMI), as it is a general measure of weight and size. It is computed by dividing body weight in kilograms by height in meters squared. Thus

$$\text{BMI} = \frac{\text{Weight}}{(\text{Height})^2}$$

(Seidell, 2001). According to the World Health Organization (WHO), the normal range for BMI is between 18.4 and 24.9 kg/m$^2$, with BMI values under 18.5 kg/m$^2$ being considered underweight. It seems that the healthiest range for BMI is between 20 and 22 kg/m$^2$. Thus, anything over or equal to a BMI of 25 kg/m$^2$ is considered overweight. After this cut-off point there are several categories of obesity, namely pre-obese (25–29.9 kg/m$^2$), obese class I (30–34.9 kg/m$^2$), obese class II (35–39.9 kg/m$^2$), and obese class III ($\geq$40 kg/m$^2$). The widespread use of BMI to measure body weight is not without criticism. It has been argued that better approaches towards the measurement of obesity are abdominal fat distribution or skinfold-thickness measures, but these are much more onerous measures in field studies than are the simple anthropometrics required for the computation of BMI. Moreover, data on the BMI are available for many populations, facilitating comparisons across groups and across different time periods. Indeed, at the time of writing, the WHO is compiling a global database on BMI, which can be found at www.who. int/nut/db_bmi.htm.

Whether the BMI is a valid measuring tool across populations with different body builds has also been questioned, as some heavily muscled populations will have a high BMI without being overweight because their weight reflects more muscle than fat mass (Antipatis and Gill, 2001). In addition, it has been proposed that Asian populations have higher health risks at lower BMI values than do other populations, so for the former lower cut-off points for obesity have been advocated (Seidell, 2001).

Obesity is probably best seen as a morbid state caused by an energy imbalance in which too much energy is consumed and not enough energy is spent. The cause of this imbalance is the subject of much research. For example, recent work has uncovered a few human monogenic obesity syndromes and has shown that in some cases obesity can be tied to a pathogenic mutation (Farooqi and O'Rahilly, 2004). It has been suggested that elevated plasma levels of leptin, a hormone which is secreted by fat cells and affects the control of energy balance, might result in obesity (Fulton and Kohl, 1999). Another hormone related to energy and appetite balances, known as gherlin, has a role in the pathophysiology of human fat deposits and has been proposed to be a contributor to obesity (del Giudice *et al.*, 2004). It has also been suggested that the melanocortin-4 receptor (MC4R) is an important regulator of food intake and energy homeostasis and that a mutation in this receptor is responsible for severe obesity (Donohoue *et al.*, 2003).

Although there are strong indications that obesity may have a genetic basis (Comuzzie *et al.*, 2001), the alarming rate at which obesity has increased is doubtless tied to environmental changes. A cursory search of health advisories published by organizations such as the WHO and Pan American Health Organization (PAHO) will confirm that obesity is becoming a major health problem in most of the world (Antipatis and Gill, 2001). The Caribbean, as will be seen below, is no exception (Fraser, 2003; Teelucksingh, 2003).

### 2.1.3   Diabetes

There are many Internet resources on this disease. Two very helpful sites were those of the American Diabetic Association (www.diabetes.org/home.jsp) and the Endocrine Disorders and Surgery group (www.endocrineweb.com/diabetes/index.html).

Diabetes is probably best understood as a disease of altered fuel metabolism. There are two major forms of the disease, although only one of them is truly of interest to us, as it is related to the same environmental changes that are linked to the obesity and hypertension worldwide epidemic (Chaufan, 2004). Type-I diabetes used to be called insulin-dependent diabetes mellitus (IDDM) or juvenile-onset diabetes. This form of the disease is typically associated with an autoimmune destruction of specialized cells in the pancreas and is commonly developed in the teenage or early-adult years. The disease has been proposed to have a genetic basis, as individuals with a specific genetic make-up (more clearly, specific human leukocyte antigen [HLA] haplotypes), after having been infected by some pathogens, develop the disease. If the pathogen "mimics" the genetic make-up of the host, then an immune reaction of the host would attack both pathogen and self-cells, resulting in an autoimmune disease which destroys the pancreatic cells. Other forms of type-I diabetes, however, are not associated with autoimmune responses. Most patients with type-I diabetes need to take insulin to remain healthy (Clark, 2004; Hart, 2001).

Type-II diabetes used to be called non-insulin-dependent diabetes mellitus (NIDDM) or adult-onset diabetes, and it is the form of diabetes of interest to us. It is the form found in at least 80% of all diabetes cases, and it is usually diagnosed in adulthood. Many patients are able to control their type-II diabetes with lifestyle changes (Clark, 2004; Hart, 2001). Lindgren and Hirschhorn (2001) and van Tilburg *et al.* (2001) review the genetics of type-II diabetes. To understand the disease, it is best to review how a healthy human body maintains its sugar levels in a stable manner.

Glucose is a simple monosaccharide sugar, and it is used as a source of energy in animals and plants. In humans, the levels of glucose must be maintained within a narrow range (70–110 mg/dl; milligrams of glucose in 100 milliliters of blood), or else hypo- (too little glucose) or hyperglycemia (too much glucose) might result. This specific range of glucose levels is important for the proper functioning of the entire body but particularly for the central nervous system (Clark, 2004; Fulton and Kohl, 1999; Hart, 2001). There are two hormones which regulate the levels of glucose: insulin and glucagon. Both of them are released by pancreatic cells, hence the development of type-I diabetes in subjects whose pancreatic cells are destroyed through an autoimmune response (see German, 2004 for an update on research into pancreatic cell replacement). The cells involved in the production of insulin and glucagon are specialized pancreatic cells which are found in clusters and are referred to as islets, or islets of Langerhans. These cells are broadly divided into α- and β-cells, depending on which hormone they secrete, which they do directly into the bloodstream. Of these two hormones, insulin is the one primarily involved in diabetes, being produced by the β islet cells. When insulin is released as a response to a high level of glucose, it binds to insulin receptors on the membranes of liver, muscle, and fat cells. Here it promotes glucose uptake into the cells (thus decreasing glucose levels in the bloodstream), and it prevents the liver from making new glucose and encourages the storage of glucose in muscle and the liver in the form of glycogen. The glucose taken into the fat cells aids in fat storage. Once the glucose level is brought down by this reaction, the β-cells decrease their release of insulin. Glucagon, in contrast, is released by the α islet cells as a response to low levels of glucose, and increases glucose levels by making the liver release its stored glucose and by making muscle produce glucose by breaking down proteins. There are other hormones involved in the maintenance of an acceptable glucose level, such as the catecholamine and glucocorticoid hormones; the most active of the latter is cortisol, which elevates blood glucose. Cortisol is of interest to us as it is found in elevated levels during periods of stress, and stress is one of the commonly noted environmental risk factors for obesity, hypertension, and diabetes. Indeed, cortisol appears to influence the accumulation of adipose tissue, especially deep abdominal fat (Fulton and Kohl, 1999; Hart, 2001).

Type-II diabetes is due to both insulin resistance and lowered insulin production (as opposed to the total lack of insulin seen in type-I diabetes). Low insulin production is due to insulin resistance, β-cell dysfunction, lowered numbers of functioning β-cells, "exhaustion" of the β-cells because they were producing too much insulin (which is not effective because of insulin resistance), or a combination of these factors. Insulin resistance is a condition in which the cells that are the target of insulin function do not respond to adequate or even high levels of insulin. Given that insulin is a vasodilator, insulin-resistant individuals might have decreased insulin delivery to the skeletal and muscle tissues, which are insulin-sensitive, resulting in a decreased absorption of glucose in these tissues. As a result, the body stores less glucose and fat while the levels of glucose in the bloodstream rise, triggering an even higher insulin response and ultimately contributing to β-cell exhaustion. Since one of the tasks of insulin is to prevent endogenous production of glucose, and diabetic patients do not have an effective insulin response, they have an increased production of glucose by the liver and higher levels of lipolysis, which provides fatty acids for use by the central nervous system in the absence of usable glucose. As a result of the breakdown of lipids, ketones are produced as a by-product. But since they are toxic for the patient, the body tries to remove them by increased urination (diuresis), causing the patient to be dehydrated while depleting her/him of sodium (Clark, 2004).

Type-II diabetic patients are frequently diagnosed when the disease has done much damage; that is, overt symptoms are not recognized until the disease has progressed and the β-cells are nearly exhausted. Some patients might overlook symptoms such as tiredness, yeast infections, increased urination, and dehydration, and might seek a doctor when more severe symptoms are apparent, such as severe weight loss due to the body's inability to store glucose. A frequently diagnosed complication seen in conjunction with diabetes is arteriosclerosis, as the patient has increased lipid levels and lipoproteins, which are more likely to adhere to the arterial walls. Evidently, this condition will make the diabetic patient more likely to suffer from hypertension (Hart, 2001).

As diabetes progresses, microvascular complications are seen in some patients, due to the thickening of the capillary-wall membranes, resulting in an impairment of motor and sensory function of the feet, leading to injuries, burns, calluses, etc., and ultimately resulting in amputation (Clark, 2004; Fulton and Kohl, 1999). A similar mechanism leads to diabetes-induced blindness (proliferative retinopathy): new blood vessels proliferate around the retina and ultimately cause blindness. Another frequent sequela of diabetes is kidney malfunction, as the kidneys are being taxed by the extra effort to secrete ketones from the body through increased urination.

Type-II diabetes is a complex disease with several risk factors, primarily aging, obesity (as many as 90% of diabetic patients are overweight), and physical inactivity. The disease appears to run in families, but to what extent this is due to a genetic propensity or to a common environment is not clear. Obesity and physical inactivity as risk factors deserve some coverage, not only because they are the strongest risk factors, but also because they are better documented. For example, the data on the contribution of macronutrients (such as fiber and carbohydrates) and micronutrients (such as zinc and vitamin E) to the development of diabetes are equivocal (Fulton and Kohl, 1999). The prevalence rates of type-II diabetes in different populations will be discussed below.

Although so many diabetic patients are obese, obesity itself is neither necessary nor sufficient for the development of diabetes. Perhaps more important is the distribution of body fat, as insulin resistance has been shown to be positively correlated with abdominal or visceral obesity. Weight gain itself, whether in a previously non-obese or obese patient, appears to be linked to diabetes as well. The weakest point of the association between type-II diabetes and obesity is the precise physiological mechanism that predisposes obese patients to diabetes, a mechanism that still remains elusive (Fulton and Kohl, 1999).

Physical inactivity as a risk factor for type-II diabetes is more difficult to study than is obesity, as the former is measured mostly with self-reports instead of a precise anthropometric tool such as the BMI. The physiological mechanism for the association between inactivity and diabetes, however, is better understood than is that between obesity and diabetes: when an individual exercises, their carbohydrate metabolism and glucose tolerance are affected. As a result of long-term physical activity, the body has an increased sensitivity to insulin, thus helping to prevent the onset of diabetes. Physical inactivity as a risk factor for diabetes is independent of age and obesity, and is therefore stressed for preventive and clinical management purposes (Fulton and Kohl, 1999).

## 2.2    Obesity, hypertension, diabetes, and globalization

There are several sources that have explored how the economic capitalist expansion of the late twentieth century affected health, sources that provide a larger overview of this issue than will be given here. Thus the reader is referred to Beaglehole and Bonita (2004), Castro and Singer (2004), Fort *et al.* (2004), Lee *et al.* (2002), McMurray and Smith (2001), and Petchesky (2003). Although the term globalization is frequently used in the media and even in everyday parlance, it refers to such a large process that a succinct definition is not easy to find. In this book, we are using the term globalization to mean the process by which most of the  poor/underdeveloped/developing/peripheral/traditional/low-income/ Third World areas have been enveloped in a worldwide capitalist market/cash economy, and the sociocultural, ideological, health, and demographic effects of this incorporation. Which term is most appropriate for these countries is not within the province of this book; the term underdeveloped will be used.

The reason this process is referred to as global as opposed to international is that it is independent of the territorial or political boundaries of polities; it supersedes the political entities of states in terms of the seriousness of the problems and the solutions needed to address such problems. In other words, globalization has made political boundaries more "porous," as capitalism and its ideology require a movable workforce (which brings its own pathogens) and an international consumer market (Buse *et al.*, 2002; Petchesky, 2003). Human groups that in the past were separated due to geographical or cultural/ideological differences are becoming closer. Moreover, the pace at which these previously separated cultures become part of a global entity is very rapid, so that the socioeconomic milieu of health has changed almost instantaneously in many communities (Lee *et al.*, 2002). Another reason why health changes are global is the degree of environmental devastation associated with industrialization. Environmental concerns cannot be discussed on a country-by-country basis any longer, given that numerous rivers and forests, and, of course, the air cross political boundaries. According to Beaglehole and Bonita (2004), the most important public health hazard faced by our species is the global damage caused to the ecology of the planet, more important to health than personal behavior or genetic make-up. An interesting link between nutrition/health and ecology is the environmental degradation caused by cattle-raising, an economic activity which decreases biodiversity (forests are cut down to provide pasture land for the cattle) and produces a food that has been linked to coronary heart disease (Beaglehole and Bonita, 2004).

Under the globalization process, peripheral/non-industrialized countries have become more and more active participants in the world market economy, whether they have become industrialized or not. For example, farmers who raise cash crops and abandon subsistence agriculture are dependent on cash for purchasing their food. Although their work is not industrial, they are part of a worldwide industrialized system of agriculture. Indeed, they are likely to purchase a packaged, processed, product based on the very crops they raised. Besides participating in a cash universal economy, these same farmers are being bombarded with a consumer ideology which is associated with the world cash economy, one that makes them consumers of products which they can only get with cash. In addition, the social and cultural milieu of countries undergoing globalization is affected, as individuals migrate from rural to urban areas seeking better jobs, thus affecting traditional family structures and social roles, as well as traditional forms of social control and allegiance (Petchesky, 2003). Equally important concerning health, is the disappearance of traditional ways of handling illness, not only in terms of non-biomedical knowledge, but also in terms of social support for the ill (Buse *et al.*, 2002; Gish, 2004). Therefore, the term globalization is all-encompassing and includes economic, sociocultural, and ideological changes which affect a community's health, broadly defined (McMurray and Smith, 2001).

We differentiate the process of globalization from the industrialization process itself, which affected societies such as the USA, Western Europe, Korea, Taiwan, and Japan before globalization affected the underdeveloped countries. As a result, industrialized countries dealt with the rise of obesity, hypertension, and diabetes before the underdeveloped groups. Because industrialized countries are found in the western and eastern hemispheres, we do not see it as proper to refer to them as "western," as that would obviously exclude Japan, one of the most industrialized countries. At the same time, equating industrialized with western countries overlooks the fact that most of the countries of Latin America, whose culture and languages are western and were derived from their Western European colonizers, are not industrialized. For countries that have been called western/industrialized/rich/advanced/developed/core, we will use the term industrialized.

All indications are that, cross-culturally, a plump, non-obese, ideal of beauty is held over that of a very skinny body (McMurray and Smith, 2001). It is thus somehow ironic that by the mid 1900s, first in industrialized then in underdeveloped countries, the idea of beauty switched towards one of being skinny when the rates of obesity, hypertension, and diabetes increased at alarming rates (Chaufan 2004).

Some of the groups that first experienced rapid rises in these three conditions were migrant groups throughout the world. Recently Himmelgreen and colleagues (2004) have shown that the prevalence rate of obesity among women born in Puerto Rico who have migrated to the USA is positively correlated with length of time in the latter. The mean BMI of these women is perhaps more telling: for women who have been in the USA for 2 years or less the mean BMI is just over 25 kg/m$^2$, whereas it is more than 28 kg/m$^2$ for women who have been in the USA for 10 years or more. In a similar fashion, rises in hypertension rates and stress levels have been reported in other migrant groups (Gage, 2000). Indeed, the question as to whether migrants are better off than are their families who do not migrate is of great interest to human biologists. Although the answer to this question is probably specific to each community, there is no doubt that migrants from a more traditional area who move into an industrialized/cash-economy environment experience rapid rises in obesity, hypertension, diabetes, and stress.

In non-migrant, underdeveloped groups it has been shown that, during the initial stages of modernization, the middle and upper classes adopt the risk behaviors associated with hypertension, obesity, and diabetes, only to be followed by the lower classes (Seidell, 2001). These risk behaviors include not only nutritional and physical activity changes, but also smoking, drinking, and experiencing stress and anxiety (Ala *et al.*, 2004; Beaglehole and Bonita, 2004; McMurray and Smith, 2001). In India and China, different segments of the society experience both over- and under-nutrition (Antipatis and Gill, 2001; Seidell, 2001). Thus, it seems that initially obesity and its accompanying diseases are seen as a sign of wealth, but later, whether by the adoption of western standards of beauty or by the availability of better medical treatment, the higher classes control their obesity problem, whereas the poor become more and more obese (Anderson and Akanji, 1994).

McMurray and Smith (2001) propose that globalization of capitalism has lead to the marginalization of large segments of humans into newly disadvantaged positions, which leads them to engage in unhealthy lifestyles, while having fewer medical resources. Bezruchka and Mercer (2004) review the evidence that socioeconomic inequality is growing worldwide, and that this trend can be tied to globalization. Lack of medical resources for poor people is due to the higher expenses of biomedical services within a cash economy and also to recent decisions to privatize traditionally government-subsidized services as a result of pressures from the World Bank and the World Trade Organization, for example (Fort, 2004; Petchesky, 2003). In these conditions, the poor cannot "choose" to get expensive medical treatment, as they simply cannot afford it (Chaufan, 2004). For example, Towghi (2004) notes that in Pakistan the recent introduction of biomedicine and expensive scientific technology has not benefited the majority of the people.

Another reason why medical costs have risen and fewer medical options are open to populations of low socioeconomic status is the predominance of biomedicine tied to capitalist globalization and the disappearance of traditional healing methods. Although in most of the world people do rely to some extent on home remedies, non-western healers are being replaced by doctors at a much higher cost to the consumer (Towghi, 2004). Wherever non-biomedical approaches to health are used, they are frequently in conflict with biomedicine, often jeopardizing the health of the patient (Davis-Floyd, 2004). Evidently, the disappearance of these traditional health alternatives is a great loss to the local culture, but it is obviously part of the globalized ideology which accompanies economic globalization. Of course, this trend is not recent but can be traced to the European Imperialistic expansion which started in the fifteenth century (Gish, 2004).

McMurray and Smith (2001) also note that the fragmentation of health profiles in countries which are being globalized reflects the "piecemeal" health transitions of these countries, different from that experienced by the industrialized countries a few decades before. Given that globalization is a complex and multifaceted process we should not be surprised that its effect on the health of different segments of the globalized group differs, depending not only on socioeconomic status but also on age, ethnicity, gender, etc. (Buse *et al.*, 2002; Seidell, 2001). Petchesky (2003) looks at the effects of globalization on women's health by considering how the global process affects health within the context of gender and human rights. The importance of socioeconomic status as a risk factor for hypertension is obvious in Ala *et al.*'s study (2004) in an urban area of Brazil, in which hypertension rates varied significantly according to socioeconomic status within one geographically restricted sample.

The importance of the environment as a contributor to obesity, hypertension, and diabetes risk factors is obvious when upwardly mobile individuals are compared with those who remain in a low socioeconomic situation for their entire life, as the risk factors diminish in the former but remain high in the latter. At the same time, the importance of these risk factors is lowest in those individuals with the high socioeconomic status. Recently, in Trinidad and Tobago an inverse relation between income and hypertension was reported (Gulliford *et al.*, 2004). Lynch (2001) notes that it is accurate to make the broad statement that individuals with lower socioeconomic status have poorer psychosocial and behavior risk factors that contribute to greater rates of obesity, hypertension, and diabetes. This is more likely due to the fact that, with modernization, the establishment of a cash economy, and the abandonment of traditional food sources the least expensive foods are frequently highly refined and high in calories (Himmelgreen *et al.*, 2000). Thus, although it could be argued that poor people are not doing "their part" to improve their health because they keep eating unhealthy foods, they probably have no other option but eating such foods. These deleterious health conditions should be understood as maladaptive responses to adverse socioeconomic conditions, which are a result of the wide socioeconomic structure under which these individuals live. The maladaptive behaviors and risk factors are multifaceted, and include smoking, a sedentary lifestyle, poor nutrition, and even stress and depression. Several authors (Beaglehole and Bonita, 2004; Chaufan, 2004; Lee *et al.*, 2002) propose that individual lifestyle choices, particularly those that are deleterious, should be seen within the context of a globalized capitalist system, in which the economic and social forces supported by a consumer ideology lead the individual to make poor choices and to live in a condition that is unhealthy. For example, Fort (2004) notes that in much of the non-industrialized world the water supply is not clean, whereas canned sodas are readily available for consumption. It is not enough to blame the individuals for choosing soda. Instead, we should ask what the international forces are that are making such a deleterious product available while clean water is not. At the same time, we should ask why in industrialized countries such as the USA tobacco and alcohol advertising has been curtailed, whereas it is actively promoted in underdeveloped countries, where smoking and alcoholism are on the rise, with their accompanying health and social ill consequences (Beaglehole and Bonita, 2004). Of course, if the communities dealing with rising rates of obesity do not see being fat as a problem but as a sign of wealth, they are unlikely to control it (McMurray and Smith, 2001). The bottom line is that obesity, hypertension, and diabetes, diseases which have been called diseases of prosperity, will be disproportionably suffered by the poor in the years to follow (Chaufan, 2004; Seidell, 2001).

Lynch (2001) also argues that the effect of these risk factors on individuals of poor socioeconomic status should be seen as operating throughout their entire lifespan, beginning with the environment in utero. As will be seen below, the rapid rises in diabetes among recently modernizing

populations has been explained by the undernutrition of these populations in utero and in early childhood. But this association actually holds
for obesity and hypertension as well as for diabetes. Indeed, Barker *et al.*
(1982) propose that undernutrition in utero and infancy has a great
potential for resulting in high frequencies of hypertension, diabetes, and
obesity, and of cardiovascular disease in general. Thus, the high frequencies of these conditions in poor-socioeconomic-status segments of industrialized or modernizing communities could very well result from an
exposure to undernutrition in prenatal and neonatal life, but also from
a lifelong environment associated with risk factors for these diseases (Ala
*et al.*, 2004).

These are broad generalizations about the impact of a modernized
lifestyle on obesity, hypertension, and diabetes rates that do not apply
equally to all countries: there are very important exceptions to these
generalizations. For example, different industrialized countries have different rates of obesity, with 25% of females being obese in the USA, and
less than 3% of adults being obese in Japan. At the same time, while Japan
is the industrialized country with the highest life expectancy, it also has
the highest rate of smoking (Bezruchka and Mercer, 2004). However, the
general statement that recently modernized regions are experiencing
alarming rates of these three conditions is true in most cases, with glaring
examples such as those of the indigenous populations of Melanesia,
Polynesia, and Micronesia, where as many as 75% of women and 50%
of males in urban Samoa were classified as obese in the early 1990s
(Antipatis and Gill, 2001), or the Pima Indians, whose adult females have
rates of diabetes close to 50% (McDermott, 1998; Zimmet *et al.*, 2001).

What exactly about the lifestyle brought about by modernization contributes to the increase in obesity, hypertension, and diabetes is not so
obvious, as it might be a combination of factors. Frequently cited is the
lack of exercise associated with modernization (Beaglehole and Bonita,
2004). Whereas many rural communities incorporate physical exercise in
their daily routine, urban economies are notorious for a lack of exercise
and a sedentary lifestyle. Surely, for individuals who must work in sedentary jobs, such as in an office, few opportunities are available for physical
activities. The lack of outdoor recreation and the increased time spent in
front of the television have been blamed for the rise in childhood obesity
(Seidell, 2001). An increasingly sedentary lifestyle has been seen even in
traditionally active segments of industrial countries, such as rural areas,
or in agricultural communities in underdeveloped countries. For example,
concomitant with a greater reliance on the automobile, a rise in obesity
has been seen in the USA rural populations, who are not forced to exert

themselves to engage in social activities with neighbors, but can drive (Sobal, 2001). In underdeveloped agricultural areas, more and more farming is being mechanized, as farmers become economically dependent on banks for loans to buy expensive equipment to allow them to increase their production; equipment that limits their physical exertion.

Another frequently cited contributor to the rise of obesity, hypertension, and diabetes in recently modernized populations is the stress associated with new expectations and the severing of traditional kin ties (Antipatis and Gill, 2001). Surely, as rural communities become modernized and young people migrate to the cities, the entire family structure begins to weaken. As a result of the decreased reliance on the wisdom of the elderly for advice and the decline in the social prestige of the elderly, more and more old individuals in a recently globalized area are left without the traditional familial support they would normally get, and, as a result, they have poorer health outcomes than did their forebears (McMurray and Smith, 2001). The young migrants who leave their home in search of better jobs are not so well off either, as it has been well established that migration is associated with heightened stress, depression, and hypertension (Ala *et al.*, 2004; Gage, 2000).

An obvious factor important in the worldwide rise of obesity, hypertension, and diabetes is the overabundance of foods rich in highly refined carbohydrates, sodium, and fats, often available in a prepackaged manner, which take away nutritional benefits from the food while adding extra calories and artificial colors and flavors (Seidell, 2001). The data showing that reduced sodium intake lowers hypertension are very strong (Kaplan, 2001). Yet, more and more people, particularly children, are eating sodium-loaded foods such as potato chips and other snacks (Beaglehole and Bonita, 2004). In a nutshell, modernization has brought with it an overabundance of foods that are rich in calories, and which have supplanted less refined, high-in-fiber foods which were usually produced with more effort, requiring more energy expenditure (Seidell, 2001; Sobal, 2001); hence the energy imbalance usually called obesity. The "unnaturalness" of the modernized lifestyle and its negative effects on health have been promulgated even in popular press books (Boaz, 2002).

In conclusion, obesity, hypertension, and diabetes have become a major health problem worldwide, one that has affected human populations in a rather predictable way (with some interesting exceptions, such as Japan). Obesity is the most obvious of the three problems, as it does not require clinical tests, as do the other two conditions. The process of industrialization in the industrialized countries was associated with a rise in these conditions, and when values, foods, lifestyle, food production, and consumption patterns were exported, the receiving groups experienced explosive levels of the three conditions. The entire lifestyle appears to conspire against people's health, bringing with it an overabundance of hypercaloric foods, a decrease in physical exertion and increased stress (Seidell, 2001). At first it is the higher classes that experience the increase in obesity, frequently side to side with high frequencies of undernutrition in poor segments of the community. But after some years the lower classes are the ones with the problem of obesity, as they are unable to afford healthy foods, and have been removed from a healthier lifestyle, whereas the higher classes adopt a better diet, increase their recreational physical activity, and even adopt western ideals of beauty.

Clearly all of these health problems should be understood within the context of a globalized capitalist economy, together with its social and ideological consequences (Beaglehole and Bonita, 2004). It is a sad commentary on the medical establishment that more economic resources are spent on understanding the genetic bases for these conditions then the environmental ones, particularly poverty (Chaufan, 2004).

### 2.3   An attempt to summarize epidemiological data from the Caribbean

Our interest in this chapter is to review the frequencies of hypertension, obesity, and diabetes in Afro-Caribbean groups and compare them with the frequencies in African and other African-derived groups. However, this is not as easy as it may seem. Firstly, a search of the data posted in websites such as those of the WHO (www.who.int/en/) or the PAHO (www.paho.org/default.htm) produces frequently disappointing results: numerous countries in both the Caribbean and Africa have rather incomplete statistics. Secondly, some countries report data divided by gender, by urbanization, and by age. Many do not. Thirdly, the definitions of hypertension, obesity, and diabetes seem to differ in virtually every country, making comparisons rather difficult. Finally, many countries do not collect their health measures by ethnicity. Thus, data from Central American countries cannot be used unless the document states that the groups are Afro-Central American. The tables in this chapter attempt to best summarize this body of data.

Table 2.1 shows the prevalence of hypertension in populations from Africa, the Caribbean, the UK, and the USA. Although the studies are not 100% comparable in terms of the age and gender of subjects or even in the definition of hypertension, the conclusion that Afro-USA populations

Table 2.1. *Hypertension prevalence rates in African and African-derived populations*

| Region | Country/population | Definition of hypertension | Gender | Age group (years) | Prevalence (%) | Source |
|---|---|---|---|---|---|---|
| Europe | Afro-Caribbeans in London | SBP >160 or taking medication | Males | Age-adjusted | 27.30 | Cruickshank *et al.* (2001a) |
| Europe | Afro-Caribbeans in London | SBP >160 or taking medication | Females | Age-adjusted | 29.00 | Cruickshank *et al.* (2001a) |
| North America | USA | SBP >140 | Males | 20–74 | 35.10 | www.cdc.gov/nchs/ products/ pubs/pubd/hus/ 03hustop.htm |
| North America | USA | SBP >140 | Females | 20–74 | 40.60 | www.cdc.gov/nchs/ products/ pubs/pubd/hus/ 03hustop.htm |
| Caribbean | Antigua and Barbuda | SBP >140 | Both | 20–39 | 1.00 | www.cvdinfobase.ca/ |
| Caribbean | Antigua and Barbuda | SBP >140 | Both | 40–64 | 13.00 | www.cvdinfobase.ca/ |
| Caribbean | Antigua and Barbuda | SBP >140 | Both | 65+ | 33.00 | www.cvdinfobase.ca/ |
| Caribbean | Bahamas | SBP >145 | Both | 21–87 | 32.30 | Halberstein and Davies (1984) |
| Caribbean | Barbados | SBP >160 | Males | Age-adjusted, 25+ | 18.00 | Cooper *et al.* (1997a) |
| Caribbean | Barbados | SBP >160 | Females | Age-adjusted, 25+ | 22.90 | Cooper *et al.* (1997a) |

| Region | Location | Definition | Group | Age | Value | Reference |
| --- | --- | --- | --- | --- | --- | --- |
| Caribbean | Barbados | SBP >160 | Males | 40–79 | 47.00 | Foster et al. (1993) |
| Caribbean | Barbados | SBP >160 | Females | 40–79 | 43.00 | Foster et al. (1993) |
| Caribbean | Cuba | SBP >140 or taking medication | Females | Adults, 15+ | 42.30 | Ordúñez-García et al. (1998) |
| Caribbean | Cuba | SBP >140 or taking medication | Males | Adults, 15+ | 51.40 | Ordúñez-García et al. (1998) |
| Caribbean | Grand Cayman | SBP >140 | Males | Adults, 21+ | 3.90 | Halberstein (1999) |
| Caribbean | Grand Cayman | SBP >140 | Females | Adults, 21+ | 7.70 | Halberstein (1999) |
| Caribbean | Grand Bahama | SBP >150 | Males | <20–64 | 27.10 | Moser et al. (1959) |
| Caribbean | Grand Bahama | SBP >150 | Females | <20–64 | 25.80 | Moser et al. (1959) |
| Caribbean | Guadeloupe | SBP >160 and DBP >95 | Males | 40–59 | 20.90 | Failde et al. (1996) |
| Caribbean | Guadeloupe | SBP >160 and DBP >95 | Females | 40–50 | 26.00 | Failde et al. (1996) |
| Caribbean | Jamaica | SBP >160 | Males | Age-adjusted, 25+ | 13.00 | Cooper et al. (1997a) |
| Caribbean | Jamaica | SBP >160 | Females | Age-adjusted, 25+ | 20.60 | Cooper et al. (1997a) |
| Caribbean | Jamaica | SBP >160 | Suburban males | 30–50 | 17.80 | Dressler et al. (1988) |
| Caribbean | Jamaica | SBP >160 | Suburban females | 30–50 | 15.10 | Dressler et al. (1988) |
| Caribbean | Jamaica | SBP >160 | Rural females | 45–55 | 33.80 | Miall et al. (1962) |
| Caribbean | Jamaica | SBP >160 | Urban females | 45–55 | 36.60 | Miall et al. (1962) |
| Caribbean | Jamaica | SBP >160 | Rural males | 45–55 | 16.80 | Miall et al. (1962) |
| Caribbean | Jamaica | SBP >160 | Urban males | 45–55 | 20.60 | Miall et al. (1962) |
| Caribbean | Limón, Costa Rica | SBP >160 | Both | 19–90 | 3.00 | Madrigal et al. (2004) |
| Caribbean | Nassau | SBP >150 | Males | <20–64 | 29.30 | Moser et al. (1959) |
| Caribbean | Nassau | SBP >150 | Females | <20–64 | 33.80 | Moser et al. (1959) |
| Caribbean | St. Kitts | SBP >160 | Male villagers | 40–9 | 20.70 | Schneckloth et al. (1962) |
| Caribbean | St. Kitts | SBP >160 | Female villagers | 40–9 | 40.70 | Schneckloth et al. (1962) |
| Caribbean | St. Lucia | SBP >160 | Males | 25–74 | 17.3 | www.cvdinfobase.ca/ |

Table 2.1. (cont.)

| Region | Country/population | Definition of hypertension | Gender | Age group (years) | Prevalence (%) | Source |
|---|---|---|---|---|---|---|
| Caribbean | St. Lucia | SBP >160 | Females | 25–74 | 24.7 | www.cvdinfobase.ca/ |
| Caribbean | St. Lucia | DBP >95 | NA | NA | 29.00 | Dressler (1984b) |
| Caribbean | St. Lucia | SBP >170 | Males | 55–64 | 44.00 | Khaw and Rose (1982) |
| Caribbean | St. Lucia | SBP >170 | Females | 55–64 | 19.00 | Khaw and Rose (1982) |
| Caribbean | Trinidad and Tobago | Hypertension undefined | Males | >35 | 18.20 | www.cvdinfobase.ca/ |
| Caribbean | Trinidad and Tobago | Hypertension undefined | Females | NA | 28.10 | www.cvdinfobase.ca/ |
| Africa | Cameroon, urban | SBP >160 | Males | Age-adjusted, 25+ | 8.70 | Cooper et al. (1997a) |
| Africa | Cameroon, urban | SBP >160 | Females | Age-adjusted, 25+ | 8.70 | Cooper et al. (1997a) |
| Africa | Cameroon, rural | SBP >160 | Males | Age-adjusted, 25+ | 4.70 | Cooper et al. (1997a) |
| Africa | Cameroon, rural | SBP >160 | Females | Age-adjusted, 25+ | 7.40 | Cooper et al. (1997a) |
| Africa | Ghana, rural | DBP >95 | Both | 16–54 | 2.50 | Pobee et al. (1977) |
| Africa | Ivory Coast | SBP >160 and DBP >95 | Males | 10–59 | 15.20 | Bertrand et al. (1976) |
| Africa | Ivory Coast | SBP >160 and DBP >95 | Females | 10–59 | 12.00 | Bertrand et al. (1976) |
| Africa | Nigeria | SBP >160 | Males | Age-adjusted, 25+ | 6.90 | Cooper et al. (1997a) |

| | | | | Age-adjusted, 25+ | 6.90 | Cooper et al. (1997a) |
|---|---|---|---|---|---|---|
| Africa | Nigeria | SBP >160 | Females | Age-adjusted, 25+ | 6.90 | Cooper et al. (1997a) |
| Africa | Nigeria, rural | Hypertension undefined | Both | 11–50+ | 15.20 | Okesina et al. (1999) |
| Africa | Traditional Yoruba living in urban Nigeria | SBP >140 | Both | 53.6 ± 12.6 | 23.40 | Owoaje et al. (1997) |
| Africa | Tanzania | Hypertension undefined | Both | NA | 48.90 | www.cvdinfobase.ca/ |
| Africa | Urban Zulus | SBP >140 | Males | 20–75 | 23 | Seedat et al. (1982) |
| Africa | Urban Zulus | SBP >140 | Females | 20–75 | 27 | Seedat et al. (1982) |
| Africa | Rural Zulus | SBP >140 | Males | 20–75 | 10.50 | Seedat et al. (1982) |
| Africa | Rural Zulus | SBP >140 | Females | 20–75 | 10.75 | Seedat et al. (1982) |
| Africa | Urban Zulus | SBP >140 | Males | 20–75 | 31.90 | Seedat et al. (1982) |
| Africa | Urban Zulus | SBP >140 | Females | 20–75 | 25.40 | Seedat et al. (1982) |

*Note:*
DBP, diastolic blood pressure; NA, not available; SBP, systolic blood pressure. Blood pressures are given in mmHg.

have a serious problem with hypertension is inescapable (with prevalence rates as high as 40%; Snieder *et al.*, 2003). However, some studies in London of Afro-UK groups show very high prevalence rates of hypertension, though not as high as those seen in the USA. Frequently studies with African-derived groups in London yield widely diverse results, sometimes indicating small differences in hypertension prevalence rates across different ethnic groups (Cruickshank *et al.*, 1985), and sometimes indicating rather large differences (Cruickshank *et al.*, 2001a). These studies are summarized by Agyeman and Bhopal (2003), but only one of them is included in Table 2.1

Most African samples have a rather low frequency of hypertension, with some notable exceptions, such as those collected in Tanzania (48.9%), urban Yoruba Nigeria (22.3%), rural Nigeria (15.20%), and among urban Zulus (23 and 31.9% in two different studies). Otherwise, most other studies report a frequency of hypertension below 16%. The studies by Seedat and colleagues (1982, 1993) strongly argue for an urban–rural dichotomy, with higher hypertension prevalence found in the former. Pobee *et al.* (1977) report a frequency as low as 2.5% for hypertension in a rural Ghanaian population. These data clearly show that there are African populations in which hypertension is not a problem (Ahrén and Corrigan, 1984).

It is also obvious that Caribbean groups have a hypertension prevalence that varies greatly among the different studies. On the lower end is the sample from Limón, Costa Rica, a group that descends from Jamaican migrants (Madrigal *et al.*, 2004) and has exceedingly low blood pressures (3%), even though they were sampled at a semi-urban area. Low hypertension frequencies were also reported in Antigua and Barbuda (1%), in Grand Cayman (3.9%), and in Jamaica in a 1997 report (13%). At the higher end is the population in Barbados, where hypertension was reported in 47% of women and 43% of males. Equally interesting is the rather high blood pressure in Cienfuegos, Cuba. As Ordúñez-García *et al.* note (1998), however, the difference in hypertension between Afro-Cubans and Hispanic-Cubans in this community is very low when compared with that seen in the USA. The data from St. Kitts presented by Schneckloth *et al.* (1962) are interesting in that females have a very high prevalence of hypertension (40.7%) whereas males have a frequency of only 20.7%. In St. Lucia, several studies report a rather high hypertension prevalence, with Khaw and Rose (1982) finding a higher prevalence in males (44%) than in females (19%) aged 55–64 years, and with the WHO's cardiovascular infobase (www.cvdinfobase.ca/) reporting the opposite (males, 17.3%; females, 24.7%). Halberstein and Davies (1984) note a prevalence rate of hypertension of 32.3% in their sample from the Bahamas, and Moser *et al.* (1959) report a high frequency in males and females in Grand Bahama (27.1 and 25.8%) and Nassau (29.3 and 33.8%). In Guadeloupe Failde *et al.* (1996) report a hypertension prevalence rate of 20.9% for males and 26.0% for females.

Simmons (1983) does not report the prevalence of hypertension in a "Creole" group in Belize, but the systolic blood pressure means of 124.2 mmHg in males and 115.8 mmHg in females do not suggest this is a hypertensive community. Data from Nassau reported by Johnson and Remington (1961) cannot be entered into the table either because they do not present hypertension prevalence rates. However, the mean systolic blood pressures for 40–44-year-old males of 142.09 mmHg and of 149.61 mmHg for 40–44-year-old females are rather high. However, we can't tell if these means are driven high because of a few outliers.

The data reported in 1962 by Miall *et al.* are surprising in that the rural and urban Jamaican female samples have very high frequencies of hypertension (33.8 and 36.6% respectively). The frequencies in rural and urban males are lower although still much higher (16.8 and 20.6% respectively) than those reported in Jamaica by Cooper *et al.* (1997a) and Dressler *et al.* (1988). Given that Jamaica was much less modernized in the 1960s than in the 1970s and 1980s it is conceivable that such glaring difference might be due to instrument differences between Miall's early study and the two later studies, and not to an actual decrease in hypertension from the 1960s and 1970s to the 1980s. That the means presented in 1961 in Nassau (Johnson and Remington, 1961), in 1962 in Jamaica (Miall *et al.*, 1962) in 1959 in Grand Bahama and Nassau (Moser *et al.*, 1959), and in 1962 in St. Kitts (Schneckloth *et al.*, 1962) are so high could be taken as support for a difference in measures due to instruments used in the 1950s and 1960s. Indeed, the importance of when the research was done was noted by Khaw and Rose (1982). Alternatively, these early studies might truly indicate that hypertension was high in St. Kitts (for women), Nassau, and Jamaica in the 1950s and 1960s, and decreased afterwards, perhaps because socioeconomic status improved, regardless of the modernization process.

In his review of the hypertension literature on the Caribbean, Halberstein (1999) concludes that hypertension is endemic and prevalent in the Caribbean. Our review of the data suggests that, at least in some areas, such a high prevalence of hypertension is not new. What still remains difficult to explain is the decrease in hypertension shown in St. Kitts, Nassau, and Jamaica by studies separated by two or three decades. If this trend is real and not an artifact of the measuring instruments, perhaps it reflects a decrease in discrimination. We should not lose sight, however, of the low frequency of hypertension reported in Limón, Costa Rica (Madrigal *et al.*, 2004), Antigua, Barbuda (www.cvdinfobase.ca/), Grand Cayman (Halberstein, 1999), and Jamaica in a 1997 study (Cooper *et al.*, 1997a).

Table 2.2 shows prevalence rates of obesity in Africa, the Caribbean, and the USA. Few data could be collected from Africa, although in Tanzania and Nigeria the frequency of obesity was low (4 and 2% respectively) and in a rural region of Mali obesity was rare (0.51%). At the same time, in a semi-urban sample of South Africa, the frequency of obesity was reported to be as high as 22.2% in 2001 by Erasmus *et al.* (2001).

However, it is obvious that once again Afro-USA populations have the most severe problem with obesity (49.7% in a sample of females), although the Caribbean groups are not found necessarily between African and USA groups; rather, some are slender and some are obese. Indeed, one of the groups sampled in Haiti, that with low educational status, has a lower frequency of obesity than that in Tanzania. In Haiti, undernutrition is still a problem. Thus its populations have not transitioned into a more westernized diet and lifestyle as have those of Antigua and Barbuda (20% obesity) and Limón, Costa Rica (18% obesity). In Barbados, the frequency of obesity is rather high in women (30%) and lower in males (10%), which is interesting as this same sample had a rather high prevalence of hypertension in both genders. Frequencies of obesity under 14% are reported in samples from Barbados (Foster *et al.*, 1993), Guadeloupe (Costagliola *et al.*, 1991), and Trinidad and Tobago (www.cvdinfobase.ca/). Simmons (1983) does not report the prevalence of obesity in a "Creole" group in Belize, but the mean BMI values of 23.5 mmHg for males and 25.1 for females do not suggest that this is a group with serious obesity problems.

Table 2.3 shows prevalence rates of diabetes for Africa, the Caribbean, and the USA. Data are particularly wanting in Africa. However, the table clearly shows that the frequencies in Tanzania, Togo, South Africa, and Cameroon are exceedingly low, whereas those of the Caribbean vary but are closer to those of the USA, which are exceedingly high. Concerning the Cameroon data, Mbanya *et al.* (1999) do not explain the unexpected finding that the frequency of diabetes is higher in the rural males than in the urban males. Two other studies report a low prevalence rate of diabetes in Africa. In two West African villages, Teuscher *et al.* (1987) did not detect any cases of diabetes in a survey of 1381 subjects. In six villages in Tanzania, McLarty *et al.* (1989) report a prevalence rate of 1.1 and 8.4% for males and females respectively. In the Caribbean, at

Table 2.2. *Obesity prevalence rates in African and African-derived populations*

| Region | Country/population | Definition of obesity | Gender | Age group (year) | Prevalence % | Source |
|---|---|---|---|---|---|---|
| North America | Afro-USA, 1999–2000 | BMI >30 | Males | 20–74 | 28.10 | www.cdc.gov/nchs/products/pubs/pubd/hus/03hustop.htm |
| North America | Afro-USA, 1999–2000 | BMI >30 | Females | 20–74 | 49.70 | www.cdc.gov/nchs/products/pubs/pubd/hus/03hustop.htm |
| Caribbean | Antigua and Barbuda | NA | Both | All ages | 20 | www.cvinfobase.ca |
| Caribbean | Barbados | BMI >30 | Males | 40–79 | 10 | Foster *et al.* (1993) |
| Caribbean | Barbados | BMI >30 | Females | 40–79 | 30 | Foster *et al.* (1993) |
| Caribbean | Guadeloupe | BMI >30 | Males | Age-standardized | 2 | Costagliola *et al.* (1991) |
| Caribbean | Guadeloupe | BMI >30 | Females | Age-standardized | 12.50 | Costagliola *et al.* (1991) |
| Caribbean | Haiti, no education or primary only | BMI >30 | Females | 15–49 | 1.50 | www.cvinfobase.ca |
| Caribbean | Haiti, secondary education or higher | BMI >30 | Females | 15–49 | 9.50 | www.cvinfobase.ca |
| Caribbean | Trinidad and Tobago | BMI >30 | Males | >15 | 7.50 | www.cvinfobase.ca |
| Caribbean | Trinidad and Tobago | BMI >30 | Females | NA | 12.5 | www.cvinfobase.ca |
| Caribbean | Limón, Costa Rica | BMI >30 | Both | 19–90 | 18 | Madrigal *et al.* (2004) |
| Africa | Tanzania | NA | Both | Total | 29.80 | www.cvinfobase.ca |
| Africa | North western Tanzania | BMI >27 for males, BMI >25 for females | Both | <9–70 | 4 | Ahrén and Corrigan (1984) |
| Africa | Nigeria, rural | BMI >25 | Both | 11–50+ | 2 | Okesina *et al.* (1999) |
| Africa | Traditional Yoruba living in urban Nigeria | BMI >31.1 | Males | 53.6 ± 12.6 | 3 | Owoaje *et al.* (1997) |
| Africa | Traditional Yoruba living in urban Nigeria | BMI >32.3 | Females | 53.6 ± 12.6 | 16 | Owoaje *et al.* (1997) |
| Africa | Peri-urban South African sample | BMI >25 | Both | Standardized to world population | 22.20 | Erasmus *et al.* (2001). |
| Africa | Mali, rural | BMI 25–26.9 | Both | 15–≥70 | 0.51 | Fisch *et al.* (1987) |

*Note:*
NA, not available. **BMI** values are given in $Kg/m^2$.

Table 2.3. *Diabetes prevalence rates in African and African-derived populations*

| Region | Country/population | Definition of diabetes | Gender | Age group (year) | Prevalence % | Source |
|---|---|---|---|---|---|---|
| North America | USA | Diagnosed diabetes | Male | 45–64 | 14.10 | www.cdc.gov/diabetes/statistics/prev/national/f5dt2000.htm |
| North America | USA | Diagnosed diabetes | Female | 45–64 | 16.60 | www.cdc.gov/diabetes/statistics/prev/national/f5dt2000.htm |
| North America | USA | Diagnosed diabetes | Male | 65–74 | 23.00 | www.cdc.gov/diabetes/statistics/prev/national/f5dt2000.htm |
| North America | USA | Diagnosed diabetes | Female | 65–74 | 25.40 | www.cdc.gov/diabetes/statistics/prev/national/f5dt2000.htm |
| North America | USA | Diagnosed diabetes | Female | 65–74 | 32.00 | http://diabetes.niddk.nih.gov/dm/pubs/africanamerican/#2 |
| Europe | Manchester, UK | Diagnosed diabetes or impaired glucose-tolerance test | Female | Adults, age-standardized | 14.00 | Mbanya *et al.* (1999) |
| Europe | Manchester, UK | Diagnosed diabetes or impaired glucose-tolerance test | Male | Adults, age-standardized | 15.30 | Mbanya *et al.* (1999) |
| Caribbean | Antigua and Barbuda | FBS >160 mM | Both | 20–39 | 0.30 | www.cvdinfobase.ca/ |
| Caribbean | Antigua and Barbuda | FBS >160 mM | Both | 40–64 | 5 | www.cvdinfobase.ca/ |
| Caribbean | Antigua and Barbuda | FBS >160 mM | Both | >65 | 15 | www.cvdinfobase.ca/ |
| Caribbean | Barbados | Fasting glucose over 7.8 mM or self-reported history | Male | 40–79 | 15 | Foster *et al.* (1993) |
| Caribbean | Barbados | Fasting glucose over 7.8 mM or self-reported history | Female | 40–79 | 18 | Foster *et al.* (1993) |

| Region | Country | Criterion | Sex | Age | Value | Reference |
|---|---|---|---|---|---|---|
| Caribbean | Guadeloupe | Fasting plasma glucose ≥8.0 mm | Male | 40–49 | 7 | Costagliola et al. (1991). |
| Caribbean | Guadeloupe | Fasting plasma glucose ≥8.0 mm | Female | 40–49 | 6.70 | Costagliola et al. (1991). |
| Caribbean | Jamaica | Diagnosed diabetes or impaired glucose-tolerance test | Female | Adults, age-standardized | 30.10 | Mbanya et al. (1999) |
| Caribbean | Jamaica | Fasting plasma glucose ≥7.8 mM | Male | 25–74 | 9.80 | Wilks et al. (1999) |
| Caribbean | Jamaica | Fasting plasma glucose ≥7.8 mM | Female | 25–74 | 15.70 | Wilks et al. (1999) |
| Caribbean | Jamaica | Diagnosed diabetes or impaired glucose-tolerance test | Male | Adults age-standardized | 22.80 | Mbanya et al. (1999) |
| Caribbean | Trinidad and Tobago | Self-reported | Men | >35 | 9.60 | www.cvdinfobase.ca/ |
| Caribbean | Trinidad and Tobago | Self-reported | Female | N/A | 12.60 | www.cvdinfobase.ca/ |
| Africa | Tanzania | Glucose conc. ≥11.1 mM | Men | 45–49 | 2.50 | www.cvdinfobase.ca/ |
| Africa | Tanzania | Glucose conc. ≥11.1 mM | Men | 50–54 | 2.10 | www.cvdinfobase.ca/ |
| Africa | Tanzania | Glucose conc. ≥11.1 mM | Female | 45–49 | 0.70 | www.cvdinfobase.ca/ |
| Africa | Tanzania | Glucose conc. ≥11.1 mM | Female | 50–54 | 1.40 | www.cvdinfobase.ca/ |
| Africa | Tanzania | Criterion of 11.1 mM | Male | Age-adjusted to the USA population | 1.10 | McLarty et al. (1989) |
| Africa | Tanzania | Criterion of 11.1 mM | Female | Age-adjusted to the USA population | 8.40 | McLarty et al. (1989) |
| Africa | Northwest Tanzania | Criterion of ≥5.5 mM | Both | Total | 0.70 | Ahrén and Corrigan (1984) |
| Africa | Cameroon, rural | Diagnosed diabetes or impaired glucose-tolerance test | Female | Adults, age-standardized | 3.60 | Mbanya et al. (1999) |
| Africa | Cameroon, rural | Diagnosed diabetes or impaired glucose-tolerance test | Male | Adults, age-standardized | 7.60 | Mbanya et al. (1999) |

Table 2.3. (*cont.*)

| Region | Country/population | Definition of diabetes | Gender | Age group (year) | Prevalence % | Source |
|--------|-------------------|------------------------|--------|------------------|--------------|--------|
| Africa | Cameroon, urban | Diagnosed diabetes or impaired glucose-tolerance test | Female | Adults, age-standardized | 7.50 | Mbanya et al. (1999) |
| Africa | Cameroon, urban | Diagnosed diabetes or impaired glucose-tolerance test | Male | Adults, age-standardized | 2.10 | Mbanya et al. (1999) |
| Africa | Togo | Blood glucose criterion of 11.1 | Both | NA | 0 | Teuscher et al. (1987) |
| Africa | Nigeria, rural | Fasting glucose over >7.00 mM | Both | 11–50+ | 3 | Okesina et al. 1999 |
| Africa | Peri-urban Black South Africans | 120-min plasma glucose value ≥11.1 | Both | Standardized to world population | 4.50 | Erasmus et al. (2001) |
| Africa | Mali, rural | Fasting glucose over 7.00 mM | Both | 35–44 | 0.80 | Fisch et al. (1987) |
| Africa | Traditional Yoruba living in urban Nigeria | Fasting glucose over 6.700 mM | Both | 53.6 ± 12.6 | 2.80 | Owoaje et al. (1997) |

*Note:*
FBS, fasting blood sugar; NA, not available.

the lower end are Antigua and Barbuda (prevalence rate of 5% or less) and Guadeloupe (prevalence rate of 6.6%). At the higher end is Barbados, where diabetes was found in 17% of all subjects. Between the two extremes is Jamaica, with prevalence rates of 9.8% among males and 15.7% among females. Gulliford and Mahabir (1999) note that diabetes has become a major health problem in Trinidad and Tobago.

In conclusion, the data shown in Tables 2.1–2.3 indicate that obesity, diabetes, and hypertension are found in relatively low frequencies in Africa, intermediate-to-high frequencies in the Caribbean, and in high frequencies in the USA. There are exceptions, such as those of the Limón population, which has a very low frequency of hypertension, or that of low-socioeconomic-status Haiti, with low levels of obesity. Moreover, the data from Africa show that urbanized populations have higher prevalence rates of these conditions than do rural populations. But the Afro-USA populations have a clearly high prevalence rate when compared with other groups. This gradient from Africa–Caribbean to USA has been discussed by Cooper *et al.* (1997b), Forrester *et al.* (1998), Luke *et al.* (2001) and Sobngwi *et al.* (2001). In his summary of hypertension studies in Africa during the first part of the twentieth century, Akinkugbe (1985) notes that hypertension has become the most important cardiovascular problem in Africa but notes that there are African populations without hypertension and in which blood pressure does not rise with age. Prineas and Gillum (1985) rightly call attention to the fact that the distribution of hypertension is not uniform in the USA. For example, the study by Burns *et al.* (1980) shows that in Dayton, Ohio, urban Afro-USA teenagers had higher blood pressure than their suburban counterparts. In the same manner, Langford *et al.* (1968) demonstrated that in rural Mississippi girls had higher blood pressure than did their urban counterparts.

An interesting study compared the diet of an African, a Caribbean, and a UK African-derived group. Contrary to expectations based on the prevalence of chronic diseases in these three sites, Mennen *et al.* (2001) report that saturated and polyunsaturated fat intake and alcohol intake were highest in rural Cameroon, intermediate in the UK, and lowest in Jamaica. These authors (Mennen *et al.*, 2001) explain the relatively low cardiovascular disease prevalence in Cameroon and the intermediate cardiovascular disease prevalence in Jamaica by the higher physical activities of these two sites. In particular, Mennen *et al.* (2001) emphasize the strenuous physical activities which not only rural, but even urban (though less frequently), people of Cameroon are engaged in. This study emphasizes the importance of physical activity to explain the Africa–Caribbean–USA/UK gradient of obesity/hypertension/diabetes noted above. The importance of physical activity is also made clear by Sobngwi *et al.* (2002), who show that obesity, diabetes, and hypertension prevalence is higher in urban than in rural Cameroon subjects, and that physical activity is significantly lower in the former than in the latter.

## 2.4   The thrifty-genotype and the thrifty-phenotype hypotheses: a review

We now present a review of attempts to explain in an evolutionary manner the high frequency of diabetes and obesity in rapidly modernizing populations. The initial proposal of the thrifty-genotype hypothesis is due to James V. Neel in 1962 (Williams, 1993). Neel (1962) proposed that a quick insulin trigger was adaptive in environments with unreliable food sources, but that such a trigger became maladaptive in environments characterized by overnutrition. When Neel's paper was published, the difference between type-I and type-II diabetes had not been established (King and Roglic, 1999). Moreover, the initial proposal focused on the high incidence of diabetes in Amerindian groups, not on African-derived populations.

It is now understood that obesity and diabetes affect virtually all human groups who have experienced recent modernization, with the adoption of western-style diets and a reduction of physical activity as described above (Baschetti, 1998; King and Roglic, 1999; Lev-Ran, 1999; McDermott, 1998; Williams, 1993; Zimmet, 1999; Zimmet and Thomas, 2003). Groups particularly affected are Native American communities, Pacific and Indian Ocean island populations, and East Indian, African-derived and Australian Aboriginal communities (McDermott, 1998; Zimmet *et al.*, 2001). Neel *et al.* (1998) reviewed the evolution of the thrifty-genotype hypothesis, and stressed that type-II diabetes, hypertension, and obesity are best understood together, although the diseases do not constitute a true syndrome; that is, they do not share a common genetic underpinning. As Zimmet *et al.* (2001) and Zimmet and Thomas (2003) note, type-II diabetes is often a manifestation of a much broader underlying disorder, sometimes called syndrome X or the metabolic syndrome, which includes a cluster of cardiovascular diseases, glucose intolerance, hyperinsulinemia, hypertension, dyslipidemia, and visceral and general obesity. The so-called New World syndrome, proposed by Weiss *et al.* (1984) includes early-onset gallbladder disease with the formation of cholesterol gallstones (Lieberman, 2003).

Neel *et al.* (1998) also clarify that the hypothesis concerns the type-II diabetes that is not of simple genetic etiology, but rather of complex multifactorial genetic basis; that is, about 90% of the type-II cases. Neel *et al.* (1998) conclude that ". . .the concept of a thrifty genotype remains as viable as when first advanced . . ." (p. 50). Indeed, the literature following the hypothesis' proposal in 1962 is very long, and the reader is directed to Neel *et al.* (1998), Lieberman (2003) and West (1978) for a list of it. Allen and Cheer (1996) refer to the thrifty-genotype hypothesis as an "orienting concept" in the fields of anthropology and nutrition. Certainly, the epidemiological data strongly support the notion that, with modernization, type-II diabetes, obesity, and hypertension rise to epidemic proportions (King and Roglic, 1999; Lev-Ran, 1999; McDermott, 1998; Zimmet, 1999; Zimmet and Thomas, 2003), as was reviewed above.

An interesting twist to the question of what evolutionary entity should be studied is presented by Allen and Cheer (1996), who argue that the non-thrifty genotype is the derived, not the primitive, state in our species. They propose that populations of northern European descent, upon the adoption of farming, started consuming milk, a sugar-rich food. Allen and Cheer (1996) argue that it was selection for the ability to consume milk that made the non-thrifty genotype so frequent in populations of northern European descent. This proposal is a powerful explanation for the virtually universal occurrence of type-II diabetes, obesity, and hypertension in rapidly modernizing populations, not only among Amerindians, as was initially proposed (King and Rewers, 1993). It also brings to our attention that scientists tend to view the European state as that which is normal for our species, when in the case of lactose absorption and low frequencies of type-II diabetes in an industrialized-diet environment, the contrary is the case (King and Roglic, 1999; Lev-Ran, 1999). Wendorf and Goldfine (1991) still insist on explaining the evolution of the thrifty genotype, even when it had been well established that most human populations have it, and will express it under overnutrition conditions. In contrast, Baschetti (1998), not unlike Allen and Cheer (1996), attempts to explain the European condition of low frequencies of diabetes by proposing that these populations evolved through natural selection for adaptation to the consumption of certain foods. These foods are not clearly specified, as is milk in Allen and Cheer's proposal (1996).

Another important theoretical contribution to the high frequency of type-II diabetes, hypertension, and obesity in rapidly modernizing populations was the proposal of the thrifty-phenotype hypothesis by Hales and Barker (Barker, 2001; Barker *et al.*, 1982, 2000, 2001; Hales and Barker,

1992, 2001; Hales *et al.*, 1997), who propose that poor nutrition in fetal and early infant life may predispose an individual to these conditions later in life. Certainly, there would be strong selection for the thrifty genotype during the neonatal and infancy periods in low-nutrition environments. Kuzawa (1998) proposes that the selective pressure for a quick insulin trigger and enhanced fat storage during the infancy and childhood period protects from undernutrition later in life. A review of existing literature on the connection between birth weight and later glucose tolerance by Newsome *et al.* (2003) finds an overall inverse relationship between them, thus providing support for the thrifty-phenotype hypothesis. However, Newsome *et al.* (2003) caution that in some papers there was more than one direction to this relation. McDermott (1998) reviews epidemiological data of Australian Aborigines, and proposes that these populations experienced malnutrition and an immediately subsequent adoption of western diet and lack of exercise. He notes that the emphasis on the presumed genetic basis of type-II diabetes instead of the environmental component does a disservice to the affected groups, since it can result in a fatalistic view in healthcare providers and sufferers, a sentiment also voiced by Cruickshank *et al.* (2001b). Thus McDermott (1998) favors the thrifty-phenotype over the thrifty-genotype hypothesis, although others have pointed out that there is no conflict between the thrifty-genotype and thrifty-phenotype hypotheses (Neel *et al.*, 1998; Williams, 1993).

As with most populations in the world, non-pastoral African groups should be expected to be lactose-intolerant and to have the thrifty genotype. But unlike most human groups, African-derived Caribbean groups were subjected to extreme conditions of low nutrition and excessive workloads during the trans-Atlantic passage and as slaves. These extreme conditions have been invoked by the "slavery hypothesis" as possible causes of high hypertension rates in African-derived groups.

### 2.5   The slavery hypothesis for hypertension among African-derived populations

Even though the slavery hypothesis has centered on the problem of hypertension in Afro-USA populations, it is certainly relevant to Caribbean groups, as much of the historical evidence cited by its proponents derives from Caribbean data. According to Wilson (1987) and Wilson and Grim (1991), the high frequencies of hypertension found in Afro-USA groups are due to a genetic propensity which evolved as a result of natural selection leading to adaptation to low-salt and dehydration conditions. In the 1991 paper Wilson and Grim did not emphasize their earlier proposal that African groups in general had exposure to low-salt environments, an untenable statement according to Curtin (1992). Instead, Wilson and Grim emphasize that during the trans-Atlantic trade, mortality due to vomiting, heat, diarrhea, and general dehydration would have selected for a metabolism that allowed surviving slaves to conserve water and salt. Once the slaves were delivered to the plantations, the same conditions of low water supply and profuse sweating would have exerted further selection for water and salt conservation. Wilson and Grim (1991) emphasize the high mortality and low fertility of Caribbean slaves, to pinpoint the extreme natural selection under which the slaves lived. The slavery hypothesis has had other proponents, such as Dimsdale (2000, 2001) and Diamond (1991), who presented it in the medical and public press respectively. Jackson (1991) agrees that the trans-Atlantic middle passage was a severe selective force on African slaves, but notes that it alone cannot account for the high frequency of hypertension in Afro-USA groups. She stresses the importance of considering culture, genetic variation, and ecology when studying hypertension in Afro-USA groups (Jackson, 1993a, 1993b).

   In a 1992 paper, Curtin presents a rather negative critique of the slavery hypothesis. Briefly, he proposes that Africa had plentiful supplies of salt, that there are African populations with low blood pressure, that USA slave populations did not have the severe low fertility and high mortality seen in the Caribbean, but rather grew healthily, and that there is no evidence of high mortality due to dehydration in either the slave ships or the plantations. Cooper and Rotimi (1994) agree with Curtin that African populations with hypertension are found in highly urbanized environments only, and refer to the slavery hypothesis as highly speculative. Cooper and Rotimi (1994) make the point that the rapid and unquestioned acceptance of this proposal reflects the bias in the scientific community towards genetic explanations for "racial" differences as opposed to sociocultural and psychological ones. Kaufman (2001) refers to the slavery hypothesis as "incompatible with historical data," and as "pseudoscientific". Shaper (1997) notes that there is little evidence in support of the slavery hypothesis and that although it might appeal to the historical imagination, it diverts attention from health issues posed by environmental factors. Dressler and Bindon (2000) note that the notion that high blood pressure among Afro-USA groups is a result of genetics has been discredited. In 1996, Grim and Robinson presented a further defense of the slavery hypothesis and insisted on continuing using racial terms as valid *biological* entities, and cite the "obvious" difference

between Blacks and Whites in frequencies of hemoglobin S. They overlook, of course, that some Mediterranean and East Indian populations
have frequencies of hemoglobin S as high as those of African populations
(Serjeant, 1992).

The strongly worded debate about the slavery hypothesis had its most
recent presentation in the journal *Epidemiology*, where Kaufman and Hall
(2003a, 2003b) presented a criticism of the hypothesis, followed by com-
mentaries by Blackburn (2003), Grim and Robinson (2003) and Weiss
(2003). To summarize, Kaufman and Hall (2003a, 2003b) present the
above-noted arguments (plus the fact that the hypothesis has rarely been
published in a peer-reviewed journal). Grim and Robinson defend it and
accuse Kaufman and Hall of calling for the end of all genetic research that
might stigmatize certain groups. Blackburn calls for a toning down of the
rhetoric, and Weiss ventures the guess that the frequencies of hypertension in Afro-USA groups are so high that a gene–environment interaction
might best explain it. Weiss then cautions us not to discard the slavery
hypothesis altogether.

Grim and Robinson's (1996) liberal use of the race concept contrasts
sharply with a virtually overwhelming agreement in recent medical and
epidemiological literature with the proposition that human races are not
biological entities. For example, Lin and Kelsey (2000) state that the
groups traditionally used to classify humans in the USA are a result of
the history of the country, and have no biological foundation. In an
editorial for the journal *Epidemiology*, Kaufman (1999) refers to groups
such as "Blacks" and "Whites" as absurdly heterogeneous. In an editorial
in *Archives of Pediatric and Adolescent Medicine*, Rivara and Finberg
(2001) ask authors not to use the terms race/ethnicity, variables that lack
any scientific basis, when variables such as educational level, household
income, etc., can be measured directly. Anderson *et al.* (2001) note that in
the USA before 1989 a baby born to a "White" and a "Non-White"
parent would have been assigned the race of the "Non-White" parent,
but that after 1989 s/he would have been assigned the race of the mother.
Clearly, this change in racial assignment indicates that race is not a
biological entity, but a social construct (Anderson *et al.*, 2001). Kaplan
and Bennett (2003) argue that because race is socially constructed, it
should not be viewed as an inherent attribute of an individual in epidemiological studies. Perhaps the strongest statement about epidemiology and
medicine's rejection of races as biological entities is the Institute of
Medicine's (IOM's) recommendation to the National Institutes of Health
(NIH) that the latter reevaluate its use of the term race because it lacks
scientific validity (Oppenheimer, 2001).

As biomedical and epidemiological workers appear to be ready to discard race as a biological entity, several researchers emphasize that, just the same, ethnicity is a powerful social category which affects people's health (Brondolo *et al.*, 2003; Jones, 2001; Kaufman and Cooper, 2001; Krieger, 2000). In the USA in particular, groups labeled by terms such as Hispanic, African-American, Euro-American, Amerindian, etc., are valid terms for epidemiological studies. But writers such as Jones (2001), who argue for the continued research of ethnicity-associated health disparities, stress that race is a social not a biological construct and that there is more genetic diversity within than among "racial" groups. Root (2001) notes that even when epidemiologists have controlled for variables such as education and socioeconomic status, they should not assume that different health outcomes in different groups are best explained by genetic differences. On the contrary, he argues that the genetic data show that there is more variation within than among groups, whereas socioeconomic variables do show more variation among than within these groups. Of course, Grim and Robinson are not the only authors to use racial terminology. Even if other authors do not invoke the slavery hypothesis when they argue that "Black race" is a predisposing factor for the high frequency of hypertension in African-derived groups, they are invoking a biological/genetic, not a sociocultural or psychological, reason for this frequency (Weinberger, 1996). A more recent paper has examined the proposition that USA-born populations of African ancestry are significantly different from African-born USA migrants and found that none of the hypertension-related loci had significantly different frequencies between groups (Poston *et al.*, 2001). Thus, Poston *et al.* propose that differences observed in hypertension between both groups are best explained by sociocultural and psychological causes.

## 2.6   Conclusion

A review of the theoretical literature on hypertension, obesity, and type-II diabetes allows us to conclude the following: the thrifty genotype is likely the primitive state in our species; that is, it should be found in most populations. The non-thrifty genotype evolved under specific conditions, such as where milk became plentiful and there was selection for lactose absorption, a sugar-rich food. But certainly the thrifty genotype appears to have been adaptive for most of our evolution, under diverse ecological settings. In the last century, however, as populations reduced their activity levels and adopted a diet rich in sugar and fat, the thrifty genotype did become maladaptive, resulting in high frequencies of obesity and type-II diabetes. At the same time, in these conditions of rapid change, individuals who suffered from undernutrition in utero and during infancy are more likely to develop obesity, hypertension, and type-II diabetes. In the Caribbean, these three conditions have become major health problems, although their prevalence rates are not as high as those of the USA. Moreover, there are populations with low hypertension rates such as that of Limón, Costa Rica. An interesting case outside of the Caribbean is that of Brazil, where Palatnik *et al.* (2002) report a virtually identical frequency of diabetes in Afro- and Euro- Brazilian subjects. Palatnik *et al.* (2002) propose that such equality in frequency could result from the higher gene flow between the two ethnicities as well as from their more equal socioeconomic status.

As for the slavery hypothesis, a review of the strongly worded proposals and counter-proposals leads this writer to side with its critics rather than with its proponents. That race has been so clearly shown to be a sociocultural, not a biological, entity, and that some Caribbean groups have intermediate or even low rates of hypertension, argue for sociocultural and psychological reasons for the high frequencies of hypertension in Afro-USA and other Afro-Caribbean groups. Indeed, research with other African-derived groups in Latin America who do not suffer from the inequalities that Afro-USA groups do indicates that the former do not have hypertension levels such as those of the USA (Frisancho *et al.* 1999). Dressler *et al.* (1999) also favor a sociopsychocultural explanation for the fact that darker Afro-Brazilians of lower socioeconomic status have higher blood pressure than do darker Afro-Brazilians of higher socioeconomic status. Indeed, the work of Dressler and colleagues strongly argues for a socio/psychocultural cause to the high blood pressure observed in Afro-USA and Afro-Brazilian groups with few psychosocial resources (Dressler and Bindon, 1997, 2000; Dressler *et al.* 1986, 1987, 1995, 1998; Dressler 1983, 1984a, 1984b, 1995, 1996). In particular, Dressler (1990) emphasizes the importance of recurring frustrating social interactions. Garn *et al.* (1988) warn that it is difficult to ascertain whether it is poverty or obesity that relates to blood-pressure readings in Dressler *et al.*'s work.

In their review of hypertension studies on people of African ancestry, Bowman and Murray (1990) conclude that the mental and social stress of urbanized life, in particular in racist environments, must have influenced the high blood pressure of certain African or African-derived groups, particularly in the USA. Indeed, the importance of the environment is emphasized by Cruickshank *et al.* (1985), who found no significant Black/White difference in hypertension rates in the UK. Their results led

Cruickshank *et al.* to propose that the similar social class of the subjects in the UK probably accounts for their similar hypertension rates. The importance of the environment is also advocated by Hoosen *et al.* (1985) for explaining the great difference in hypertension rates of urban and rural Zulus. Robinson *et al.* (1980), however, caution us against assuming that a traditional rural lifestyle will always result in low blood pressures and an urban one will always result in hypertension. Indeed, Beiser *et al.* (1976) note that rural migrants to urban areas in South Africa initially exhibit elevated rates of hypertension, but that as acculturation takes place such rates decrease.

As appalling as the conditions were during the middle passage, they did not result in a uniformly high prevalence of hypertension in all Afro-New World populations. Indeed, some Caribbean groups, such as that described by Madrigal *et al.* (2004) in Limón, Costa Rica, have frequencies of hypertension more in line with those of rural Africa and less in line with those of urban Jamaica, the place of origin of the Costa Rican group. This, despite the fact that 18% of the sample had a BMI value of greater than 30 kg/m$^2$. This case argues for a very strong environmental component to blood pressure variation. In their survey of literature on hypertension and coronary artery disease in Africa, Akinboboye *et al.* (2003) also conclude that, in Africa, high frequencies of hypertension are best explained by changes in lifestyle associated with modernization. They note that the rise in hypertension is associated with urbanization, and that there are still African communities with low frequencies of hypertension in which there is no rise of hypertension associated with aging.

All indications are that, with increased urbanization and modernization, obesity, diabetes, and hypertension are already becoming, and are likely to become, a serious healthcare issue in Afro-Caribbean groups (Gulliford, 1996). Dressler (1995) discusses the changes associated with modernization which might lead to an increase in cardiovascular morbidity, including urbanization, migration, cultural change, new modes of subsistence, low physical activity, westernized diet, language change, severance of kinship ties, the adoption of new prestige ranking, and exposure to new belief systems and ideologies, including a more individualistic form of interpersonal relationships, etc. All of these factors could very well explain the rise in hypertension seen in rapidly modernizing communities such as those of the Caribbean or those of urban Africa. Dressler (1984a) poses that in the Caribbean cardiovascular disease is as much a sociocultural as a biomedical phenomenon. As such, the hypertension, diabetes, and obesity problem should be confronted by considering the sociocultural milieu that is raising the frequency of these conditions.

# 3 Infectious disease epidemiology and Afro-Caribbean populations

In this chapter, we cover the main infectious diseases that have plagued Afro-Caribbean populations since the first African slaves were brought to the region. Unfortunately, our discussion will be centered on the Caribbean islands and will not include the Atlantic coast of Central America except on rare occasions. Epidemiological data for the Afro-Caribbean groups of the latter region are very difficult to find and are not included in the data reported by the Caribbean Epidemiology Center (CAREC; Le Franc, 1990).

Our theoretical framework is a biocultural, evolutionary one. That is, we will be looking at disease by considering the biology of the human host and of the pathogen, but we will also consider the cultural context of disease. For example, we will discuss the human-induced environmental changes which have led to the creation of propitious environments for the spread of disease (Krumeich *et al.*, 2001; Manderson, 1998). The evolutionary approach will be of importance when we look at human–pathogen coevolution, as well as to the origin of new diseases. Besides the evolutionary and biocultural approaches, we will be relying on the epidemiological approach to disease. Therefore, in the first section we define a few epidemiological terms, and in the rest of the chapter, we review the major infectious diseases that have affected Afro-Caribbean groups. The only sexually transmitted disease reviewed in this Chapter is AIDS. All other venereal diseases are discussed in Chapter 5, under the section on fecundity.

## 3.1 An introduction to epidemiology

Infectious diseases are those that are caused by infectious organisms or particles. In contrast with non-infectious diseases such as obesity, diabetes, and hypertension, infectious diseases result from the invasion of the human **host** (the patient) by the **pathogen**, or the disease-causing agent. The latter are commonly agreed upon to belong to one of the following groups.

- Bacteria and rickettsiae. These organisms are similar in that they lack a nuclear membrane but only the latter require living within a host cell. Not all bacteria are harmful, as humans carry useful bacteria in their intestinal and respiratory tracts. Various acute respiratory infections, tuberculosis, several diarrheal diseases, whooping cough, and tetanus are all bacterial. *Rickettsia prowazekii* causes louse-borne typhus.
- Viruses. Protein envelopes of DNA or RNA which cannot reproduce outside of a host. For this reason, they are considered not to be alive. Viral human infections range from the mundane to the deadly; for example, from the common cold to HIV.
- Prions. Non-living pieces of protein which insert themselves into the host cell's genetic material. Diseases caused by prions are slow-acting and usually fatal. In humans, Creutzfeldt–Jakob disease and probably Kuru are caused by prions.
- Protozoa/protists. Single-celled organisms, more similar to animals than to plants because they lack a cell wall. The malaria parasite is a protozoan.
- Fungi. Multicellular decomposers which produce spores. Athlete's foot is of fungal origin. Some fungi are innocuous inhabitants of the human body which nonetheless can grow out of control and cause disease. This is the case with *Candida*, which causes vaginal yeast infections.
- Metazoa. Multicellular organisms such as intestinal worms.

Whereas metazoa are large entities and commonly called macroparasites, the other infectious agents are considered microparasites because of their small size (Jackson, 2000; Sattenspiel, 2000a; www.cdc.gov/ncidod/index.htm; www.paho.org/default.htm). An accessible source on the evolution of human pathogens and the importance of this evolution to human health is Nesse and Williams (1996).

Infectious diseases can be *endemic*, *epidemic*, or *pandemic*. An endemic disease is one which is found at relatively low but constant levels in a region. Thus, a good number of people are continuously affected by the disease. For example, in Haiti malaria is endemic. An epidemic disease is one that moves into a region where it was not prevalent before, and affects a large number of people. Malaria can also exist in epidemic form, when it is brought by migration into a new region where susceptible hosts live. Other diseases such as rubella, mumps, and chickenpox can affect a population in epidemic fashion, after a large enough cohort of new susceptible hosts has accumulated. Finally, a pandemic disease affects a large area, such as a continent or even the world. AIDS is currently a pandemic, having affected the entire world (Sattenspiel, 2000a).

The *mode of transmission* of the pathogen can be direct, from host to host, or it might be indirect, in which case a vector or a vehicle is required. Direct transmission of an infectious disease can occur through droplet (influenza), fecal–oral (giardia), sexual (genital herpes), congenital (HIV), or skin-to-skin (yaws) transmission. Vehicle indirect transmission requires agents such as needles or water to transmit the pathogen. Vector-borne diseases require an arthropod such as mosquitoes (yellow fever) or fleas (lyme disease; Jackson, 2000; Sattenspiel, 2000a).

A detailed description of the *human immune response* is out of the bounds of this book. However, a short description is necessary for understanding the human response to the infectious diseases discussed below. A more in-depth description of human immunity can be found in Marieb (2004). A nice and easy-to-read account of viral and bacterial evasions of human immunity is provided by Goodenough (1991). An immune response is provoked by the presence of a foreign substance called an antigen. Antigens can be viruses, bacteria, pollen, etc. The host has his/her own antigens which identify his/her tissue as being their own. The beauty of the immune system is that it is able to distinguish between invading and self-antigens, and attack the former. Of course, there are autoimmune diseases in which an individual builds up an immune response against his/her own tissues. The autoimmune basis of type-I diabetes was discussed in Chapter 2.

The immune response is usually divided into cell-mediated and humoral or antibody-mediated immunity. There are three types of cell involved in *cell-mediated immunity*: B lymphocytes or B cells, T lymphocytes or T cells, and macrophages. Both B and T lymphocytes are produced in the bone marrow, but each one matures and develops immunocompetence at a different site: B cells in the bone marrow, T cells at the thymus. Upon maturation, both types of cell migrate to lymphoid organs, where they bind with antigens and complete their differentiation into fully functional T and B cells. A form of T cell to be discussed later is the CD4+ T cells, which bind to antigens presented by antigen-presenting cells (APCs), like macrophages. The T cells then release lymphokines that attract other cells to the area. The result is inflammation, an immune response which seeks to destroy the invading antigen. Macrophages are also produced in the bone marrow and are found in the lymphoid organs. Their role is to engulf foreign particles and to present fragments of the foreign antigens on their own surfaces to the T cells. Macrophages also secrete soluble proteins that activate T cells, which in turn release chemicals that cause the macrophages to become more active. Evidently, the three types of cell work together when an immune response is mounted.

The *humoral immune response* cannot be separated from the cell-mediated immune response. When a B cell is activated, it grows and multiplies rapidly, so that many cells (clones) with the same antigen-specific receptor are produced. Most of these clones become plasma cells, which secrete antibodies at a tremendously high rate. These secreted antibodies circulate in the lymphatic and blood systems, where they bind to the free foreign antigens and mark them for destruction. The activated B cells that did not become plasma cells become long-lived memory cells, which can mount a virtually immediate humoral response should the host be infected by the same pathogen again (Marieb, 2004).

An adequate immune response however, requires a well-fed host. If an individual is undernourished, s/he will not be able to protect her/himself from infection, as s/he does not have enough amino acids (the building blocks of protein) available to produce antibodies. Thus it has been documented repeatedly that infection and undernutrition have a synergistic effect, in which the presence of one condition worsens the other. If a child is undernourished, s/he will not be able to respond to the infection, which will cause havoc in the child. Thus, slightly undernourished children are severely affected by what would normally be a simple, easy-to-overcome infection such as the common cold. When these children are finally able to fight the infection off, they are in even worse nutritional shape than at the beginning of the infection (Butcher, 1998).

The *host's reaction* to the infectious agent is not equal across different human beings and is not the same even in the host throughout his/her life (Pozos and Ramakrishan, 2004). Indeed, age, gender, pregnancy status, nutrition, presence of other infections, socioeconomic status, and stress are all contributors to the immune response of a host to an infection, and to his/her recovery from it. The immune response of someone who is undernourished, pregnant, breast-feeding, and under severe stress will be different from the response of the same person when well fed, not pregnant, not breast-feeding, and not under severe stress. Indeed, when a disease such as the common cold affects the same individual twice, both occurrences involve a host in two different physiological states, and in different environments. Equally important for some diseases is the host's genetic make-up: the reaction to malaria of individuals with "normal" hemoglobin (Hb AA) and individuals who are carriers of sickle-cell anemia (Hb AS) will be radically different, as will be discussed in Chapter 4.

When different ethnic groups have different *prevalence rates* of diseases (the total number of cases of a disease during a specified time period relative to the number of persons at risk for the disease during that time period), a genetic predisposition might or might not be the cause of this difference. Whereas there is very good evidence of a genetic reason for higher levels of sickle-cell anemia among African, East-Indian and Mediterranean human groups, the evidence in support of a sociocultural underpinning to the higher levels of obesity, hypertension, and diabetes among Afro-USA groups is stronger.

Another factor outside the host, the vector, and the pathogen which influences disease transmission is the surrounding *ecology* broadly defined, including not only the physical, but also the cultural environment. Thus, it is well known that humans create vector-friendly microhabitats which impact disease prevalence. For example, leaving standing pools of water in dengue-prone regions is an invitation for mosquitoes to reproduce. Whoever is exposed to vectors because s/he goes outdoors at dusk and dawn might impact disease distribution by gender and age. Finally, cultural transformations of the environment such as the cutting down of trees in slash-and-burn agricultural areas, or the construction of dams, has been shown to increase prevalence rates of malaria and schistosomiasis respectively. It has also been shown that when humans begin to move into forests, they can easily acquire *zoonotic diseases*; that is, diseases caused by pathogens that specialize in non-human hosts (Jackson, 2000; Sattenspiel, 2000a). The displacement of large numbers of people in Colombia, for example, as a result of political strife, has caused the clearing of the forests and high morbidity and mortality due to malaria. Civil strife in Africa has caused massive population movements and poverty and is linked to epidemics of malaria and Ebola virus. Thus we cannot look at the resurgence of malaria or the appearance of Ebola in isolation from the region's economic and political realities (Jackson, 2000).

### 3.2 The Caribbean climate, population movements, and infectious disease

According to Sattenspiel (2000b), a tropical climate in an exceptionally pathogen-friendly environment. As in other tropical regions, the Caribbean experiences heavy rainfall (often times in the form of a hurricane) and warm temperatures, both ideal for mosquitoes and flies. Rainfall is associated with an increased number of diarrhea-related deaths because the water supply is contaminated with fecal matter (Madrigal, 1994). The constant warm temperature in the tropics does not eliminate vectors during winter, as occurs in colder climates. The Caribbean region then, provides an excellent environment for the growth of the mosquito population, to the detriment of the human population's health. Given that Afro-Caribbean populations experienced generations of substandard diet and were exposed to inhumane work conditions, it is to be expected that human hosts would not be in a position to mount an effective immune response to infectious diseases.

Another factor which has contributed to the spread of infectious disease in the Caribbean is the steady stream of migrants coming from and going to the Caribbean, as will be discussed in Chapter 5. Besides the steady flow of migrants that started moving through the region as soon as the Europeans invaded the area, and subsequently when emancipation was proclaimed, tourists now provide an excellent transport agent for infectious disease. Particularly important is sexually transmitted disease in islands in which many tourists are buying sex from local sex workers (Lawless, 1991; Wheeler and Radcliffe, 1994). It is obvious that a prostitute, whether male or female, is not in a position to request the use of condoms for her/his protection, given the power differential between the sex worker and her/his client. Sex tourism is particularly of concern when discussing the AIDS epidemic (Alleyne and Sealey, 1992; Morrison, 2001; Quinn, 1995; Wasserheit, 1995; World Bank, 2001). It has been noted that sex tourists frequently prefer to hire children, with the assumption that the latter are unlikely to be infected with sexually transmitted diseases. Such children are obviously at high risk from infection of lethal and non-lethal sexually transmitted diseases, not to mention deep psychological wounds (Feldman and Miller, 1998).

### 3.3   The epidemiologic transition in the Caribbean

As Armelagos *et al.* (1996) so well illustrate, many human populations have moved through an epidemiological transition from a preponderance of infectious to a preponderance of non-infectious diseases. Afro-Caribbean populations have indeed experienced different disease profiles through time. As discussed in Chapter 1, mortality was very high during the middle passage across the Atlantic and at the plantations. It is to be expected that a vulnerable host, such as a slave, should not be able to adequately respond to infections. Thus many infectious diseases severely affected the slaves and their immediate descendants. After emancipation, the Caribbean as well as the rest of Latin America experienced a period in which childhood mortality was high, particularly due to infectious diseases. The result of this epidemiological situation was a low life expectancy. But in the 1900s much was achieved towards the eradication of infectious pathogens and their vectors in the Caribbean. Indeed, in many islands (though not in the Atlantic coast of Central America), malaria and several childhood diseases such as whooping cough, poliomyelitis, and diphtheria have been eradicated. In a review prepared by the Pan American Health Organization (PAHO, 1994) infectious diseases are noted to have continued to decrease into the 1980s. Indeed in most of the Caribbean region infectious or parasitic diseases are not major causes of death (Alleyne and Sealy, 1992). Therefore, during the twentieth century, life expectancy increased as a result of declining infant and childhood mortality, and Afro-Caribbean groups transitioned into a low-mortality demographic profile. As a result, many of the Caribbean nations started having to deal with diseases typical of more economically advanced countries, such as cardiovascular and malignant diseases (Alleyne and Sealey, 1992).

However, not all sources are as positive about the eradication of infectious disease, as some pathogens have come back to the region, beginning in the 1970s. Previously rare (such as dengue) or unknown (such as AIDS) diseases have affected the region, or old ones (such as malaria, Chagas' disease, and tuberculosis) have come back, with pathogens and vectors resistant to drugs (malaria) and arthropod-control measures (mosquitoes). There are many reasons for this resurgence: poor use of antibiotics and the fact that pathogens and vectors evolve quickly in response to human measures (Nesse and Williams, 1996). But without a doubt, poverty, a decline of socioeconomic conditions, lack of funding for healthcare preventative and clinical strategies, increased urbanization in the form of shanty towns without running water and proper sewage disposal, malnutrition, and inadequate garbage disposal are to be blamed for this situation (Alleyne and Sealey, 1992; Guzmán and Kourí, 2002; Le Franc 1990; McGranahan *et al.*, 1999; PAHO, 1994; Rawlins, 1999). An obvious disease of poverty which has made a comeback in many areas is gastro-intestinal infection, which produces diarrhea (Le Franc, 1990). Gray (1999) notes that in the entire English-speaking Caribbean economic growth was negative from the 1970s through the 1990s, and that such economic decline impacted childhood health. It is during this time that HIV and tuberculosis became important contributors to childhood morbidity and mortality. Indeed, the Caribbean during the last decades of the 1900s presents an interesting epidemiological situation: whereas much of the population has transitioned into a low-mortality profile, and chronic diseases have became a more important concern for public health officials, declining economic conditions have brought about a return of infectious diseases (Gray, 1999; Holder and Lewis, 1997; Le Franc, 1990; McGranahan *et al.*, 1999). The question of why the health status of the region has declined in a few years, while it took so many decades to improve it, is interesting. As Le Franc (1990) notes, although it took 20 to 30 years to battle polio, typhoid, tetanus, malaria, etc., it has taken as little as less than 5 years for health status to deteriorate, even in some cases with a parallel build-up of expensive health-specialist clinics. The answer to this apparent paradox is that the economy itself appears to have had a greater impact on the health status of the population than did expenditure on health services. If, for example, a family's ability to purchase good food, obtain clean water, and dispose of sewage is compromised, then infectious diseases will affect its members easily. Thus we see that in the Bahamas, Grenada, Trinidad and Tobago, and Guyana, infant mortality rates actually increased during the 1980s. After 2000 the life expectancy of Haiti decreased from 54 to 50 years (Farmer and Castro, 2004). Moreover, the expensive health facilities being built in the islands are not available for the use of the local population, but are for so-called health tourists, who come for health treatments at a lower price than would be obtained for example in the USA. Obviously, these expensive medical clinics are out of the reach of the local population, who might be struggling just to obtain clean water and food (Le Franc, 1990). Farmer and Castro (2004) assert that the neoliberal health policies in place since the 1980s in the Caribbean have only removed from most people the scientific advances in healthcare and made them inaccessible to the masses because of their high cost, while these advances are reserved for the economic elite. As they (2004:18) aptly put it, "The wealth of the world has not dried up; it has simply become unavailable to those who need it most."

A very unfortunate contributor to rising infectious diseases among infants and young children is the continuing abandonment of breast-feeding in favor of infant formula. It has been well shown that mothers are bombarded with media propaganda about the supposed benefits of infant formula, and that many are turning towards an earlier and earlier weaning age, or even choosing not to breast-feed at all, and adopting baby formula (Betrán *et al.*, 2001; Campbell, 1988; Krumeich *et al.*, 2001). Baby formula is never a good substitute for mother's milk, but if it is used with contaminated water, it can be deadly (www.lalecheleague.org/).

The following sections analyze the impact of several infectious diseases on the health of Afro-Caribbean groups. The medical treatment of these diseases is not covered in this chapter, as it is outside of the aims of the book.

### 3.4   Malaria

There are many species of malaria which favor non-human hosts. *Plasmodium falciparum* and *Plasmodium vivax* more frequently affect humans, but *Plasmodium malariae* and *Plasmodium ovale* also do on occasions (Breuer, 1985; Green and Danubio, 1997). Sallares (2002) and Ewald (1994) discuss the evolution of the pathogens. Figure 3.1 shows a diagram of the malaria life cycle. The disease is caused by protozoa transmitted by mosquitoes of the *Anopheles* genus, a vector that is essential to the pathogen's life cycle. Humans are infected when they are bitten by a female mosquito, which injects motile sporozoites that migrate to the liver. After a few days, the sporozoites divide asexually to form merozoites, which erupt from the liver and invade the host's blood system. Once in contact with the red blood cell, the parasite enters it, "hiding" itself from the immune system (Aikawa and Miller, 1983; Breuer, 1985; Ewald, 1994; Klemba *et al.*, 2004; Pasvol, 2001a, 2001b; Taylor and Siddiqui, 1982). Entry into the red blood cell takes about 10–20 s, and requires specific ligands or receptor sites on the surface of the red blood cell (Hadley *et al.*, 1986; McGregor, 1983; Pasvol, 2003; Pasvol *et al.*, 1978; Pasvol and Wilson, 1982). For example, *P. vivax* requires that the Duffy blood-system antigens be present (FyA and/or FyB) on the red blood cell's surface to enter it, and absence of these antigens provides nearly total protection from infection (Aikawa and Miller, 1983; Hadley *et al.*, 1986). In the same manner, *P. falciparum* binds to glycophorin C on the red blood cell's surface, and its absence in Melanesian populations has been proposed to be a genetic protection from the disease (Pasvol, 2003).

After invasion, the cell recovers to such an extent that it can be invaded again by another pathogen (Garnham, 1988). However, parasitized red blood cells have a tendency to bind to uninfected red cells (resetting) or to endothelial cells in deep tissues (cytoadherence), explaining the absence of parasitized red blood cells in peripheral blood (Pasvol, 2001b). For most of its life cycle within humans, the *Plasmodium* pathogen lives inside the host's red blood cells, consuming by endocytosis 25–75% of the host's hemoglobin and possibly glucose-6-phosphate dehydrogenase (G6PD) as well (Fletcher and Maegraith, 1972; Klemba *et al.*, 2004; Perrin *et al.*, 1982). Pasvol (2001a) describes the pathogen as having a voracious appetite. Inside the red blood cell, the pathogen develops sequentially into three morphologically distinct forms (rings, trophozoites, and schizonts), and after a species-specific number of days, it causes the cell to rupture and floods the circulatory system with new merozoites, which in turn

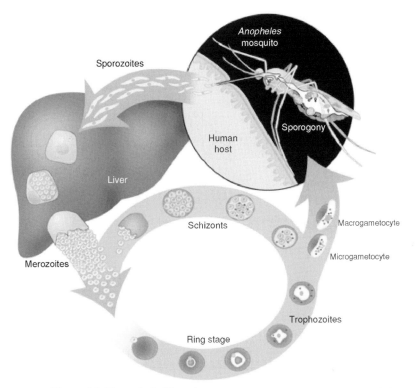

Figure 3.1. The malaria life cycle.

invade new red blood cells. When the red blood cells rupture and release the merozoites, the host suffers from an elevated fever, an attempt to rid itself of the infection (Breuer, 1985; Deans and Cohen, 1983; Garnham, 1988). According to Pasvol (2001b), the acute rigor which is associated with the elevated fever is highly suggestive of a physiologic response to a toxin, but the nature of this malarial toxin has not been resolved.

Malaria is a deadly disease for many children, especially those who are being weaned. During the breast-feeding period, the child receives passive immunity from mother's milk and has the opportunity to slowly build up its immunity. Children take years to develop immunity and require constant exposure to the pathogen (Cohen, 1977; Taylor and Siddiqui, 1982). True immunity for malaria does not exist, so the term *premunition* (Allison and Eugui, 1983; Cohen and Butcher, 1972; Playfair, 1982; Struik and Riley, 2004) is sometimes used to indicate a state of antibody production in the presence of a constant antigen insult. In other words, premunition requires that the host be exposed to malaria on a constant basis. Malarial immunity does not protect from infection from other species or even other strains of the same species (Allison and Eugui, 1983; Cohen and Butcher, 1972; Deans and Cohen, 1983; Struik and Riley, 2004). This explains why malarial areas suffer from malaria epidemics on occasion, following the importation of a new strain. That the pathogen presents the host with several different antigens (each one associated with a different life stage), and that it mutates rapidly, make it a very difficult pathogen against which to mount an immune response (Playfair, 1982). Immune individuals carry antibodies against merozoites and sporozoites, against infected erythrocytes, and against soluble parasite antigens (Breuer, 1985; Boonpucknavig and Udomsangpetch, 1983; Playfair, 1982; Taylor and Siddiqui, 1982). However imperfect the immune response to malaria might be, in endemic areas many asymptomatic individuals carry the parasite and do not suffer from the disease (McGregor, 1983; Struik and Riley, 2004).

Malaria was one of the deadliest diseases to the American Indian population following the European invasion. The disease was endemic in much of southern Europe and in Africa, and brought by both slavers and slaves. Once in the New World, it simply ravaged the Caribbean Amerindian populations (DeSantis, 1997; Kiple, 1988). Not only did it find ready vectors in the Caribbean mosquito populations, but it also thrived in the tropical ecology of the Caribbean. As Merbs (1992) so aptly notes, the European slavers quickly noticed that whereas the Amerindian populations were being decimated by disease in general, and malaria in particular, many African slaves suffered much less than the former. This resistance to malaria was a very good reason for the slavers to prefer Africans over Amerindians (Curtin, 1968; DeSantis, 1997; Kiple, 1988; Miller, 1995). The genetic basis of the African slaves' resistance to malaria will be discussed in Chapter 4 (Pasvol, 1996).

Perhaps no other disease contributed so much to the transformation of the genetic make-up of Caribbean human groups; malaria, a strong selective agent, brought the Amerindians to the brink of extinction, while naturally selecting the genetic resistance already present in some of the African slaves. But such genetic protection did not shield the slaves from the disease. First of all, not everybody has the genetic make-up that protects against malaria. Secondly, true malarial immunity does not exist. On the contrary, premunition protects from a specific malaria strain within a species, and requires constant contact with the parasite. Thus, it comes as no surprise that malaria, having killed off the Amerindian population, extracted a heavy toll from the slaves. These slaves, who had developed antimalarial immunity in their home country, were brought to the Caribbean to be exposed to different strains of the pathogen, while undergoing most inhumane conditions. After crossing the Atlantic, and eventually making it to the plantations, the slaves were in no condition to face a new malaria strain. And indeed, malaria was one of the top killers, contributing disproportionately to a very high mortality rate in the islands (Curtin, 1968; DeSantis, 1997; Kiple, 1988). A large body of epidemiological data on the 1800–1900s comes from Curtin's work with mortality and morbidity data of African recruits (former slaves) housed in the Caribbean.

Curtin (1988) notes that during 1817–36 mortality of recruits in the Caribbean was very high (40 per 1000) when compared with that of Sierra Leone (30 per 1000) and Ghana (20 per 1000). Malaria was largely responsible for these deaths. Before 1859, malaria was classified as "fevers," together with typhus, typhoid, and yellow fever. Together, these diseases caused close to 170 admissions per 1000 per year, just under the main cause of admissions, abscesses and ulcers, at 180 per 1000 per year. From 1859 to 1864, malaria was classified as "paroxysmal fevers," separate from typhoid, typhus, and yellow fever, and it contributed to 71% of deaths from "fevers". For the rest of the 1800s malaria contributed between 53 and 92% of fever deaths. During the latter part of the 1800s, when other infectious diseases were being controlled as a result of a cleaner water supply, malaria remained stubbornly difficult to control, and it was not until the 1900s that the disease became less important. Curtin (1988) proposes that a more effective use of quinine and possibly mosquito control caused this decrease.

Malaria was effectively eradicated sometime during the first half of the 1900s in most of the islands of the Caribbean (Nicolas *et al.*, 2003; Poinsignon *et al.*, 1999; Rawlins, 1993, 2000). However, it remained a common disease in the Atlantic areas of Central America inhabited by Afro-Central Americans. For example, in Costa Rica, perhaps the country with the most advanced infectious disease program in Central America, there were 1210 cases reported as recently as 1964 (Malaria Action Programme, 1987). Unfortunately, malaria was one of several infectious diseases that re-emerged after the 1980s in the entire Caribbean area (DeSantis, 1997; PAHO, 1994). However, this resurgence is not homogeneous throughout the region but is centered in French Guiana, Guyana, Suriname, Haiti, and the Dominican Republic. In the early 1990s the highest risk of contracting malaria occurred in Guyana and French Guiana (Poinsignon *et al.*, 1999; Rawlins, 1993). This resurgence is most likely a result of antimicrobial resistance of malaria parasites and pesticide resistance of mosquitoes (DeSantis, 1997).

The role of political and socioeconomic upheaval in the resurgence of malaria in the Atlantic coast of Central America is more important than it is in the Caribbean islands (PAHO, 1994). During the 1980s, various political and armed conflicts occurred in several countries in Central America, which contributed to the rise of malaria. Indeed, the situation which afflicted the Central American Afro-Caribbean groups in the 1980s was not very different from that which is affecting politically displaced people in Colombia at the time of writing. For example, during the US-led insurgence against the democratically elected *Sandinista* government of Nicaragua, people were forced to migrate, and malaria outbreaks occurred in the Bluefields region of eastern Nicaragua. Given that the Afro-Caribbean populations of the Bluefields and Limón regions of Nicaragua and Costa Rica respectively have a long history of migration and inter-marriage, population movements from Bluefields to Limón intensified, and the Atlantic coast of Costa Rica experienced several outbreaks of malaria (Madrigal, 1988, 1989).

On occasions there have been cases reported in Caribbean islands where malaria has been eradicated, but to where migrants from malarial endemic areas move. Given that various potential mosquito vectors are endemic to the entire Caribbean area (*Anopheles albimanus, Culex quinquefasciatus, Aedes aegypti*), it is not surprising that new cases arise because a mosquito bit an infected migrant and then bit someone else (Poinsignon *et al.*, 1999; Rawlins, 2000). Indeed, it is not practical to think of the different islands as epidemiological islands isolated from others, given the tremendous population movements which are traditional to the area and the popularity of the area with tourists.

Without a doubt, malaria has been eradicated from most of the Caribbean islands. However, it was never eradicated from the Atlantic coast of Central America, where it slowly decreased for most of the 1900s only to increase again in the 1980s. The growing threat of resistant mosquitoes and pathogens, as well as the worsening of life conditions since the 1980s, lead us to predict that malaria will only become a more serious problem in the future for Afro-Caribbean groups. Malaria outbreaks are tied to political, economic, and environmental crises, as is obvious in the 1980s in Central America or currently in areas of South America. Holtz and Kachur (2004) note that in areas where malaria has been totally eradicated, such as the southeast USA or in Italy, the main cause of such a decrease was the reduction of poverty. An effective plan of eradication of this disease must take into account basic issues such as environmental restoration, and political and economic security of the population.

### 3.5   Dengue fever and dengue hemorrhagic fever/dengue shock syndrome

Dengue fever and dengue hemorrhagic fever (DHF)/dengue shock syndrome (DSS) are caused by four forms of the viral genus flavivirus (DEN-1, DEN-2, DEN-3, and DEN-4; Goncalvez *et al.*, 2002). Immunity against one of the forms does not provide immunity against the others. Indeed, when there have been outbreaks of the disease in endemic areas, one or more of the viral types have been isolated in addition to the one which is found in endemic form. This suggests that when a strain is introduced in an endemic dengue area, the new strain is likely to affect a great many individuals (Campione-Piccardo *et al.*, 2003). Interestingly, the probability of experiencing the most severe form of the disease is higher if the patient is being infected for a second time, because of what Monath (1995) calls "immune enhancement." Kurane and Takasaki (2001) also emphasize the importance of secondary infections as causes of hemorrhagic symptoms, which appear to result from elevated cytokines produced by the host's immune system. The virus is transmitted by a mosquito, which is referred to by most sources as a "domesticated" vector, *Aedes aegypti aegypti* (Foster *et al.*, 2004). The evolution of the dengue virus has been researched by a few groups (Foster *et al.*, 2004; Goncalvez *et al.* 2002).

Classical dengue fever does not usually cause death, but only morbidity in the form of fever, headache, malaise, and generalized body aches (Kurane and Takasaki, 2001). In contrast, DHF/DSS are much more serious conditions which involve various hemorrhagic manifestations and circulatory failure, and might result in shock, resulting in mortality of up to 20% of the affected patients (da Fonseca *et al.*, 2002; Guzmán and Kourí, 2002; Kurane and Takasaki, 2001; Mairuhu *et al.*, 2004; Monath, 1995). According to Hadinegoro *et al.* (1999), a fast clinical response to the infection is a key determinant of whether the patient will survive or not. DHF is most frequently observed in children who are being infected a second time (www.who.int/ctd/dengue/disease.htm).

In contrast with malaria, which caused much morbidity and mortality in Afro-Caribbean populations during the 1700–1800s, dengue is a disease of the second half of the 1900s and of the present (Carme *et al.*, 2003; da Fonseca *et al.*, 2002; Guzmán and Kourí, 2002). Apparently few cases or outbreaks ever occurred before the Second World War (Monath, 1995). The appearance of dengue fever during the second part of the 1900s in the Caribbean is mirrored in other areas, most notably southeast

Asia. The historical process that lead to this increase in the disease in both areas is, however, not terribly different: it can be linked to the ecological, sociocultural, and economic process of urbanization and its many effects on humans. Given that the disease is transmitted by a "domesticated" mosquito, it benefited from the rise in urbanization which took place through the Caribbean region in the second half of the 1900s (Strobel and Lamaury, 2001). With increased urbanization, the vector had a virtually unlimited source of food (human blood) and the pathogen of non-immune hosts. Particularly important have been the innumerable breeding grounds provided by humans to their domesticated mosquito: abandoned tires, containers, and even potted plants provide stagnant pools of water in which the vector can lay its eggs. Equally important are cultural behaviors which promote the availability of breeding grounds for the mosquitoes. For example, if someone is saving water for drinking purposes, s/he might not see this water as "stagnant" (Carme *et al.*, 2003; Guzmán and Kourí, 2002; Mairuhu *et al.*, 2004; Monath, 1995; PAHO, 1994). Whiteford (1997) looked at the management of water for household use in the Dominican Republic, and concluded that gender roles in the management of water were important issues in the creation of mosquito breeding pools. It is indeed sad that a 1947 campaign of the PAHO to eradicate *A. aegypti*, successful in 73% of the region originally affected, eventually failed so that in the 1970s much of the Americas had been re-colonized by the vector (Ewald, 1994). The evolution of resistance on the part of the mosquito cannot be discounted when discussing the failure to control it. According to DeSantis (1997), the entire English-speaking Caribbean was undergoing a dengue and DHF/DSS epidemic in 1997. Equally worrisome is the importation from Asia to the Americas of another potential vector, *Aedes albopictus* (the tiger mosquito), which appears to thrive in proximity to humans (Monath, 1995).

The evolution of outbreaks in the Caribbean has been traced by Campione-Piccardo *et al.* (2003), who find that some outbreaks are experienced by one single island, whereas others are experienced by several islands. Sometimes the same strain is involved in the outbreaks; sometimes several different strains are involved. Campione-Piccardo *et al.* (2003) conclude that the Caribbean should not be considered as a single epidemiological entity with respect to dengue.

Dengue and its more dangerous DHF/DSS forms are infectious diseases of recent concern to Afro-Caribbean populations. It is clear that the eradication of the vector, a domesticate of humans, is not the only component to the eradication of the disease. The proper disposal of old tires and containers, and the elimination of culturally desirable objects such as plants, are all necessary cultural changes towards the elimination of this disease. It is disheartening that whereas the campaign to eradicate the vector took decades to achieve its goal in much of the region, it failed in a matter of a few years, and the mosquito re-colonized the entire region. Dengue is one disease that clearly shows that the conditions which have lead to a decline in health through a rise of infectious disease are multifactorial, and include socioeconomic, cultural, and ecological components. The current growth of shanty towns in much of the world, be it the Caribbean, Central America, or southeast Asia, is associated with deteriorating health conditions. Hence, the rise of dengue and its more serious form in the Caribbean and southeast Asia. As long as the epidemiological conditions of these expanding shanty towns are not changed, the disease cannot be hoped to be eradicated (Strobel and Lamaury, 2001).

### 3.6   Gastrointestinal infectious diseases

Under this heading, we are including a large number of pathogens which cause a broad range of gastrointestinal maladies, such as cholera, typhoid fever, amoebiasis, and geohelminth (intestinal worm) infections. We do not include gastrointestinal infections which cause chronic infections such as peptic ulcer disease, as the clinical manifestation of these infections is very different (see Lee *et al.*, 2001, for a review of *Helicobacter pylori* infections in the Caribbean).

Diarrheal diseases might result from bacterial infections from the following organisms: *Salmonella typhi* (which causes typhoid fever), *Shigella, Escherichia*, and *Vibrionaceae*. Typhoid fever is endemic in Haiti, and appeared in an epidemic manner in Jamaica. In Haiti, it reached epidemic proportion in the early 1990s because of the political upheaval of those years and a concomitant concentration of people in urban areas without a clean water source (DeSantis, 1997). *Campylobacter jejuni* is another bacterium that has been reported in Curaçao, associated with contaminated water from a well (Endtz *et al.*, 2003).

*Vibrio cholerae*, the bacterium which causes cholera, was terribly deadly during the 1800s, when the Caribbean was devastated by repeated epidemics of cholera, which apparently killed Afro-Caribbeans preferentially. Kiple (1985) proposes that the slaves or free Afro-Caribbeans' inadequate diet and poor access to water account for the disproportionate mortality of these groups. Specifically he suggests that Afro-Caribbeans did not have an adequate stomach lining to avoid infection with *Vibrio,* as a result of poor diet. During the 1990s cholera did not reach the Caribbean despite the South American pandemic of that decade (Theodore-Gandi, 1991).

Diarrheal diseases might also result from protozoan infections, such as that of *Giardia lamblia*, which was detected in 10.5% of a recent sample of children in Guyana (Lindo *et al.*, 2002). Another common protozoan is *Entamoeba histolytica*, which causes amoebiasis, thought to have been eradicated in Jamaica, but recently reported in more than one case (Williams *et al.*, 1989).

In the Caribbean, intestinal worms or geohelminths have been particularly prevalent. The most common of these worms are *Ascaris lumbricoides*, *Trichuris trichiuria*, and *Necator americanus*. *Ascaris* is one of the largest (females can measure up to 45 cm) intestinal worms that infects humans. *Trichuris* is not as large as *Ascaris*, and is known as human whipworm. Infections with *Trichuris* are more likely to be asymptomatic than are *Ascaris* infections. Infections by *Necator*, also known as hookworm, might be accompanied by anemia, as the host suffers from blood loss. All of these macroparasites are transmitted through contaminated water or food and by lack of basic hygienic measures such as hand-washing (www.biosci. ohio-state.edu/~parasite/ascaris.html; www.nematodes.org/nematodeESTs/ Necator/Necator.html). Several surveys demonstrate the prevalence of these three geohelminth infections in the Caribbean. In two samples of children taken in high-risk areas of Jamaica, 38.3 and 42–47% were infected with *Trichuris* and 19.4 and 15–37% with *Ascaris* (Wong *et al.*, 1994). In one of the samples, intestinal worm infection and anemia were both associated with lower achievement in school (Hutchinson *et al.*, 1997). In Guyana, *Necator* was found to be most common, in 28.2% of children, whereas the frequency of *Ascaris* was 18.8% and that of *Trichuris* was 14.1% (Lindo *et al.*, 2002).

Although all of these gastrointestinal pathogens are plentiful, ranging from macro- to microparasites, from bacteria to viruses, they tend to produce intense diarrhea and to affect children, who succumb quickly to dehydration. Water or food contaminated with fecal manner is the usual mode of transmission. The water does not need to be drunk, as infection can occur while bathing or walking in contaminated water. A frequently overlooked cultural factor that might enhance diarrheal diseases is shortened breast-feeding, as mother's milk includes antibodies against pathogens to which mother and baby are exposed, and babies who are weaned do not have passively acquired immunity (Campbell, 1988; Krumeich *et al.*, 2001; Levine and Levine, 1995).

Diarrheal diseases such as cholera, dysentery, typhoid fever, and macro-parasitic intestinal infections are diseases of poverty (Theodore-Gandi,

1991). As such, we can expect them to have been major killers of African slaves and their descendents until rather recently. Particularly affected should have been children, whose nutritional status is compromised by any of these ailments. Indeed, the synergistic effect of undernutrition and infectious diarrheal diseases has already been noted (Käferstein, 2003). Not surprisingly, diseases of the "stomach and bowels" made an important contribution to the morbidity of African troops serving in the West Indies in 1819–36, having been responsible for about 90 admissions per 1000 per year (Curtin, 1988). Moreover, there is evidence of diarrhea, dysentery, the "bloody flux," and various intestinal worms in the medical writings from plantations. It is also clear that slavers were concerned about the effects of "dirt-eating" on slaves, as this was a practice much prosecuted by the slavers. What is not understood is whether this was a cultural practice of the slaves with which they sought to alleviate undernutrition or even to de-parasitize themselves (Kiple, 1988).

According to DeSantis (1997), diarrheal diseases remain a major child killer in the Americas as a result of contaminated water and food. In the Caribbean, however, the number of deaths attributed to gastrointestinal infections decreased between the 1980s and the 1990s. This decrease is most likely due to a cleaner water supply and more readily available oral rehydration therapy. Indeed, the control of gastrointestinal infections probably contributed in great part to the epidemiological transition of the region. Despite this decrease in mortality due to diarrheal diseases, large segments of the Afro-Caribbean population get contaminated water and are exposed to improper solid-waste disposal. In addition, the indiscriminate use of antidiarrheal drugs might have led to the rise of drug-resistant strains (PAHO, 1994).

As diseases of poverty, gastrointestinal infectious are some of the easiest to eliminate. Clean water and appropriate sewage disposal are two key, relatively low-cost, elements. An important point, however, is that individuals need to be educated in the adequate use of latrines, hand-washing, and cooking. Any educational campaign towards eliminating gastrointestinal diseases through behavioral changes such as these must be done within the culture of the educational subjects: changing people's behavior is not easy, and it is nearly impossible if it conflicts with their own cultural values (Krumeich *et al.*, 2001; Manderson, 1998).

In conclusion, all indications are that for several centuries, from the beginning of the slave trade until the 1900s, Afro-Caribbean populations suffered greatly from gastrointestinal infections. All the diseases discussed above, whether caused by macroparasites, bacteria, or protozoans, are associated with contaminated water and food supply. It is not difficult to imagine that such would be the case in a plantation. Great strides were made in much of the Caribbean as a result of a clean water supply during the 1900s. It is quite obvious that groups that still suffer from these infections are those living in conditions of poverty, not only in the countryside, as perhaps was the case in the 1900s, but in shanty towns around large urban areas. Indeed, this is the case with Haiti, where rural-to-urban migration has brought many people to live in crowded conditions without an adequate water supply. Thus it is probably not appropriate to speak broadly of "the food- and water-supply situation in the Caribbean." Whereas some segments of the population have benefited from clean water and food, and have been without major gastrointestinal disease burdens for several generations, others have not.

### 3.7   HIV infection and AIDS

There are so many sources available on the human immunodeficiency virus (HIV-1) and acquired immunodeficiency syndrome (AIDS) that it is not possible to offer an exhaustive literature review on these subjects. The Internet provides numerous sites to get updated information on the virus and the syndrome, such as www.niaid.nih.gov/factsheets/hivinf.htm, www.cdc.gov/hiv/bscience.htm, www.nlm.nih.gov/medlineplus/aids.html, and www.tulane.edu/~dmsander/garryfavweb.html. Petchesky (2003) provides an excellent account of the struggle by underdeveloped countries to obtain anti-HIV medicines. To this issue, Davis and Fort (2004) add that the staggering number of AIDS deaths in underdeveloped countries illustrates how transnational pharmaceutical companies have negatively impacted the health of the world's poor.

There is broad agreement in the scientific community that the causal agent of AIDS is HIV-1, a slow retrovirus. Outside of the traditional, well-established scientific community there are challenges to the proposition that HIV is the causal agent of the disease AIDS. These alternative views will not be reviewed in this book. Instead, the reader is directed to websites such as www.virusmyth.net/aids/.

Figure 3.2 shows a diagram of the HIV life cycle. The HIV retrovirus is a simple infective agent whose genetic material is in the form of RNA enveloped by a capsid. The capsid is surrounded by an envelope, which is derived from the host-cell plasma membrane and is acquired when the virus buds through the cell membrane. The envelope also contains viral-derived glycoproteins such as gp120 and gp141. When a retrovirus invades a host cell, it injects into the cytoplasm both its RNA and its

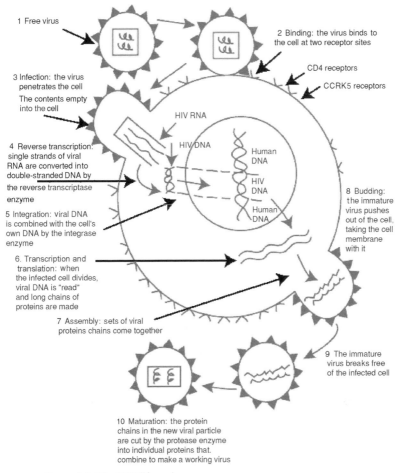

1 Free virus

2 Binding: the virus binds to the cell at two receptor sites

CD4 receptors

3 Infection: the virus penetrates the cell

The contents empty into the cell

CCRK5 receptors

HIV RNA

4 Reverse transcription: single strands of viral RNA are converted into double-stranded DNA by the reverse transcriptase enzyme

HIV DNA

Human DNA

HIV DNA

Human DNA

5 Integration: viral DNA is combined with the cell's own DNA by the integrase enzyme

8 Budding: the immature virus pushes out of the cell, taking the cell membrane with it

6. Transcription and translation: when the infected cell divides, viral DNA is "read" and long chains of proteins are made

7 Assembly: sets of viral proteins chains come together

9 The immature virus breaks free of the infected cell

10 Maturation: the protein chains in the new viral particle are cut by the protease enzyme into individual proteins that combine to make a working virus

Figure 3.2. The HIV life cycle.

enzymes (reverse transcriptase, integrase, and viral protease), which allow the RNA to produce a complementary DNA (cDNA) molecule, which is then inserted into the host's own DNA. This viral DNA contains the information for the production of viral proteins and all the components of the viral capsid. As part of the host's chromosomes, the viral DNA is replicated and passed on to daughter cells.

The target cells of the HIV are macrophages and T cells which carry the CD4+ antigen, whose immune role is to present foreign antigens to other cells to precipitate an immune reaction. It seems that to enter a cell, the virus requires two receptors: CD4 and CCRK5 as shown in Figure 3.2

(also known as CCR5). HIV entry into a host cell requires an initial attachment of one of its envelope glycoproteins (gp120) to the cell's CD4 receptors. This initial attachment enables the viral envelope to bind to a coreceptor, such as CCRK5. At this point, another viral glycoprotein (gp41) brings both viral and cellular membranes into close proximity and facilitates the actual merger. It seems that there is another factor involved in HIV entry, the host cell's oxido-reductase protein disulfide isomerase (PDI). This review of cellular entry is based on papers published during the year of the writing of this book (Markovic and Clouse, 2004; Nguyen *et al.*, 2004), but the reader is cautioned to keep in mind that knowledge about HIV infection changes constantly, and that newer sources should be found.

Since the host antigen CCRK5 is involved in viral entry, the possibility that host mutations in this protein might affect viral entry has been researched extensively. The polymorphisms in the CCRK5 and other linked receptors have been investigated, leading to the classification of CCRK5 alleles into nine distinct human haplogroups, all characterized by polymorphism at different positions in the CCRK5 promoter region (Nguyen *et al.*, 2004). It now appears that if individuals inherit two copies of the CCRK5 gene which contains a 32-base-pair deletion (in the open reading frame, CCRK5-Δ32), they are relatively resistant to HIV infection. It has been proposed that mutations that offer resistance to HIV infection are more commonly found in European-derived populations because they also offered resistance from the pathogen that caused the Black Death in Europe. Perhaps the best articulation of this viewpoint is to be found in the book by Scott and Duncan (2001) entitled *Biology of Plagues*, in which the authors convincingly argue that the Black Death was not caused by *Yersinia pestis*, the pathogen that causes bubonic plague. On the contrary, Scott and Duncan argue that the Black Death was a severe hemorrhagic illness, not unlike Ebola viral infections, and whose extreme virulence was a strong selective agent for resistant individuals; that is, individuals with the CCRK5-Δ32 mutation. The work of Libert *et al.* (1998) provides the basis for this suggestion, since they proposed that most CCRK5-Δ32 mutations arose from a single event in Europe, where their current distribution could not be explained by random genetic drift but most likely by positive selection. Further, Stephens *et al.* (1998) dated the mutation to about 700 years ago, and offer support for a strong selective agent similar to HIV to be responsible for the presence of the mutation in northern Europeans. Since the CCRK5-Δ32 mutation is not common in human populations outside of Europe, its absence has been proposed to be responsible for the rapid spread of HIV infection in Africa and in African-derived groups such as those of the Caribbean (Scott and Duncan, 2001).

Two groups of researchers have recently tested in mice whether the presence of the deletion ($CCRK5^{-/-}$) inhibits *Y. pestis* infection. Both groups found that there was no survival difference in control and $CCRK5^{-/-}$ mice, although one group found an in-vitro difference in the infection of macrophages by *Yersinia,* suggesting that the relation between the pathogen and the mutation is not altogether simple (Elvin *et al.*, 2004; Mecsas *et al.*, 2004). Whereas this recent work puts in doubt the suggestion that the CCRK5-Δ32 mutation offers resistance to *Yersinia* infection, it does not address Stephen *et al.*'s (1998) and Scott and Duncan's (2001) suggestion that the Black Death was not caused by *Yersinia* but was caused instead by a viral agent similar to the Ebola virus. Of course, since such a virus is presumably not alive any more, it is difficult to perform in-vivo and in-vitro tests with it.

Ancient DNA work has added more fuel to the debate on the identity of the plague pathogen: Raoult *et al.* (2000) isolated *Y. pestis* from the teeth pulp of three skeletons presumably at a plague common grave, and suggest that the debate can now end: the medieval Black Death *was* caused by *Yersinia*. Such strong conclusion is contested by Wood and DeWitte-Aviña (2003, 2004), who argue for a pathogen different from *Yersinia*, unlike anything alive to date. Whether the high frequency of the CCRK5-Δ32 mutation is due to selection by an Ebola-like pathogen during the Middle Ages in northern Europe is unclear. What is clear is that this mutation is rare to non-existent in African-derived populations.

Infection with HIV-1 produces strong immune responses, involving both cytotoxic T lymphocytes (CTLs) and antibody responses, responses that keep the virus at a stable level during a prolonged asymptomatic period. Recent work has shown that there are also intracellular immune reactions which protect the host (Navarro and Landau, 2004). As the HIV infection progresses, more and more CD4+ cells are killed off by the virus, and the patient's immune status declines. Eventually, the clinical manifestations of AIDS are apparent, most conspicuously an inability to fight HIV-1 and other infections. Although the patient's immune response with CD4+ is compromised, his/her response with B cells and CD8+ T cells continues to be vigorous.

A host is not affected by one single population of HIV but actually contains viral populations of great genetic diversity, mainly as a result of the virus' high rates of mutation and immense population size. An important force determining the evolution of HIV-1 within a host is her/his drug therapy, as drug-resistant strains become more frequent within a host if s/he is exposed to drugs (Leal *et al.*, 2004). See Bailey *et al.* (2004) for a recent overview of viral mechanisms of immune avoidance and Buckheit (2004) for a review of HIV drug resistance.

When the syndrome of acquired immunodeficiency first received attention from the medical profession and from the public in the early 1980s, the Caribbean became virtually attached to it as a risk factor. Retrospectively, it seems that the first case in the region occurred in Haiti in 1978, although the first properly diagnosed case occurred in Jamaica in 1982.

Without a doubt, the Caribbean region which received the most negative press as a risk factor and a depository of the disease was Haiti. Reviewing the popular press from the 1980s, Pape (1999) finds it obvious that at the time there was fear of the unknown, and even a demonization of Haitians, and their sexual and cultural practices. The fear of AIDS and Haiti was in agreement with popular-press reports of Haiti as an exotic place, where cannibalism, voodoo, and zombies were everyday occurrences (Conner and Sparks, 2004; Lawless, 1991). This is particularly ironic in that the virus was probably introduced into Haiti through contact with the homosexual community of the USA, since the first case of AIDS in Haiti appeared 1 year later than the first case in the USA (Lawless, 1991; Lewis *et al.*, 1997; Wheeler and Radcliffe, 1994). As Lawless (1991) notes, Haiti was openly promoted in the New York gay community during the 1970s and 1980s as a great destination for gay sex tourists.

In most of the Caribbean, HIV initially was transmitted through male homosexual and bisexual sex, supporting the 1980s notion that AIDS was a "homosexual" disease. As recently as 1997, Lewis *et al.* reported that 67% of all cases in the Caribbean were of male subjects. However, the demographic profile of those affected has changed since that time, and the disease is now primarily transmitted through heterosexual sex (Camara, 1999; Quinn, 1995; Wasserheit, 1995; World Bank, 2001). Transfusion infections do not contribute an important proportion of cases in the Caribbean, as effective screening of the blood supply started in the mid 1980s. Women are becoming a particularly vulnerable segment of the population to infection, and, as a result, female and pediatric cases are both on the rise. Thus most children infected with HIV received the virus in utero or through mother's milk. In 2001, the number of pediatric cases in some of the Caribbean regions was among the highest in the entire American continent: 18.2% of HIV/AIDS cases in the British Virgin Islands occurred among children (Camara, 1999; Lewis *et al.*, 1997; Quinn, 1995; Sobesky *et al.*, 2000; World Bank, 2001). The problem of transmission from mother to baby through breast-feeding is not a simple one: whereas it is much better for a baby to be breast-fed so that s/he is protected from most infectious diseases, it *might* be best for him/her not to be breast-fed if the mother is HIV-infected, as long as clean water is available for affordable formula (World Bank, 2001). The fact that the AIDS epidemic has become a heterosexual and not a homosexual problem has actually had the unforeseen effect of obscuring the still fairly high prevalence rate of the infection in homosexual males. Indeed, it was not until 2002 that a United Nations AIDS initiative on HIV in men who have sex with men in the Caribbean and Latin America was established (Cáceres and Stall, 2003).

Another aspect of the AIDS epidemic in the Caribbean, which has changed, is that because of effective use of chemotherapy, the incidence of full-blown cases of AIDS has decreased in some regions, for example French Guiana. For this reason, an accurate count of the epidemic is best obtained not from the clinical cases, but from surveys such as those done at maternity clinics, where most patients are routinely tested (Sobesky *et al.*, 2000).

The great majority of affected individuals are of productive age; that is, between 20 and 44 years. Farmer and Castro (2004) fear that parts of the Caribbean might suffer from the "missing generation," as is happening in Africa. This possibility of course, raises the specter of a large number of orphans in the near future, not to mention the productive costs to the economy of the region (Pape, 1999; Wheeler and Radcliffe, 1994; World Bank, 2001).

Despite similarities across the Caribbean region in that most patients are between 20 and 44 years of age and had a greater probability of acquiring the disease heterosexually, the region is not homogeneous in terms of the extent of the epidemic (Camara, 1999; Farmer and Castro, 2004). Some countries have the highest prevalence of HIV/AIDS among adults in Latin America and the Caribbean, such as Haiti, the Dominican Republic, the Bahamas, Barbados, and Guyana, with a prevalence rate between 2 and 5%. In contrast, Cuba has an exceedingly low prevalence rate (0.02%), reflecting a government policy, which though effective, has been the focus of human-rights criticisms (Conner and Sparks, 2004). Moreover, whereas some countries have a generalized epidemic, affecting broad sections of the population (Haiti, Dominican Republic, Barbados), others have a "concentrated" epidemic, affecting primarily homosexual and bisexual males (Guyana), and still others have a significant population of intravenous drug users who are particularly at risk (Puerto Rico and Bermuda; Farmer and Castro, 2004; Morrison, 2001; Sobesky *et al.*, 2000; World Bank, 2001).

The relationship between drug use and HIV infection is not simple. The Caribbean has been a stop point for cocaine traffickers for a long time, so that this drug is not unusual in the region. The adoption of crack cocaine in some areas of the Caribbean is linked to AIDS in that it is tied to poverty, and unprotected sex in exchange for the drug. On the other hand, Puerto Rico and Bermuda, with their sizeable population of intravenous drug users face a different problem, namely the sharing of contaminated needles. Therefore, whereas crack cocaine is linked to high risk of HIV infection because it is associated with unprotected sex, heroin is associated with HIV infection because its users might share contaminated needles (Bastos *et al.*, 1999; Wasserheit, 1995). Therefore, any government efforts to stop the spread of HIV among drug users need to consider that the route of transmission of the virus differs in the different drug-user communities.

Haiti is the area in the Caribbean with the largest AIDS problem, being the only country in the Americas in which AIDS is the number one cause of all adult deaths (Farmer and Castro, 2004). The common use of injections in the island's folk medical system appears to be tied to the generalized epidemic seen there. Given that the needles and other items used for these injections are unlikely to be sterilized, and given that injections are very popular, they provide an exceptionally effective transmission route for the virus (Lawless, 1991). In Haiti, AIDS is frequently seen as the result of a black magic spell, so that patients tend to seek help from non-biomedical practitioners. Perhaps as a result of the lack of understanding of the epidemiological basis of the disease, but also because of the bad press received during the 1980s, there are few community-support systems for AIDS sufferers in Haiti (Conner and Sparks, 2004).

The impact of AIDS on the demographic profile of the Afro-Caribbean population is already being felt, having started to change mortality and morbidity profiles of the area (Holder and Lewis, 1997). Indeed, it is an infectious disease that has gained in prevalence rates and as a cause of mortality, surpassing chronic, cardiovascular diseases in importance. It is no overstatement that the AIDS epidemic will affect population growth in the region as it becomes the main cause of death of young adults. But it will do so differently from most other infectious diseases, which usually affect the younger age groups. Instead, AIDS will remove a sizable portion of working-age individuals, and leave the elderly and the young without traditional family support. The economic impact of the disease can also not be overstated. Not only will the governments need to step up to take care of the dependent age groups, but they will also have to divert precious resources towards the control and prevention of the disease (Camara, 1999; Lewis *et al.*, 1997; Morrison, 2001).

Much of the governments' efforts to stop the epidemic have focused on stopping the sexual, perinatal, and blood supply transmission of the virus, with the use of condoms being the main focus of efforts (Camara, 1999). Throughout the world, public measures against the AIDS epidemic stumbled with the problem of a reluctance to discuss sexual behavior openly, including homosexual and commercial sex. For this reason, promoting the widespread use of condoms is not easy (Farmer and Castro, 2004; Morrison, 2001). As Stuart (1999) notes, there are cultural reasons why condom use is not adopted as much as it should be. Even with information about the risks of unprotected sex, males do not adopt it, and females are not in a position to ask it, resulting in a continuing heterosexual spread of the disease. Thus, the problem with lack of condom use is clearly not one of lack of information, but of the culture surrounding the transmission of HIV. Several authors note that the widespread Caribbean acceptance of concurrent relations and of serial monogamy provides an ideal cultural milieu for the spread of sexually transmitted diseases (Camara, 1999; Lewis *et al.*, 1997; World Bank, 2001). But most important is the widespread fact that if a woman requests the use of a condom she would offend her partner (Feldman and Miller, 1998; Morrison, 2001; World Bank, 2001). Thus even if a woman knows that her husband or boyfriend has not protected himself in the past, or is not even currently protecting himself when having sex with other women or with men, she might not feel that she can request him to use a condom. As a result, we see women becoming more and more the victims of AIDS.

Teenage girls might be particularly vulnerable, as they might have even less power than adult women in their relations. Interestingly, it has been shown that adolescent women who engage in high-risk sexual behavior do not see themselves to be at high risk. It appears that even if these women have access to information, they have not interiorized it, and put it into action. It is well known that adolescent pregnant girls are a high-risk category for both themselves and their babies: since pregnant teens are still growing, they are in actual competition for resources with their fetuses. And babies born to teenage mothers have a high probability of being premature or of low birth weight (Frisancho *et al.*, 1983). With the threat of AIDS, the high-risk status of these mothers and babies has only risen (Yinger *et al.*, 1992).

In conclusion, the culture surrounding sexual relations in the Caribbean might interfere with an effective implementation of condom use as a deterrent to HIV infection. Not only does the status of women need to be addressed, but also the status of sex workers, particularly when it comes to dealing with foreign sex tourists (World Bank, 2001). It is evident that if an individual, whether male or female, is in a disadvantaged position, s/he will be unable to insist on the use of condoms, even if s/he knows that s/he is engaging in high-risk sexual behavior (Feldman and Miller, 1998). Another concomitant problem that is only likely to increase is the use of crack cocaine, associated with poverty and use of sex for obtaining the drug. In this case, a broader social approach towards eradicating the drug and alleviating poverty needs to accompany efforts to implement condom use. A further problem is that because individuals infected with HIV are afraid of social ostracism, they might not communicate their HIV status to new or current partners (Camara, 1999). Or even further, infected individuals might be unaware of their HIV status as they might not seek to be tested as a result of the ostracism towards AIDS patients (World Bank, 2001). In terms of education, several authors note that it should be targeted to specific groups, for example women in stable relations, parents of sexually active teenagers, sex workers, and even children (Morrison, 2001; Walrond, 1999; Wheeler and Radcliffe, 1994). As Krumeich *et al.* (2001) note, changing people's health behavior is not easy. Only a culturally sensitive approach, which considers the socio-cultural, ethnic, and economic circumstances of the subjects, will be successful.

Given that the epidemiologic AIDS situation in specific Caribbean regions is different, sometimes affecting the general population, some-times the gay and drug-using population, even with diverse rates of increase, we should not look at the Caribbean as a homogenous epidemi-ological AIDS region, but as one that is undergoing several different epidemics (Bastos *et al.*, 1999; Lewis *et al.*, 1997; Wheeler and Radcliffe, 1994; World Bank, 2001).

### 3.8    Tuberculosis

Tuberculosis (also known as TB) is caused by the air-borne bacterium *Mycobacterium tuberculosis*, which is spread through air droplets. On rare occasions, other species of *Mycobactorium* infect humans (Iseman, 1995; Legrand *et al.*, 2000). The pathogen is an obligate aerobe, which grows successfully in tissues with a high partial pressure of oxygen, such as the lungs. It is also a slow-growing organism, which accounts for the fact that many human lesions are either subacute or chronic. Other infectious diseases, such as measles, have much higher rates of transmission than does tuberculosis, which might infect only one-third of individuals in close contact with the patient. Whereas the mode of transmission of tuberculosis is well understood, it is not clear why some individuals become infected, and of those infected, why some develop the disease while others keep a latent infection for many years. But the proportion of infected individuals who are free of symptoms can be as high as 90% (Strull and Dym, 1995).

If the pathogen is not eliminated by the host upon initial infection, there can be a progressive disseminated disease affecting different tissues. Spread of the disease can occur by the lymphatic or the blood system. In this manner, tuberculosis can affect several different tissues, hence the tuberculosis classification system by location of disease: pulmonary, pleural, lymphatic, bone and/or joint, genitourinary disseminated (miliary), meningeal, peritoneal, etc. The most obvious sign of pulmonary tuberculosis, and that which is in the popular mind, is the strong, frequent bouts of cough together with "consumption," or a general wasting of the individual. In its more advanced forms, tuberculosis can involve the bones, and leave a distinct mark in the thoracic vertebrae spines (Pott's disease) or in other areas such as the hips, knees, and phalanges (Goodman *et al.*, 1984; Perzigian *et al.*, 1984; www.orthoteers.co.uk/Nrujp~ij33lm/Orthtb.htm).

Alternatively, the initial infection can be asymptomatic, later progressing to overt clinical expression. This "latent" infection appears to be contained in granulomas, which are structures consisting of various immune cells (Pozos and Ramakrishan, 2004). If the granulomas do not heal, they are also characterized by necrosis; but if they do heal, they do so by encapsulation, calcification, and scar formation.

Primary tuberculosis is the childhood infection, which usually has no major clinical manifestations, and is recognized by a skin test. This primary infection is usually resolved without therapy. Postprimary tuberculosis is the adolescent/adult infection, which can result in more significant symptoms, such as high fever, cough, and pleuritic chest pain and occasional shortness of breath (Strull and Dym, 1995). Approximately 60% of postprimary infections will resolve spontaneously. These postprimary infections will usually occur because the disease is reactivated (after a latency period) or because the patient is exposed to the pathogen again. This exposure to a new inoculum has become a frequent cause of postprimary infections, as more and more individuals are being exposed to the pathogen. The human immune response to the bacterium appears to involve CD4 T cells, which explains why HIV and tuberculosis are so deadly together (Iseman, 1995; Lauzardo and Ashkin, 2000).

Genetic studies of the pathogen have indicated that the human bacterium originated relatively recently, probably as recently as 15–20 000 years ago, having speciated from bovine tuberculosis. The most plausible site for the origin of the human pathogen appears to have been Europe, with a subsequent, recent spread to the rest of the world (Sola *et al.*, 1997, 1999; Sreevatsan, 1997). Recent molecular studies of the tuberculosis bacterium in the Caribbean have shown the importance of human migration in the introduction of this pathogen to the region. Sola *et al.* (1997, 1999) have noted that after the introduction of the parasite only about 500 years ago, in Guadeloupe it has remained similar to pathogens isolated in settings as far away as Polynesia and South Africa.

Before the pathogen for tuberculosis was isolated in 1882 by Koch, the disease was known to be associated with poor living conditions (Sola *et al.*, 1997), as dramatized in Puccini's *La Bohème*. Even in paleopathological studies, tuberculosis has been shown to be a problem among settled agriculturalists with a relatively poor-quality diet as opposed to mobile hunters and gatherers, with a more variable and qualitatively better diet (Perzigian *et al.*, 1984).

Although in any discussion about the resurgence of infectious disease, tuberculosis is presented as the classical example of a disease that was controlled and virtually eliminated but came back, this representation is being challenged. Thus, on one hand we see statements that as recently as the 1980s in medical schools in the USA tuberculosis was presented to students as a disease on the verge of eradication (Iseman, 1995; Lauzardo and Ashkin, 2000; Strull and Dym, 1995), and on the other hand some authors note that tuberculosis never came close to being eradicated in the majority of the world, only in wealthy sections of wealthy nations. It has been argued that what has prompted the acceptance that the disease is making a comeback after the 1970–80s is simply the fact that there has been more migration, which has brought the previously hidden disease to a more public sphere. Currently the disease, whether caused by a drug-resistant or milder pathogen, is killing more humans than it ever did (Porter *et al.*, 2002). But tuberculosis was always present in poor areas of the world (Farmer, 1996); not only this, but also it was never eradicated in poor sectors of wealthy nations. For example, tuberculosis was rampant in the adult homeless population of large urban areas in the USA (Strull and Dym, 1995). The differential distribution of tuberculosis between wealthy and poor countries not only affects the rising number of cases in migrant-receiving countries such as the USA and the UK, which have witnessed a tremendous increase of cases, many of them among migrants (Strull and Dym, 1995). Instead, these migrant-brought cases are also seen within the Caribbean. For example, in Guadeloupe, where the number of cases had decreased from 25 in 100 000 inhabitants in 1982 to 10 in 100 000 inhabitants in 1988, 18% of all cases from 1982 to 1994 were found in Haitian migrants (Roussel *et al.*, 1996). Clearly, the relationship between migration and the rise in tuberculosis cannot be overlooked, not even within the Caribbean region. Porter *et al.* (2002) see the rise of tuberculosis worldwide as part of the globalization of the capitalist economy, a process reviewed in Chapter 2.

The resurgence of the threat of tuberculosis is not only due to the heightened world migration which has brought poor people into more visible places, but also due to the HIV-infection epidemic (Porter *et al.*, 2002). In the USA, for example, two main subpopulations are suffering tuberculosis. First are the poor, including the urban homeless population as well as immigrants. This group, then, encapsulates the tuberculosis cases which existed before the 1980s but were "hidden" from the public's notice, as well as the cases brought by poor migrants. Second are the AIDS patients. In the initial stages of the AIDS epidemic, this second group of tuberculosis sufferers were very different from the first, as they were not indigent, they were mostly gay, and lived in cities with large gay communities such as San Francisco, New York, and Miami. As the profile of the AIDS epidemic changed, and because AIDS became a heterosexually transmitted disease, the AIDS/tuberculosis patients are a more general sample from the population, including women and children (Strull and Dym, 1995). Outside of the USA, in Africa for instance, HIV and tuberculosis co-infection is rampant. In Malawi for example, the rate of HIV infection among tuberculosis patients was as high as 70% (Ridzon, 2004). In reality, neither disease should be viewed in isolation, and medical practitioners are thus trying to design the best chemotherapy for patients infected with both pathogens, while trying to spare the patient from severe secondary effects of the medicines.

It is unfortunate that not much information is available on the evolution of the disease in the Caribbean prior to the 1900s. However, it is fair to venture that Afro-Caribbean populations, during and after slavery, living in cramped conditions, with poor diet and excessive amounts of physical work, would be at great risk of the disease.

As Curtin (1988) notes, it is very difficult to determine from slaver's reports whether African slaves suffered from pneumonia or tuberculosis, or yet another "disease of the lungs." Be that as it may, both pneumonia and tuberculosis were the most likely to account for most of such "lung" morbidity and mortality. Indeed, "diseases of the lungs" were a chronic problem of the slaves and their descendants for centuries (Curtin, 1988).

Tuberculosis in particular was deadly for the African slaves in the New World. The disease was relatively rare in Africa in comparison with Europe, and the living conditions of the slaves made them highly vulnerable to the disease.

In the Caribbean, tuberculosis remained a disease without proper care until the 1940s, when sanatoria and special hospital wards were established, and new drugs were introduced. In the 1950s and 1960s a more aggressive response to the disease with chemotherapy, and an incorporation of the tuberculosis programs into the general health services of the various countries, resulted in a lowering in morbidity and mortality. Richardson (1979) calls the 1970s the decade of tuberculosis complacency in the Caribbean, as it was in the wealthy nations (www.carec.org/data/tb/tb_cases_chart_80_20.html). According to Werker *et al.* (1994), the efforts to control drug-resistant tuberculosis and tuberculosis and AIDS co-infection in most of the English-speaking Caribbean region are inadequate. In 1994, 19% of 204 isolates in the Caribbean were drug-resistant, and in 1998–9 11% of 90 isolates were drug-resistant (Prabhakar, 2000). Thus, resistant tuberculosis pathogens are an important problem in the Caribbean, particularly when the migration patterns of the area are considered. In Haiti, multidrug-resistant strains are associated with patients who did not comply with therapy (Ferdinand *et al.*, 2003).

The difference in the number of cases of tuberculosis between different countries of the Caribbean region is quite startling. For example, for the year 2000 CAREC reports two cases in Antigua and Barbuda and 210 in Guyana (www.carec.org/data/tb/tb_80_00.html). These numbers are not adjusted for population size, and as such they are not prevalence rates. Perhaps the most ominous number we found is the prevalence rate in Haiti: in 1999, Pape (1999) reported that 80% of the adult population in Haiti was infected with the tuberculosis bacterium. In a report from the French Guiana, the principal AIDS-defining diagnosis was presence of tuberculosis, which was found in 20% of AIDS cases (Sobesky *et al.*, 2000). Equally distressing is a recent report that in Guadeloupe, several AIDS patients were infected with the usually opportunistic pathogen *Mycobacterium simiae*. Most patients shared a specific type, which is very similar to one found in Cuba, but two even had a previously unreported type (Legrand *et al.*, 2000). The co-infection of HIV and *Mycobacterium* confirms how weakened the immune system of AIDS patients becomes, and how prone they are to other opportunistic infections, even those caused by unusual human strains.

In conclusion, tuberculosis was a disease that caused much mortality and morbidity among the African slaves and their descendants for hundreds of years. Given that it is a disease of the poor, it affected the overworked and undernourished Afro-Caribbean peoples. Tuberculosis was not on the verge of eradication in the "decades of complacency," be that the 1950s, the 1960s, or the 1970s. It was hidden, concentrated among the poor, whether inside rich nations such as the USA (among its homeless urban population) or in the Caribbean, in islands such as Haiti. Since tuberculosis is a disease with very low rates of clinical manifestation among those infected, its active morbid state is tied to the conditions of poverty to which it is so obviously linked. The recently seen increase in tuberculosis cases in the Caribbean and in large migrant-receiving centers such as the USA or the UK reflect both the increase of migration-related cases as well as the increased frequency of AIDS cases. Among some Afro-Caribbean groups such as those of Haiti, AIDS and tuberculosis are tightly linked. In other, wealthier areas of the Caribbean, where tuberculosis had been nearly eradicated, migration from poorer islands has brought tuberculosis back. The difference is that the pathogen is now likely to be drug-resistant, and much more difficult to treat. As long as the poverty surrounding tuberculosis patients continues and effective chemotherapy programs are not in place, the disease is unlikely to disappear from the Caribbean. On the contrary, given the high prevalence rates of AIDS, the costs associated with tuberculosis chemotherapy, the problems delivering it, and the lack of prospects for the eradication of poverty in areas such as Haiti, the Caribbean is likely to see an increase in the severity of the problem of tuberculosis. Porter *et al.* (2002) conclude that the eradication of tuberculosis will only succeed if a global control strategy is adopted, in which the principles of social justice and equity address the socioeconomic causes of the disease.

## 3.9   Yellow fever

Yellow fever is a viral, vector-borne disease which afflicted Afro-Caribbean populations for several centuries and has been largely brought under control. The virus belongs to the Flaviviridae family and is transmitted by *A. aegypti*, just like dengue, another member of the same viral family. However, in most cases yellow fever does not cause as severe a pathology as dengue. Patients usually experience flu-like symptoms and recover quickly. On some occasions however, individuals might suffer from internal bleeding, kidney failure, meningitis, hepatitis (resulting in the yellow color taken by the patient's skin), and a high fever. If a patient suffers from the disease as a child, the morbidity is usually milder, and the infection results in lifelong immunity. Currently, yellow fever is found in South America and in Africa, and only occasionally in the Caribbean. It is not found in Asia, despite the presence of available vectors (Parker and Parker, 2002; www.netdoctor.co.uk/travel/diseases/yellowfever.htm).

The virus is heterogeneous between South America and Africa and even within Africa, several strains are present (Cockburn, 1963; Wang *et al.*, 1997). Much has been written about the history of yellow fever in North, Central, and South America, and a cursory search on the Internet will provide many historical accounts of the disease in the USA. These are not cited because they are mostly non-refereed pieces of work, but they do show a keen interest in the history of the disease. Concerning the disease's importance in Central America, much has been written about its medical understanding and about its importance in the construction of the Panama Canal (Delaporte, 1991). But when it comes to a review of yellow fever in the Caribbean, not much information is found, whereas (non-informative) controversy about the disease abounds.

The protagonists of the controversy surrounding yellow fever in the Caribbean are Sheldon Watts (2001) and Kenneth Kiple (2001). Only two of their writings are cited here, as they contain citations of the authors' earlier works. Kiple's position is that "Blacks" have an inherited protection from yellow fever, which is according to him a disease of African origin. In this manner, he explains the much higher yellow fever mortality of "Whites" in the Caribbean. Watts questions Kiple's position about the origin of yellow fever, and notes that most likely the virus originated in the New World, as is suggested by Mayan documents, and that it was imported to Africa as late as the 1760s. He goes on to note Kiple's poor use of human classification terms such as "Blacks," his lack of substantiation of an inherited protection, and his over-reliance on southern USA medical writings. According to Watts, these medical writings stress the low yellow fever morbidity and mortality of "Blacks" not because these people did not get the disease, but because the documents' authors wanted to show the descendents of African slaves to be beasts of burden who did not get sick like "White" people.

Our purpose in this book is of course not to arbitrate between Watts and Kiple but to present a review of yellow fever's effect on the evolution of Afro-Caribbean populations. Concerning the origin of the disease, there is evidence in support of both the New and Old World as places of origin for the disease. For example, Monath (1994) cites the same Mayan manuscripts noted by Watts, manuscripts that describe an epidemic of black vomit, typical of yellow fever. Besides this manuscript, there is evidence that yellow fever affected broad areas of the New World, and European ports of call, which traded New World goods. Wilkinson (1995) supports a New World origin to the disease (or less likely that the pathogen was endemic in both Europe and the Americas) and proposes that yellow fever is responsible for the collapse of the classic lowland Maya civilization. On the other hand, a phylogenetic analysis of the flaviviruses indicates that yellow fever is of African origin, lending support to Kiple's position (Gaunt *et al.*, 2001; Lepiniec *et al.*, 1994).

A thorough search of the scientific literature indicates that whereas there is abundant evidence of the presence of acquired immunity in individuals previously exposed to the disease (indeed Thonnon *et al.*, 1998, note that lack of immunity was the greatest risk factor associated with infection during an epidemic in Senegal), no evidence is found of any inherited or genetic protection or immunity from yellow fever, besides Kiple's proposal, written from an historian's viewpoint. For example, two recent reviews of the genetic basis for susceptibility to and protection from infectious disease do not mention yellow fever as a disease to which there is a demonstrable inherited protection (Cooke and Hill, 2001; Hill, 2001). Thus, whereas there is clinical, in-vitro, and population and molecular genetic data showing that some humans have a genetic protection from malaria, no such data are found when it comes to yellow fever.

An additional point about epidemiological units of study is relevant here: in Chapter 2 we reviewed the so-called "slavery hypothesis," which proposes that descendants of African slaves have an inherited propensity to hypertension as a result of their suffering from vomiting and excessive sweating during the middle passage. One of the strongest criticisms we offered of this hypothesis is the use of "Blacks" or "Whites" as valid biological entities. Given what we know about the distribution of human genetic variation and ethnic groups' differential exposure to disease ecology, there is no justification for using, a priori, a genetic explanation for differences in disease frequencies between different ethnic groups. Statements about "Blacks" and "Whites" having differential genetic propensity to disease in the absence of any molecular or physiologic explanation for this difference reflects authors' lack of understanding of the distribution of human variation, and their assumption that their own folk classification of humans has a genetic basis, which it does not.

That yellow fever was an important disease for Afro-Caribbean groups, one to which they had no genetic or acquired immunity upon first confronting it, is not in dispute. And if Lewis' list of Caribbean epidemics is any indication, the disease was a frequent unwelcome guest in many Caribbean islands for several centuries (Lewis, 1991; also see Downs, 1991). But it is even difficult to obtain agreement about when the disease became a problem in the Caribbean islands. For example, Curtin (1988) states that yellow fever started affecting the Caribbean quite late, in 1860s and the 1870s, during which decades the disease appeared in epidemic form and usually affected migrants to the region. However, Lewis (1991) notes that there were several yellow fever epidemics as early as 1620 in Cuba, 1635 in Guadeloupe, and many others through the islands and up to the early 1900s.

Interestingly, the more recent history of yellow fever is very different from that of its close cousin, dengue fever. Whereas dengue is a disease associated with recent urban growth and ecology, yellow fever has been virtually eliminated from most of the Caribbean islands, despite the presence of the vector, which continues to spread dengue. The difference between the epidemiology of both diseases apparently results from the successful elimination of the virus in heavily human-populated areas when the campaign to eliminate the domesticated Caribbean mosquito *Aedes* appeared to have been won (see Section 3.5 on dengue). Thus when the vector came back with a vengeance, dengue took advantage of this oversupply of vectors, but yellow fever was no longer present. However, yellow fever has a sylvatic cycle, one for which the primary hosts are monkeys, so that new urban epidemics might occur after someone has ventured into the forest. This explains the continuing threat of yellow fever in parts of the South American and Central American Caribbean, and the virtual elimination of the disease in the Caribbean islands, where few forests remain. Trinidad is the one Caribbean island in which yellow fever cases have continued to be reported with frequency, prompting specula-tion that perhaps another mammal besides monkeys is the alternative host to humans. Although yellow fever is much more under control than is dengue, it has had its own increase, though at a much more modest rate since the 1980s, throughout the Caribbean area. Most likely, this increase in numbers is the result of sylvatic-acquired yellow fever, and not a result of the reintroduction of yellow fever as an urban disease such as dengue (Goncalvez *et al.*, 2002; Lewis, 1991; Monath, 1994; www.netdoctor.co. uk/travel/diseases/yellowfever.htm). For example, the first case of yellow fever in French Guiana since 1902 was reported in 1999, and it was a case of sylvatic-acquired yellow fever (Heraud *et al.*, 1999).

In conclusion, there is conflicting evidence about the origin of yellow fever, although phylogenetic work strongly indicates an African origin. But there is no evidence in support of the suggestion that people of African ancestry have genetic protection from the disease. On the contrary, all indications are that the disease ravaged Afro-Caribbean populations for several centuries. The temporary control in the mid

1900s of the *Aedes* mosquito successfully eradicated yellow fever in most of the Caribbean islands, where it is currently a sylvatic-origin disease. Given the greater contact of humans with tropical forest vectors and alternate hosts in Central and South American Caribbean regions, the sylvatic-acquired outbreaks have become more important and frequent in these regions since the 1980s. However, the disease is clearly less important than is its close cousin, dengue.

### 3.10   Conclusion

In this chapter we have reviewed the infectious diseases that have afflicted Afro-Caribbean groups for most of their history. The epidemiological data are neither large nor very clear when it comes to discerning the infectious diseases that plagued the slaves. For example, we don't know to what extent "diseases of the lung" among the slaves were truly dominated by tuberculosis, but we assumed that they were. Nor do we know to what extent yellow fever affected the slaves, as there are contradictory statements about when the disease became important in the Caribbean.

The general theme that emerges out of our research with infectious disease among the slaves and their immediate descendents after emancipation is that the slaves were in such a poor health and nutritional state, that they would have been very unlikely to be able to fight off infection effectively without dramatically deteriorating their already-poor nutritional status. Thus, the classical epidemiological state that we see in much of the underdeveloped world today, in which children die of a simple infection because they are severely undernourished, would probably be very common among the slave children. Adults as well would be at high risk of mortality and morbidity due to infection.

During the 1900s the Caribbean, more so than much of Latin America, was able to effectively control many of its main infectious-disease killers. The best examples of this are malaria and yellow fever, which were totally or virtually eradicated in much of the Caribbean, but which remained endemic in much of the Atlantic coast of Central America. As a result of this infectious-disease control, much of the Caribbean transitioned into an epidemiological pattern of chronic diseases with low morbidity and mortality due to infectious diseases. This state of affairs, however, deteriorated dramatically sometime around the 1980s, when many governments instituted neoliberal policies which restricted government-supported healthcare and promoted private healthcare initiatives (Farmer and Castro, 2004). It was during this decade that a number of infectious diseases became a serious concern again not only for the Caribbean but for all of Latin America. For example, gastrointestinal infections, which result in diarrhea and dehydration, and are easily avoided with a clean water and food supply, became a concern to the area once more. Malaria and tuberculosis are being seen in not-so-infrequent "rare" cases in areas where they were eradicated years ago. Dengue has become an important cause of mortality and morbidity and together with AIDS and tuberculosis is perhaps the most aggressive of the new infectious diseases. All of these diseases – tuberculosis, dengue, malaria, and gastrointestinal infections – are diseases associated with the urban ecology of shanty towns. It is no surprise that two of them require a mosquito vector, which thrives in such environments. It is no surprise either that gastrointestinal infections have made a comeback, since clean water and proper sewage disposal are rare in these urban environments of poverty.

Another major contributor to the rise in infectious diseases in the Caribbean is, of course, AIDS. AIDS has contributed to the number of deaths itself, but has also contributed indirectly, by weakening the hosts' immune system, rendering him/her at the mercy of other infectious diseases. The epidemiological pattern of the AIDS epidemic, however, is different from what has been generally observed in other infectious diseases: AIDS is killing mostly individuals of the productive-age category, who will leave the elderly and very young without support. For most of the diseases we covered in this chapter, we see that it is not reasonable to discuss the Caribbean (let alone the Caribbean islands and the Atlantic coast of Central America) as a single epidemiological unit. Thus whereas malaria became a very serious problem in the Limón region of Costa Rica during the 1980s, it had been eradicated in most of the islands by that time. Whereas some sectors of the Afro-Caribbean population have not had to confront problems with gastrointestinal maladies, recent samples of at-risk children in Jamaica show them to have a significant load of intestinal worms. For AIDS, the situation is very complex, with some regions having an epidemic circumscribed to gay males, others with a general population epidemic, others with an epidemic associated with intravenous drug use, and yet others with crack cocaine use. In all of this discussion, Haiti occupies a special place. As the poorest country in the western hemisphere, Haiti did not transition into a low-mortality population which suffers from chronic diseases. The epidemiological situation of Haiti is truly unique in that it has endemic levels of malaria, tuberculosis, and AIDS, together with an urban and rural ecology that lacks clean water and sewage disposal, one which provides breeding grounds for mosquitoes, the vectors of malaria, yellow fever, and dengue.

Another "theme" that runs throughout this chapter is the importance of migration for the introduction and spread of disease. The Caribbean has had a long history of migration, which is truly integral to its culture and history. At the same time, the area has become a popular tourist attraction, bringing tourists who act as disease carriers to or from the Caribbean. It was through forced migration that the African slaves came to the Caribbean. It was through migration that malaria was introduced to the region. Most likely, it was through sex tourism that AIDS was introduced to Haiti. And through labor migration, malaria and tuberculosis have spread through the region. The infectious-disease epidemiology of the Caribbean is nothing short of complex. Whereas for all of the diseases discussed each island or region is unique, having its own epidemic of AIDS, for example, the entire region is united by migration. Most Caribbean islands have significant out- and in-migrant communities, which act as an epidemiological bridge among the islands. The Afro-Caribbean communities of the Atlantic Central American coast are in constant flux, exchanging marriage partners or laborers, both within Central America and with the islands. To understand the infectious-disease epidemiology of the Caribbean, we need to look at each population in isolation from, and together with, the rest of the region.

# 4    *Population genetics of Afro-Caribbean groups*

The broad purpose of this chapter is to use population genetics research to unravel the origin in Africa and subsequent microevolution in the New World of Afro-Caribbean populations. The chapter will heavily favor research with abnormal hemoglobins, which features prominently in the Afro-Caribbean genetics literature. This body of literature is disappointingly small, however. Whereas much research has been done on the population genetics of Afro-South American groups, not much work has been done with Afro-Caribbean groups. Crawford's project with the Garifuna or Black Caribs stands out in a rather sparse literature (Crawford, 1983, 1984; Crawford *et al.*, 1981, 1984). This chapter is divided into the following sections: first, the malaria hypothesis and hemoglobin S in the Caribbean; second, β-globin gene studies and the origin in Africa of Afro-Caribbean groups, and third, microevolution and genetic maps of Afro-Caribbean groups.

We take for granted that the reader has had a basic exposure to Mendelian genetics inheritance, as well as to the inheritance of mitochondrial DNA (mtDNA) and the Y chromosome. We also assume that the reader is familiar with the production of proteins in general and of hemoglobins in particular, and that the reader understands how restriction fragment length polymorphism (RFLP) analysis of DNA works. An excellent recent review of basic genetics in the human biology literature is to be found in Weiss (2000). We also assume that the reader has a basic understanding of evolutionary theory. Otherwise, see Section 5.1 for a review of evolutionary forces.

Population genetics is a branch of biology in which statistical methods are used to test hypotheses about the distribution of genes within a population. The most fundamental subject of interest is to establish if the population is undergoing evolution and, if so, by which evolutionary force. The usual first step in population genetics research is to test if the gene frequencies are at equilibrium or if they are changing/evolving, for which the Hardy–Weinberg equilibrium is used. See Madrigal (1999/2000) for a review of the statistical methodology to test Hardy–Weinberg equilibrium. If a sample is found not to be at equilibrium, the population geneticist would be interested in finding out if the population is changing because it is undergoing natural selection, because it is receiving many migrants who are affecting it through gene flow, or because it is experiencing genetic drift as a result of its small size and isolation (O'Rourke, 2000). This chapter gives examples of these three evolutionary processes occurring on the population genetics of Afro-Caribbean populations. We will discuss natural selection in the form of malaria, the results of African, European, and Amerindian gene flow in the formation of new populations, and the effect of genetic drift in the evolution of small groups.

### 4.1   The malaria hypothesis and abnormal hemoglobin polymorphisms in the Caribbean

#### 4.1.1   A review of human hemoglobins

Humans have several types of hemoglobin (Hb for short), each one of which has four polypeptide (long protein) chains. Most adults produce Hb A, which has two $\alpha$ and two $\beta$ chains ($\alpha_2\beta_2$). The $\alpha$ chain is produced by the $\alpha$ gene, which is located in a gene cluster of $\alpha$-like genes and pseudogenes located on chromosome 16. The $\beta$ chain is produced by the $\beta$ gene, located in the $\beta$-like gene cluster, found on chromosome 11. Adults also have a very small amount of Hb A2, which consists of two $\alpha$ and two $\delta$ polypeptides ($\alpha_2\delta_2$). Figure 4.1 shows the $\alpha$-like and $\beta$-like gene clusters.

Abnormal hemoglobins are produced by mutations in the $\beta$ or $\alpha$ alleles. Some mutations involve a single substitution (for example, Hb S and Hb C), some a double substitution (for example, Hb C-Harlem and Hb S-Travis), and yet others a frameshift mutation (for example, the $\alpha$ chain Wayne). Serjeant (1992) provides an excellent review of hemoglobin mutations and hemoglobin production. Hb S is the result of a substitution at the sixth place in the $\beta$ chain, where valine replaces glutamic acid. Hb C results from a substitution at the sixth place as well, but lysine replaces glutamic acid. There are other mutations that occur in both the $\alpha$ and $\beta$ chains affecting the production of hemoglobin, broadly placed under the term $\alpha$ or $\beta$ thalassemia (Serjeant, 1992).

#### 4.1.2   The malaria hypothesis

The course of a malarial infection in humans, its transmission, and the host immune reaction were covered in Chapter 3. In this section we look

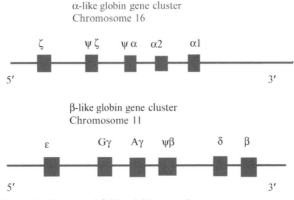

Figure 4.1. The α- and β-like globin gene clusters.

at the importance of malaria as a selective agent in human evolution, a selective pressure which is associated with the occurrence of high frequencies of abnormal hemoglobins in endemic malarial areas (McQueen and McKenzie, 2004; see Miller, 1995 and Weiss, 1993 for reviews of other possible human polymorphisms associated with malaria). Malaria is probably the disease that has killed more humans in our entire evolutionary history than any other, and as a result it has had a profound impact on human variation (Greene and Danubio, 1997). On its website, the WHO reports that malaria is currently the principal cause of at least one-fifth of all young child deaths in Africa (www.rbm.who.int/amd2003/amr2003/summary.htm). In 1988, Garnham estimated that nearly 100% of children under the age of 1 year in holoendemic areas of Africa were infected with malaria.

Malaria as a selective agent in human evolution became important only after populations adopted agriculture under certain environmental conditions. Livingstone (1976) notes that malaria was present in Africa before it became a human disease. However, it was probably restricted to forest areas, where it affected apes and monkeys. Only when high-density human groups moved to these areas and altered the ecology through slash-and-burn agriculture did humans become a major host of the malaria pathogen. In addition to Africa, this situation took place in the Mediterranean, the Middle East, and India (Greene and Danubio, 1997). Moreover, it is presently occurring in areas of South America, Central America and southeast Asia. In Costa Rica, for example, during the last 20 years malaria has moved from one region to another, wherever deforestation is most acute (see Chapter 6).

The malaria hypothesis states that some abnormal hemoglobins (such as Hb S and Hb C), the thalassemias, G6PD deficiency, and Duffy (Fy⁻ Fy⁻) variants are held at polymorphic levels (the variants are at a frequency of at least 1%) by the action of malaria (Agarwal *et al.*, 2000; Ashley-Koch *et al.*, 2000; Clegg and Weatherall 1999; Flint *et al.*, 1998; Greene and Danubio, 1997; Hill, 1996; McQueen and McKenzie, 2004; Ockenhouse *et al.*, 1984; Pasvol and Wilson, 1982, 1989; Roth *et al.*, 1983a, 1983b). In other words, these polymorphisms are a genetic adaptation, brought about by natural selection, to the disease malaria. Simply put, the malaria hypothesis states that Hb S heterozygotes are resistant to malarial infection. In contrast, individuals who only carry Hb A have a higher risk of dying of malaria. Many, though not all, homozygous Hb SS individuals die before reproduction. Since natural selection favors the heterozygote over either homozygote, the hemoglobin system is considered to be a balanced polymorphism. This balance is one in which the fitness for the entire population is at a maximum. The cost of the adaptation, however, is the number of individuals with sickle cell anemia, who suffer from a painful and often fatal disease (Ashley-Koch *et al.*, 2000). This is not advantageous from the perspective of the individual with the disease, but it is from the perspective of the entire population. Since the malaria hypothesis was first proposed by Haldane (1949) a considerable body of evidence confirming the malarial connection has been accumulated (Allison, 1954, 1956, 1956/7, 1960, 1975; Beauvais and Beauvais, 1986; Colombo and Felicetti, 1985; Livingstone, 1957, 1958, 1971, 1976, 1989a, 1989b; Rucknagel and Neel, 1961).

According to Charmot-Bensimon (1999), the Hb S polymorphism is the only one that can be explained solely in terms of malarial selection. Hb S has been proposed to be an adaptation to the deadliest species of the pathogen, *P. falciparum*, and Duffy Fy⁻Fy⁻ to its mildest form, *P. vivax*. In this chapter we focus on Hb S and not on the other polymorphisms.

The earliest proposed evidence in support of the malaria hypothesis was the overlap of endemic malarial areas and of populations with high frequencies of Hb S. This distribution suggests that natural selection had acted upon the system to maintain the frequencies. Basically, there are no indigenous populations with polymorphic levels of Hb S who have not been exposed to endemic malaria. Polymorphic frequencies of Hb S are found in African, East-Indian, and some Mediterranean populations (Serjeant, 1992). The distribution of malaria in the Old World before major eradication programs took place in the mid 1900s and of the Hb S allele are shown in Figure 4.2.

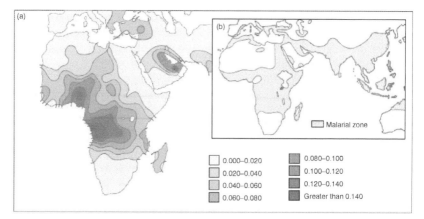

Figure 4.2. Maps of the Old World showing (a) the frequencies of the Hb S allele and (b) malarial areas.

Epidemiological and clinical studies have provided clear evidence for the malaria hypothesis. In general, this line of research looks at the parasitemia density and incidence of infection in individuals with the Hb AS and Hb AA genotypes, especially during childhood, when individuals have not developed premunition. Most of these investigations indicate that heterozygotes suffer lower levels of parasitemia in comparison with controls. Several studies also indicate that Hb AA subjects suffer more frequent and more severe infections (Colombo and Felicetti, 1985; Fleming *et al.*, 1985; Perrin *et al.*, 1982). According to Hill (1992), the protection of Hb S is most obvious at the clinical level rather than at the parasite-density level.

Further evidence for the malaria hypothesis is found in studies performed in vitro (Friedman, 1983). This line of research has provided valuable data on the actual cellular mechanism that protects heterozygotes from malarial infection. Sickling occurs readily in red blood cells with Hb S that are infected with the younger stages of the pathogen. Host cells infected with older forms do not sickle, or take longer to do so but contain polymerized hemoglobin, which inhibits *P. falciparum* growth. Sickling results in parasite death and puts a stop to the infection (Pasvol, 2003; Pasvol and Wilson, 1982, 1989; Pasvol *et al.*, 1978; Roth *et al.*, 1978). Perrin *et al.* (1982) also suggest that parasite death might result from loss of intracellular potassium rather than from sickling. Pasvol and Wilson (1982) state that metabolic and physical mechanisms independent of sickling might interrupt malarial infection in an Hb AS individual. Hebbel (2003) proposes that the instability of Hb S is the mechanism for

Table 4.1. *A comparison of the reproductive performances of Hb AA and Hb AS females*

|  | Genotype | | | | |
|---|---|---|---|---|---|
| Reproductive variable | AA (*n* = 108) | AS (*n* = 22) | *t* | *P* | df |
| Mean number of pregnancies | 6.74 | 6.30 | 0.34 | ns | 123 |
| Mean number of live births | 6.12 | 5.77 | 0.36 | ns | 128 |
| Mean completed family size | 5.00 | 4.68 | 0.38 | ns | 128 |
| Mean number of abortions | 0.72 | 0.66 | 0.20 | ns | 123 |
| Mean age at menarche | 14.13 | 14.25 | −0.25 | ns | 110 |

*Note:*
df, degrees of freedom; ns, not significant.
*Source:* Madrigal (1989).

protection from malarial infection. Greene and Danubio (1997) suggest that oxidant stress to the pathogen accounts for the antimalarial protection in most if not all erythrocyte abnormalities associated with malaria. They also note that the same oxidant stress can be achieved via diet, and is part of the traditional African antimalarial medicine.

In addition to greater survival of heterozygotes in malarial environments, a higher fertility of heterozygote females has been proposed to account for the elevated frequencies of Hb S in endemic regions. In an early paper, Livingstone (1957) proposed that the high frequency of Hb S in malarial environments could be the result of both differential mortality and differential fertility. In 1987, I collected data to test the differential-fertility hypothesis in Limón, Costa Rica (Madrigal, 1989). The hypothesis of differential fertility was tested by comparing the reproductive careers of homozygous Hb AA and heterozygous Hb AS females of at least 40 years of age. The mean completed family size and the numbers of live births, abortions, and total pregnancies of both groups were compared. A discriminant function analysis was applied to the fertility data to determine whether it were possible to separate the normal homozygotes from heterozygotes using one or more linear combinations of the original variables. Table 4.1 shows the comparison of the reproductive performance of Hb AS and Hb AA females from Limón. The two groups do not have significantly different numbers of pregnancies, live births, or abortions, or a significantly different completed family size. All *t* scores are below 1, and are clearly not significant. A stepwise discriminant function analysis of the reproductive variables listed in Table 4.1 was performed. However, no variable contributed significantly to the discrimination, and none was entered into the model. From a multivariate perspective, the homozygous Hb AA and the heterozygous Hb AS women do not differ reproductively, thus confirming the results of the univariate analysis.

More recently however, Hoff *et al.* (2001), working with an Afro-USA group in a non-malarial area reported that Hb AS females had higher fertility, in support of Livingstone's (1957) early proposal. The results of Hoff *et al.* (2001) call into question Madrigal's (1989) conclusion.

In conclusion, many data support the hypothesis that Hb S is held at polymorphic levels by the action of natural selection. It should be noted that despite the virtual agreement among researchers about this explanation, Bowman (1990) stands in sharp disagreement. Bowman favors other explanations for the high frequency of Hb S in African groups, including polygamy. Besides Bowman's position, there is little controversy about malaria acting through differential mortality. Whether malaria acts through differential fertility as well is more controversial, with Madrigal (1989) and Hoff *et al.* (2001) presenting the most recent opposing positions about it.

### 4.1.3   Hb S in the Caribbean

As reviewed in Chapter 1, the native Caribbean population was quickly decimated after the European invasion, and rapidly replaced by the forced importation of African slaves. That the African slaves could adapt well to the tropical Caribbean climate was rapidly noted by the Europeans (Kiple and Ornelas, 1996). Malaria was probably the main selective agent to which the Africans had a genetic adaptation. Crawford (1983, 1984) emphasizes the importance of abnormal hemoglobins in the successful adaptation of the Black Caribs (Garifuna) to highly malarial areas of the Central American Atlantic coast. Besides Hb S, Hb C, Duffy Fy- Fy-, hereditary persistence of fetal hemoglobin, G6PD deficiency, and thalassemia are also present in Afro-Caribbean populations (Collier and de la Parra, 1952; Halberstein *et al.*, 1981; Higgs *et al.*, 1981; Kéclard *et al.*, 1996, 1997; Madrigal *et al.*, 1990; Monplaisir *et al.*, 1986; Montestruc *et al.*, 1959; Nickel *et al.*, 1999; Romana *et al.*, 1996, 2000; Serjeant and Serjeant, 1972; Serjeant *et al.*, 1968, 1973a, 1973b). Lisker (1983) provides a summary of abnormal hemoglobin studies in Latin America and the Caribbean.

It is fascinating that malaria, an Old World disease, was so successful in the New World, and spread quickly through tropical and semi-tropical regions. It is equally fascinating that the Hb S polymorphism (and probably others as well) conferred protection to the African slaves in a foreign land, where they had been forcefully taken. Certainly, Hb S contributed greatly to the survival of the slaves and subsequent population growth of the slaves' descendants. The Garifuna in particular provide an example of great demographic success in an endemic malarial area (Crawford, 1983).

## 4.2   β-Globin gene studies and the origin in Africa of Afro-Caribbean groups

In the 1980s a new laboratory technique contributed to a greater understanding of the evolution of the Hb S gene. The technique of RFLPs consists of digesting a section of DNA with restriction enzymes with the purpose of uncovering polymorphisms. The variants or alleles here are defined by the presence ($+$) or absence ($-$) of a restriction site; that is, the site where the enzyme can cut (Williams, 1989). The set of alleles in a section of DNA is referred to as a haplotype.

RFLP analysis of the sickle hemoglobin gene ($\beta^S$-globin) has shown that in Africa alone there are four common haplotypes: haplotype 19 or Senegal type, haplotype 20 or Central African Republic (CAR)/Bantu type, haplotype 3 or Benin haplotype, and haplotype 17 or Cameroon type. Outside of Africa is haplotype 31 or the Arab-Indian haplotype (Excoffier *et al.*, 1987; Pante-de-Sousa *et al.*, 1999; Ramsay and Jenkins, 1987; Trabuchet *et al.*, 1991). The distribution of the African haplotypes is shown in Figure 4.3. These data offer overwhelming support to the idea that the mutation for Hb S occurred at least five times, on chromosomes with different haplotypes. Later the mutation was selected for by the action of malaria (Antonarakis *et al.*, 1984; Nagel, 1984; Nagel and Labie, 1985; Nagel *et al.*, 1985; Pagnier *et al.*, 1984; Wainscoat *et al.*, 1986). Other haplotypes do occur, but at much lower frequencies. Romana *et al.* (2000) look at atypical haplotypes in Hb SS patients in Guadeloupe. Currat *et al.* (2002) propose that the Senegal $\beta^S$ haplotype is of rather recent origin. It should be noted that among the virtually universal acceptance that several mutations of Hb S have occurred, Livingstone (1989a, 1989b) offers a contrasting view, proposing that one and not several mutations occurred.

RFLP analysis of the sickle cell gene can provide an innovative tool to answer important historical and anthropological questions about the African slave trade and diaspora. Indeed, Pagnier *et al.* (1984) indicate that the analysis of haplotypes associated with this DNA region provides

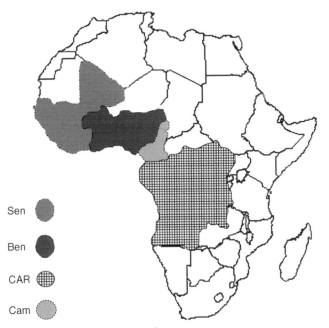

Figure 4.3. Distribution of the $\beta^S$-globin gene haplotypes in Africa. Ben, Benin type; Cam, Cameroon type; CAR, Central African Republic/Banto type; Sen, Senegal type.

an objective tool to determine the place of origin of Afro-American populations.

Nagel (1984) compared the results of Curtin's historical research (Curtin, 1969) on the origin of slaves with the results of RFLP analysis in Jamaica. He computed the expected proportions of slaves brought from different parts of Africa based on the observed frequencies of the major African haplotypes in a sample of Jamaican Hb SS patients. A remarkable agreement between the projections generated by the haplotype frequencies and the historical expectations generated by Curtin was obtained. Thus, about 72% of slaves were predicted to have come from central West Africa, based on a frequency of 72% of the Benin haplotype, whereas the prediction was 68% based on historical reconstructions. Similarly, Rodríguez-Romero *et al.* (1998) note that in the Limón (Costa Rica) group, which descends primarily from Jamaican founders, the frequency of the Benin haplotype is very similar to that of Jamaica; that is, 73.3%. Interestingly, Rodríguez-Romero *et al.* (1998) mention that the frequency of the Bantu or CAR haplotype is higher in the Pacific coast of

Costa Rica among the descendants of the early African slaves who came with the earliest Spanish colonizers. Nagel (1984) reports similarly good agreement between historical data and genetic predictions on the origin of the African slaves brought to Cuba, a proposition later supported by data reported by Muñíz-Fernández *et al.* (2000). In contrast, work in Guadeloupe by Kéclard and collaborators (1997) shows that the results of RFLP analysis do not agree with the expectations generated by historical work. They conclude that the African component of Guadeloupe is different from that of Brazil and Cuba but similar to that of Jamaica. Reviewing previous work, Kéclard *et al.* (1997) conclude that in regions dominated by the British and French slave trade the Benin haplotype is prevalent (USA 50–60%, Jamaica 70%, and Guadeloupe 75%), whereas in regions dominated by the Spanish and Portuguese trades the Bantu haplotype has a greater frequency (Brazil 62%, Cuba 39%, and Surinam 30%). Indeed, the different frequencies of the Hb S haplotypes in Costa Rica appear to reflect the different European powers which brought the African slaves to the country: the descendants of the Spanish slaves have higher frequencies of the Bantu haplotype than do the descendants of the British slaves, who have higher frequencies of the Benin haplotype.

Studies of the haplotypes of Afro-Brazilian sickle cell anemic patients indicate that the distribution of haplotypes is different from that observed in the United States or Jamaica, probably because of different origins of slaves brought to North and South America (Zago *et al.*, 1992). The distribution of Hb S haplotypes in Afro-Amazonian Venezuelan, and Brazilian groups has been explained by different origins of the slaves, but also by genetic drift of these small groups. Since some of these populations descend from small numbers of runaway slaves, genetic drift must have had a strong effect on their evolution. In some cases, neighboring groups have significantly different haplotype frequencies without any evidence that the founding members of the groups had different origins. Genetic drift is most likely responsible for such differentiation (Bortolini *et al.*, 1998; Pante-de-Sousa *et al.*, 1999; Vívenes de Lugo *et al.*, 2003)

In addition to contributing to the historical work on the origin of the African slaves, RFLP research has added valuable insight into sickle cell anemia's clinical manifestations (Pagnier *et al.*, 1984). The clinical profile of sickle cell anemia has been researched at length by Serjeant and colleagues in Jamaica (Serjeant *et al.*, 1968, 1973a, 1973b; Serjeant and Serjeant, 1972). Even in very early studies, Serjeant and colleagues called attention to the relatively benign clinical outcome of many Jamaican patients in comparison with that of the USA patients. Madrigal (1988) observed the same situation in the Limón population, which descends from Jamaican migrants. Wierenga *et al.* (2001) also note that many Jamaican patients survive well into their 30s and 40s. RFLP analysis provides a powerful tool to understand the genetic causes of the different clinical presentation of Hb SS patients. Specifically, the Senegal haplotype appears to be of a more benign clinical course, and according to Pante-de-Sousa *et al.* (1999) might be underrepresented in samples obtained at clinics, as these Hb SS patients are not sick as often. Zago *et al.* (1992) indicate that such underlying DNA differences are likely to account, at least in part, for the differences in the clinical manifestations observed between patients of the USA and Brazil. In Cuba, the frequencies of patients with the Senegal haplotype increase after age 20, due to a lower mortality of this in contrast to the other haplotypes (Muñíz-Fernández *et al.*, 2000).

A more recent attempt to study the origin of the African slaves by genetic means is to be found in the work of Bandelt *et al.* (2001) with mt DNA. By sequencing and performing RFLP analysis of mitochondrial DNA (mtDNA), Bandelt *et al.* (2001) concluded that the descendents of African slaves in Brazil and Santo Domingo have a different mtDNA haplotype, reflecting their different points of origin. Specifically, the Santo Domingo samples were very similar to non-Atlantic western Africa, whereas those from Brazil resemble all areas of Africa except Senegambia. Salas *et al.* (2004a), using mtDNA from several African-derived groups through the Americas, propose that the African slaves whose descendents are found in North and Central America were brought from western Africa. Further work on mtDNA by Salas *et al.* (2004b) and Bortolini *et al.* (2004) strongly indicates that the presence of an unusual East African mtDNA haplotype in some South American individuals could be explained not by direct slave importation from East Africa but by gene flow from East Africa into western Africa, from where the slaves were taken.

In conclusion, the development of RFLP analysis of the sickle cell gene has had important consequences for the study of the African slave trade and subsequent diaspora in the Americas. It allows researchers to test hypotheses generated by historical documents about the place of origin of the African slaves. The data reviewed here indicate that sometimes the population genetics results confirm, but sometimes challenge, the predictions put forth by historians of the slave trade. Data on mtDNA have been exceedingly successful in pinpointing the area in Africa where the slaves originated, even tracing migration routes within Africa. Trachtenberg *et al.* (1996) note that genetics studies using the HLA system might be able to pinpoint in a finer manner the place of origin in Africa of the slaves. In addition, RFLP analysis has the ability to substantially improve the diagnosis and clinical understanding of sickle cell anemia, a common disease among the descendents of the slaves. It is for this rather practical reason that more research on the $\beta^S$-globin gene cluster is highly desirable, besides the fact that it provides a deeper understanding of the origin of the African slaves. Unfortunately, population genetics research in the Caribbean has been lacking when compared with research in Afro-South American groups (da Silva *et al.*, 1999; Jaramillo-Correa *et al.*, 2001; Martinez-Labarga *et al.*, 1999). Indeed, in her paper on admixture studies in Latin America, Sans (2000) provides a table of admixture studies in 14 Afro-Latin American groups. Of these, two are from Crawford's study on the Garifuna, and one is from a study in Nicaragua. All others are from South American groups, and no other is from the Caribbean.

### 4.3   Microevolution of Afro-Caribbean groups

Population genetics research on African-derived New World groups has shed much light into the evolution of these populations by genetic drift and gene flow in the American continent. Studies on the action of natural selection through malaria have already been reviewed above. Unfortunately, we see again a great gap in research on Afro-Caribbean groups when compared with research on Afro-South American groups.

Research with South American groups has been ample, and studies attest to the population-specific evolution of various African-derived groups (da Silva *et al.*, 1999; Jaramillo-Correa *et al*, 2001; Martinez-Labarga *et al.*, 1999). For example, different Afro-Colombian groups have different frequencies of Amerindian mtDNA haplotypes, as a result of their differential gene flow with Amerindian or "Mestizo" groups (Rodas *et al.*, 2003). In Uruguay, Bravi *et al.* (1997) investigated the differential contribution of African, European, and Amerindian parental groups to a group of Afro-Uruguayans. Their conclusion was that there was an important contribution of maternally inherited Amerindian mtDNAs, whereas no Amerindian paternally inherited Y chromosomes could be found in the sample. This research strongly suggests that female and not male Amerindians contributed to the Afro-Uruguayan gene pool, although Bravi *et al.* (1997) caution that the Y chromosome is less informative than is mtDNA. Bortolini *et al.* (1997a, 1997b) found African and Amerindian-derived mtDNA haplotypes in three Afro-Brazilian groups. They also found significant heterogeneity among three Afro-Brazilian groups, heterogeneity which could not be explained in terms of geography. Bortolini *et al.* (1999) propose that differences in the

Y-chromosomes and mtDNAs found at different Afro-South American groups are best explained by the unique history of each population. A population-specific history which leaves its own signal on each population is also proposed by Abe-Sandes *et al.* (2004), who, working with Y-chromosome polymorphisms, found very different levels of genetic diversity within two Afro-Brazilian groups. The cause of this diversity was African and European-derived Y chromosomes, not Amerindian ones. These data confirm the proposition that Amerindian males contributed very little to the formation of the current Brazilian population.

Only one paper could be found that looks at differential male–female gene flow in the formation of an Afro-Caribbean group. Parra *et al.* (1998) report data on the Y chromosome, mtDNA haplotypes, and biparentally inherited genetic markers for a Jamaican and several Afro-USA groups. Based on biparentally inherited information, the percentage of European ancestry in the Jamaican group was only 6.8%, a rather low percentage in comparison with the Afro-USA groups. When looking at maternal and paternal contributions from the founding populations, Parra *et al.* (1998) conclude that the European component is higher in the male than in the female lines. In other words, more European males than females contributed to the Afro-Jamaican gene pool. This fits well with what we know about the Europeans who had most contact with the African slaves. Not only were males found in slaving ships and in charge of the sale of slaves, but they were usually the slave drivers at the plantation. In the home, European females would have been assisted by female, not male slaves, as was discussed in Chapter 1. Thus, opportunities for gene flow between European females and male African slaves would have been rather limited, a conclusion confirmed by the genetic data. Parra *et al.* (1998) also note an absence of Amerindian mtDNA haplotypes in the Jamaican group, indicating that the genetic make-up of this group is rather different from that of Afro-South American groups, which do show an important maternal Amerindian contribution.

Pereira *et al.* (2001) have looked for evidence of the Bantu expansion by looking at the mtDNA hypervariable region I of individuals from Mozambique, and then by looking for matches to the Mozambique haplotypes in Santo Domingo in the Caribbean and in Brazil. Out of the total of 109 haplotypes of African origin found in these two American samples, 15 were Mozambique haplotypes, indicating that there was an important contribution of eastern African slaves into the slave trade to the Caribbean and Brazil.

It is interesting to note that when Fernandez-Cobo *et al.* (2001) looked at admixture proportions in an Hispanic Puerto Rican group using the JC virus, they found a 26% contribution from Africa, and an unexpectedly large Amerindian contribution (61%). A similar conclusion was reached by Martínez-Cruzado et al. (2001), who using mtDNA also found a significant Native American component in Puerto Rican subjects: 69.6% of subjects who claimed to descend from a female ancestor with Amerindian facial features had Amerindian mtDNAs, whereas 52.6% of a random Puerto Rican sample did. These results indicate that the African contribution to a so-called Hispanic group is rather high (over 25%), and that when the Europeans arrived in the Caribbean they readily mated with Amerindian females. Unfortunately, similar projects with mtDNA and Y chromosomes are lacking for Afro-Caribbean populations.

The importance of gene flow in the formation of the Afro-Caribbean gene pools is stressed by Carrington et al. (2002). In their study of HLA haplotypes among various ethnic groups of Trinidad, Carrington et al. (2002) concluded that whereas New World-African-derived groups are similar in their HLA frequencies, they are different from African groups. This is probably a result of the mixing of different ethnic groups from Africa in the New World, as well as gene flow with Europeans and Amerindians.

Perhaps the largest and most comprehensive population genetics project with an Afro-Caribbean group is the Black Carib/Garifuna project, headed by Michael Crawford (Crawford, 1983, 1984; Crawford et al., 1981, 1984; Johnston and Little, 2000). This project however, took place before mtDNA and Y chromosome markers could be studied, so the project cannot offer light on the maternal and paternal contributions to the formation of this group. The Garifuna, however, have such a unique origin and history, having incorporated a large group of Amerindians, that their genetic make-up is probably not too similar to that of most Afro-Caribbean groups. Indeed, Crawford et al. (1981) report a 75% African, 22.4% Amerindian, and 2.4% European contribution to the Garifuna from Livingston, Guatemala. But these admixture estimates cannot be taken to be typical of all Black Carib groups. Indeed, the Garifuna, who are found through Guatemala, Honduras, and Nicaragua, have had a long history of population fission and isolation. Thus Crawford (1983) stresses the importance of genetic drift following population fission, and gene flow with local populations, in the microevolution of each Garifuna group. More recent work with the Black Caribs of Belize (Monsalve and Hagelberg, 1997) with mtDNA data confirms the African-slave and Amerindian origins of the Garifuna, as both Carib and Yoruba mtDNA haplotypes were detected in this population. These results show that both Amerindian and African slave females contributed to the formation of this group.

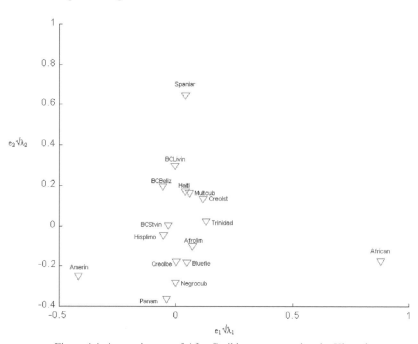

Figure 4.4. A genetic map of Afro-Caribbean groups plus the Hispanic population from Limón, Costa Rica, along the two-scaled eigenvectors (77% of the total variation explained). See Madrigal *et al.* (2001a) for details on the methodology and the populations. Spaniar, Spaniards; Amerind, Amerindians; African, Africans; BCLivin, Black Caribs from Livingstone; BCBeliz, Black Caribs from Belize; Haiti, Afro-Haitians; Multcub, "mulattoes" from Cuba; Creolst, "Creoles" from Saint Vincent Island; BCStvin, Black Caribs from Saint Vincent; Trinidad, Afro-Trinidadians; Hisplimo, Hispano-Limonenses; Afrolim, Afro-Limonenses; Creolbe, Creoles from Belize; Bluefields, Afro-population from Bluefields; Negrocub, Afro-Cubans; Panam, Afro-Panamanians.

The Afro-Caribbean group living in Limón, Costa Rica, descends primarily from Jamaican workers who migrated to Costa Rica beginning in the late 1800s. Thus it provides an interesting comparison with the Jamaican group mentioned above. In contrast with Parra *et al.* (1998), who only considered European and African parental populations, Madrigal *et al.* (2001a) considered an Amerindian parental population as well. Madrigal *et al.* reported 75% African ancestry in the Limón group, much lower than that reported by Parra *et al.* (93%). Madrigal *et al.* (2001a) also report a contribution of 11% from Europeans and 14% from Amerindians. We know not if the estimates by Parra *et al.* (1998) would have been similar to ours had they considered a tri-hybrid model, or if the

Limón population has absorbed such a large Amerindian component since its arrival in Costa Rica.

Madrigal *et al.* (2001a) place the Limón gene frequencies in the context of Afro-Caribbean groups and the three parental groups by applying a correlation analysis to genetic data obtained from a total of 16 Afro-Caribbean groups plus the "Hispanic" Limón group (for details on the methodology, and the sources of the data, see Madrigal *et al.*, 2001a). The results, shown in Figure 4.4, indicate that there is much variation in the contribution to the individual groups from the three parental populations. Some of the Black Carib groups are the closest samples to the Spaniard and Amerindian parental groups. The Limón sample appears to be more or less in the middle of the range of European contribution. If anything, Figure 4.4 emphasizes the tremendous genetic variation found among Afro-Caribbean groups.

### 4.4   Conclusion

Population genetics provides an exceptionally good tool to investigate the microevolution of Afro-Caribbean groups. It is fascinating that malaria, a disease that selected for various polymorphisms in Africa, became so well adapted to the New World. After this and other diseases had devastated the Amerindian population, the Europeans brought African slaves to replace them. It was the polymorphisms that gave these Africans protection from malaria which allowed them to survive in what became a hostile malarial environment. Indeed, throughout the Caribbean there are high frequencies of erythrocyte abnormalities associated with malaria, although here we only concentrated on Hb S. Further study of the Hb S gene through RFLP analysis has challenged or confirmed historically derived statements about the origin of the slaves in various places of the New World. The fascinating picture that emerges is one of different populations in the Caribbean who originated in different places in Africa, and whose clinical manifestation of sickle cell anemia varies.

After arriving in the Caribbean, the slave populations evolved in different directions. Some groups (such as the Black Caribs) incorporated large amounts of the Amerindian gene pool, a similar situation to that seen in South America. Evidently, groups that were small and isolated were more under the influence of genetic drift than were larger groups. To what extent, however, the Amerindians did or did not contribute to other Afro-Caribbean groups is not altogether clear. Parra *et al.* (1998) did not consider a tri-hybrid admixture model, and concluded that their

Afro-Jamaican subjects were overwhelmingly African. Madrigal *et al.* (2001a), in contrast, working with a Jamaican-derived group in Costa Rica, report a substantial Amerindian contribution. This discrepancy could simply be due to the fact that Madrigal *et al.* used a tri-hybrid model, and Parra *et al.* used a di-hybrid model, or it could be due to gene flow with Costa Rican Amerindian groups and the Costa Rican population at large.

The general conclusion to this chapter is that each group, in each region, has evolved differently. It seems that in South America African-derived groups have incorporated a large proportion of Amerindian genes and experienced a great deal of genetic drift. In North America, in the USA in particular, African-derived groups have incorporated a large proportion of European genes. In the Caribbean we see all possible combinations, from the Black Caribs with a large proportion of Amerindian genes, to the Jamaican sample, which is overwhelmingly African, to the Costa Rican group, which has a good portion of Amerindian and European genes.

The conclusion that populations of African descent in the New World are varied genetically because of their own unique evolutionary trajectories is a strong argument against racial and genetic explanations for the high prevalence rates of hypertension in "Blacks." Indeed, the group with the highest hypertension rate, that of the USA, has very high frequencies of European admixture, higher than that of Limón, Costa Rica. Yet the latter group has a very low prevalence rate of hypertension. If anything, the data reviewed in this chapter strongly show that lumping New World African-derived groups together for epidemiological studies is fallacious.

# 5  Demography of Afro-Caribbean groups

## 5.1  Demography, biological anthropology, and human biology

Demography, broadly defined, is the study of human populations, with a focus on their fertility, mortality, migration, distribution, and change in size and composition. Fertility or natality is generally defined as the act of childbearing; mortality is death, whereas morbidity is disease. Migration is the movement of people from one place to another. Fertility, mortality, and migration all affect a population's distribution, its size, and its composition (Swedlund and Armelagos, 1976). Some authors prefer to emphasize that demography is quantitative in nature (Riley and McCarthy, 2003; Swedlund and Armelagos, 1976), some that the focus on fertility, morbidity, mortality, and migration is aimed at understanding the structure of human groups (Harrison and Boyce, 1972), and others that the primary focus of demography is the study of mortality and fertility transitions (Beaver, 1975). There are many excellent books on demography and its methods, and the reader is referred to them for a background on the field (Riley and McCarthy, 2003; Rives and Serow, 1984; Shryock et al., 1976; Siegel and Swanson, 2004; Stycos, 1989). We will not discuss the computation of demographic rates or any other methodological tools.

The fields of biological anthropology and human biology have many interests that intersect with demography. Indeed, there are several sources that focus on demographic anthropology (Basu and Aaby, 1998; Dyke and Morrill, 1980; Kertzer and Fricke, 1997a, 1997b; Renne, 1994; Roth, 2004; Swedlund, 1978; Swedlund and Armelagos, 1976; Zubrow, 1976), historical/genealogical demography (Dyke and Morrill, 1980), and even on archive-based human biological research (Herring and Swedlund, 2003). Kertzer and Fricke (1997a) review the needs that one discipline satisfies in the other, and the conflicts that arise out of this sometimes less than happy marriage. Zubrow (1976) discusses the questions posed by each discipline of interest to the other one, as well as specific variables which can be used to generate testable hypotheses in both. Renne (1994) discusses the relations between demography and economic anthropology, cultural ecology, political economy, and cultural anthropology. Roth (2004) looks at demography from the perspective of evolutionary ecology. Basu and Aaby (1998) and Basu (1995) discuss ethical problems that are uncovered in demographic anthropological and applied anthropological work, such as the practice of intentional high mortality of girls. Basu and Aaby (1998) note that whereas demography has usually stressed clearly defined variables such as "wanted vs. unwanted births", anthropology, with its ethnographic methods, can uncover that human fertility and mortality are much more complex entities. All of these sources are excellent wells of information on the methodological, theoretical, and ethical growing pains of demographic anthropology or anthropological demography.

The most obvious reason why biological anthropology and human biology are interested in the demography of human populations is that the processes of interest to demographers (fertility, mortality, and migration) are part of evolutionary forces (Harrison and Boyce, 1972). There are four forces of evolution: natural selection, genetic drift, gene flow, and mutation. These evolutionary forces, in one manner or another, result in a change of gene frequencies in a population through time; evolution by its most basic definition is the change in gene frequencies across the generations in a breeding group (Harrison and Boyce, 1972; O'Rourke, 2000; Swedlund and Armelagos, 1976). The role of mutation is to introduce new variants into a population. If these variants become more frequent, and achieve a frequency of at least 1% in the population, then one of the other three forces has likely been responsible for this increase. Genetic drift encompasses all the random forces which might result in a change in gene frequencies in the population. This change usually leads towards a loss of genetic variation. Small and/or isolated groups, such as those of island populations, are particularly affected by genetic drift.

Natural selection is usually defined as differential mortality and/or differential fertility of two or more phenotypes. Anthropologists interested in determining fitness measure fertility or the number of children produced by women who have achieved the end of their reproductive period or are nearing it (see Madrigal, 1989). A classical example of natural selection was already given in Chapter 4, and that is the higher fitness of the Hb AS phenotype in malarial environments. Since fitness is measured in terms of lower mortality and/or greater fertility of one phenotype with respect to another, demography can be tremendously important in the microevolutionary study of human groups; that is, evolution over a few generations. Migration, finally, is the usual manner in which gene flow, the introduction of genetic material new to a region, takes place. The Caribbean is obviously an area where massive population movements have taken place and continue to occur. We already covered in Chapter 4 the genetic maps of Afro-Caribbean groups. We noted that whereas some Afro-Caribbean groups have benefited from little genetic contribution from Amerindian groups, others such as the Black Caribs have substantial amounts of Amerindian genes.

Demography has thus much to offer to the fields of biological anthropology and human biology. Practitioners of the latter disciplines interested in studying microevolution of living humans will usually, in one way or another, look at demographic data. This is particularly the case if evolution is occurring through gene flow, which takes place as a result of migration and/or through natural selection, which occurs through the differential mortality and/or fertility of different phenotypes.

## 5.2   Demographic transitions

According to Riley and McCarthy (2003) the most important unifying concept in demography is that of fertility and mortality transitions, usually subsumed under the concept of the demographic transition model. There are many sources on this model, and we will only cover it in the simplest forms (Beaver, 1975; Donaldson, 1991; Menken, 1989; Riley and McCarthy, 2003; Watkins, 1989). According to the demographic transition model, human populations have changed their demographic profile through a set of fertility and mortality transitions. Human populations are viewed as "starting" with high fertility and high mortality, and having stable population sizes, since many of those born also die. After this stage, human populations lower their mortality, while keeping their fertility high. As a result, the population size increases. Eventually human populations also control their fertility so that the population size remains stable, as few are born but few also die. As Handwerker (1986) notes, the demographic transition model rests upon the idealized concepts of traditional and modern societies, the former transitioning into the latter through a process of development, industrialization, westernization, and modernization.

As important as the demographic transition model is to demography, it is one of the areas of demography most attacked by biological anthropology and human biology (Beaver, 1975; Handwerker, 1986; Swedlund and Armelagos, 1976; see Riley and McCarthy (2003) for an excellent summary of these criticisms). The latter disciplines, with a strong evolutionary and cross-cultural focus, have shown evidence that it is not clear at all that all populations "started" with high fertility and high mortality.

Anthropologists in particular note the well-documented low fertility of the !Kung of the Kalahari Desert, a fertility which, according to Wood (1994), is not typical of hunters and gatherers. Handwerker (1986) notes that in cross-cultural anthropological studies the various factors that have been proposed by demographers to cause fertility decline turn out to be spurious or inconsistent across different cultures. Thus he calls for an understanding of the transition from high to low fertility as a cultural change. Zubrow (1976) also emphasizes the tremendous variation in mortality and fertility in non-industrialized groups. Anthropologists and human biologists have also argued that the demographic transition model describes the history of European and European-derived populations and is not applicable to many other regions in the world. According to Zubrow (1976) the availability of resources is a more general explanation of the variation in fertility and mortality than is the demographic transition model, as it applies to the history of European populations. To this criticism, Beaver (1975) responds that although the trends observed in European groups and explained by the theory have not been found in other populations this does not invalidate the theory. He argues that the theory should only be asked to predict that the relationships among the independent variables of the model (contraceptive technology, education, change in values, etc.) are the same, not that the change in the dependent variables (mortality and fertility) will be the same. Anthropologists and human biologists, with their focus on small human groups, as opposed to demographers with their focus on national populations, have also noted that the demographic transition model overemphasizes the homogeneity of human groups. For example, although European and USA populations can be broadly described as having low fertility and low mortality, they are not uniformly so. For example, within the USA the Amerindian reservations have different mortality and fertility profiles than the general population. Sociological studies have shown that in the USA migrant groups have remained isolated and with their own demographic profiles, even within large urban areas (Lieberman and Waters, 1989). Thus although anthropology and human biology have benefited much from the demographic transition model, they have criticized it broadly and by doing so they have contributed to its growth. Within the field of demography criticisms have been leveled against the demographic transition model, particularly on the inability of demographers to satisfactorily explain and accurately predict decreases in fertility (Handwerker, 1986; Riley and McCarthy, 2002).

Despite the many criticisms raised against the demographic transition model, it has remained a fundamental part of demography and demographic anthropology, according to Riley and McCarthy (2003), because it is broadly consistent with empirical evidence. Indeed, the demographic transition model has become virtually a universal story in demography, despite the plethora of criticisms against it. Zubrow (1976) notes that the model has remained so important because of its parsimony, simplicity, and predictability.

Our review of the literature showed that fertility transitions are more hotly debated than are mortality transitions. The reader is referred to the following sources for a more in-depth discussion. The volume edited by Handwerker (1986) contains several papers on decision-making and fertility, the biological determinants of fertility, and the culturally specific milieus of fertility. Wood (1994) provides a comprehensive treatment of the biology of fertility. In particular, he discusses the concept of natural fertility, and seriously challenges the anthropological notion of low fertility of hunting and gathering populations. Beaver (1995) reviews the specific effect on fertility of several variables which might have caused the decline in fertility, such as contraceptive technology, values and norms, kinship structure changes, etc. Beaver (1975) and Handwerker (1986) discuss at greater length the causes of fertility decline. See Rosetta and Mascie-Taylor (1996) for an excellent human biology volume on variation in human fertility.

In this chapter we will not focus on mortality and morbidity, as these have been covered in Chapters 2 and 3. Instead, our emphasis here is on the fertility and migration of Afro-Caribbean groups. Mortality will only be mentioned in terms of childhood/infant mortality, as it has been proposed to be a direct independent variable on fertility variation. Our focus on migration is on recent and current migration, as we already discussed the evolutionary processes that produced the genetic composition of Afro-Caribbean groups in Chapter 4. We will also discuss the demographic transition model as it applies – or not – to Afro-Caribbean human groups.

## 5.3 A short review of fertility trends in Afro-Caribbean populations

In this chapter we follow the demographic and anthropological definition of fertility as the total number of children produced. Fecundity is the potential for reproduction. From an anthropological perspective, it is important to ask whether human fertility is only part of the typical low hominoid (apes and humans) fertility profile, as proposed by Wood (1994). This is not an easily answered question: in comparison with orangutans, gorillas, and chimpanzees, who are our closest relatives, humans are much more fertile (Burton, 1995). At the same time, most human groups do not achieve their reproductive potential, and those with the highest fertility are usually colonizing a region that is uninhabited (Wood, 1994).

As this book has a human-biological perspective, we will look at fertility holistically. That is, we will consider biological aspects of fertility, such as sexually transmitted disease and infertility, and also cultural aspects of fertility. Therefore, prominent in this chapter will be a discussion of culturally mediated factors that affect fertility, such as age at commencement of sexual activity and mating/family types. The topic of the Afro-Caribbean family will receive particular attention.

As was noted in Chapter 1, the life conditions of slaves in the Caribbean were hardly conducive to achieving high fertility. During slavery the sex ratio was skewed (though less so towards the end of the slavery period; Knight, 1997), the life conditions of women, pregnant or not, were extremely difficult, feelings of dislocation and depression must have been rampant, miscarriages were very common, and infant and childhood mortality was very high (Bush, 1996, 1999; Craton, 1978). All in all, the Afro-Caribbean slave populations experienced low fertility. Some exceptions were seen before but usually after the abolition of the slave trade, when planters had to rely on the slave population's natural increase, and thus started promoting pronatalist practices (Knight, 1997; Morrissey, 1989).

Several specific causes for the low fertility of African slaves have been proposed. One is family type, as fertility is usually highest in nuclear families, which were infrequently found among slaves but were more frequent in the freed African-derived groups (Knight, 1997). It has also been proposed that some African women were sterile by the time they got to the New World as a result of sexually transmitted diseases (Craton, 1978). Once they arrived in the Caribbean, slave women suffered from many gynecological problems, including amenorrhea (lack of a menstrual cycle), miscarriages, and sterility (Bush, 1996, 1999). There are also some suggestions of the existence of abortifacients and contraceptives in slave medical knowledge (Bush, 1996, 1999; Morrissey, 1989). Whether slave women decreased their own fertility as an act of resistance to their dismal conditions was discussed in Chapter 1.

After emancipation, the population numbers of the former slaves increased in most colonies (Knight, 1997). The most likely explanation for the fertility increase seen in most former slave populations was an increase in fecundity of females as a result of better diet and less strenuous work

(Morrissey, 1989). Indeed, not only former slaves, but all sectors of Caribbean society, experienced higher fertility, indicating that there was a betterment of life conditions throughout the colonies (Knight, 1997). For example the population of a Jamaican plantation increased 10-fold from 1838 to 1975 (Craton, 1978). But the fertility increase seen in post emancipation islands was not universal. For example, the fertility in Jamaica and the British West Indian islands was relatively low if compared to that of Puerto Rico: the average mother aged 45 in Puerto Rico had produced an average of 6.7 children, whereas the average mother aged 45 in Jamaica had only produced an average of 4.9 children (Stycos and Back, 1964).

Crude birth rates are available from several Caribbean islands from 1950. With almost no exception, the crude birth rate has decreased throughout the region from 1950 to the present. For example, in the Bahamas it decreased from 38.6 in 1950–5 to 14.3 in 1990–5; in Guadalupe from 39 in 1950–5 to 17.8 in 1990–5; in Jamaica from 34.8 in 1950–5 to 24.1 in 1990–5; in Trinidad and Tobago from 38.2 in 1950–5 to 17.6 in 1990–5. French Guyana shows less of a decline, from 36.4 in 1950–5 to 32.3 in 1990–5, although it was 25.8 in 1975–80 (CEPAL, 2003). According to Micklin (1994), the governments of Antigua/Barbuda, the Bahamas, and Barbados stated in 1983 that fertility was too high, but in 1989 that it was satisfactory.

In conclusion, the evolution of fertility of Afro-Caribbean groups can be summarized as follows: fertility below replacement during slavery; a fertility increase after emancipation so that, when the twentieth century arrived, fertility was seen as too high by some governments. After 1950, an increasing control of fertility brought crude birth rate to what most governments currently view as acceptable levels.

### 5.4   Afro-Caribbean family structure

It should be stressed from the start that in anthropology family is not equated with a nuclear household headed by a man (Bush, 1999). Rather, anthropologists recognize a wide variety of family structures. Equally important is, that in most societies there is more than one family structure, although one of them is either more frequent or it is sanctioned as "the prefered one." There are many studies of "the Afro-Caribbean family," described in the following paragraphs. Although this might be the most studied, and perhaps the most frequent family type, of Afro-Caribbean groups, it is not and it was not the only one in the region. A problem that arises when reading the sociological, historical, and cultural anthropological literature on Afro-Caribbean families is the obvious ideology of the writers that permeates their view of the subjects. As will be seen below, Afro-Caribbean women are portrayed in very different lights by different authors.

Although different authors disagree as to whether the various components of the Afro-Caribbean family described here should be seen as one, many agree that in this family type there is a separation of marriage and reproduction; a high proportion of non-marital unions (visiting and "common-law" unions) occurring in sequence, with marriage usually occurring towards the later reproductive years after a history of several unions, each of which usually produces at least one child, high rates of birth outside of marriage, fostering of relatives' children, and female-headed families with strong networks of consanguineal female folk. Perhaps the most fundamental characteristic of this family is that households are usually headed by a grandmother who shares the house with her daughters of reproductive age and their children born to different visiting or common-law unions. Hence the name matrifocal given to these families (Abraham-van der Mark, 2003; Ariza and de Oliveira, 1999; Barrow, 2001; Blake, 1961; Gearing, 1992; Gonzales, 1984; Harewood, 1984; Henriques, 1953; Matthews, 1953; Mohammed and Perkins, 1999; Nobbe *et al.*, 1976; Ortmayer, 1997; Otterbein, 1965; Roberts, 1975; Roberts and Sinclair, 1978; Stycos and Back, 1964).

A reconstruction of the evolution of the family structure in Afro-Caribbean groups must rely on historical sources. Given that most of these records were written by the slavers, they are tinted by prejudice and might not provide an accurate description of the slave family. It should be noted that there is a recent increase in the number of sources stating that African slaves and their descendents arranged themselves in male-headed nuclear families much more frequently than previously indicated (Higman, 1975; Morrissey, 1989). Charbit (1984) notes that the importance of matrifocal families among the slaves has been overstated by sociocultural anthropological researchers. He notes that ". . .residential matrifocality is proportionally in the minority, whereas nuclear households, whether extended or confined to the biological family, are by far the most frequent." Higman (1975) also notes the existence of polygamous slave family households. He concludes that the nuclear, not the matrifocal, family was the dominant type during slavery. Bush (1999) states that both the social complexity of slave life, and the varied ethnic backgrounds of the slaves, resulted in different marital and family forms coexisting. So, it should not be assumed that matrifocal families have always been or were the most common form of family in Afro-Caribbean communities, although the literature on them is ample. Whatever forms of family life the slaves arranged themselves into, slave conjugal and familial relations were continuously disrupted by the sale and transfer of partners and kin (Barrow, 2001).

A historical review of the Afro-Caribbean family structure should first consider that the legal status of slaves was not the same throughout the Caribbean. For example, within the British colonies there were important variations, as territories that had been taken from France and Spain offered legal status and protection to their slaves which did not exist in the older British territories. Thus in the former the slaves were able to enter the contract of marriage, whereas in the latter they were not (Stark, 1999). Still, most slave unions in most colonies, whether Spanish, French, British, etc., were not sanctioned in a marriage, with either a European or an African-based ritual (Ortmayer, 1997; Smith, 1988, 1996).

After abolition, the frequency of legal marriages remained very low among the former slaves and their descendants (Smith, 1988), in part because of the high rates of migration of males to work overseas on jobs such as the Panama Canal and the Costa Rican railroad (Barrow, 2001). Bush (1999), however, sees less continuity between the family structure during slavery and afterwards. She argues that high migration upon emancipation forced the former slaves to change their family structure. O'Neal (2001) notes the high frequency of illegitimacy in the Virgin Islands during the postemancipation period. She mentions that in great part the Christian churches, and the state's insistence on abolishing African-derived rituals such as the Obeah man/woman might have contributed to the former slaves' unwillingness to marry, if a marriage was feasible.

The low frequency of marriages in the Caribbean remained and has remained quite stable until recently. For example, in 1950, two-thirds of women in the USA aged 20–24 were married, but in Jamaica the proportion of married women in this age group was 10%. In 1985 the frequency of out-of-wedlock births was as high as 84.6% in Jamaica, 85.7% in St. Lucia, 80.8% in St. Kitts, and 82.9% in Antigua (Ortmayer, 1997). In their 1997 survey, Mohammed and Perkins (1999) found that the proportion of adult female respondents who were married was 20% in Barbados and St. Lucia, and 16% in Dominica. Abraham-van der Mark (2003) notes that the frequency of out-of-wedlock births in Curaçao decreased temporarily during the years in which an international company was hiring married workers, but increased again after the company left. Thus it is fair to conclude that legal marriage is less frequent in the

Caribbean than say, in the USA or Latin America. As a result, many children are born out of wedlock.

In general, three types of union are discussed in the Caribbean demographic literature: legal marriage, common-law unions, in which the partners live together, and visiting unions, in which the partners do not cohabitate (Abdulah, 1985; Smith, 1988). It should be stressed that visiting and common-law unions are socially recognized stable partnerships that frequently result in the birth of children and which involve responsibilities from both partners (Ariza and de Oliveira, 1999). For most women, there is a chronology to these unions, starting with visiting unions, then common-law unions, and ending with marriage, usually towards the end of their reproductive career, after producing children with several partners (Gonzales, 1984; Roberts and Sinclair, 1978). For example, in Trinidad and Tobago the average age of women entering a married union was 23.2 years, 1.7 years above the corresponding figure for common-law unions, and 3.1 years above that of visiting unions (Roberts, 1975). In Jamaica marriage is not infrequent; it is simply late (Blake, 1961; Stycos and Back, 1964). Therefore, in Afro-Caribbean communities marriage is not an appropriate manner to determine commencement of sexual activity, as it is in other communities (Ariza and de Oliveira, 1999; Mohammed and Perkins, 1999; Nobbe *et al.*, 1976; Otterbein, 1965). A frequent reason given by respondents on the reason for the late age at marriage in the Caribbean as opposed to, for example, Latin America, are the economic difficulties involved in paying for a marriage (Henriques, 1953; Nobbe *et al.*, 1976). Moreover, it seems that in economic terms marriage benefits the male more than the female (Coppin, 2000b).

Many of the sociological and historical literature sources seek to "explain" the Afro-Caribbean family structure as if there were something wrong with it, as if it were aberrant. Of course, we do not take that position but see such family structure as perfectly viable and healthy. However, we are still interested in reviewing the literature on the historical roots of this family structure, and this is what we do next.

Most explanations for the Afro-Caribbean family structure have focused on the slavery legacy, the West African heritage, an imbalanced sex ratio, poverty, and the minor influence of Christian churches on the African slaves and their descendants (Ariza and de Oliveira, 1999; Matthews, 1953; Ortmayer, 1997; Otterbein, 1965; Smith, 1996). We begin with the latter proposal. To the middle-class Black and "Colored" groups, legal Christian marriage became a manner to differentiate themselves from the slaves or their poor rural descendants after emancipation.

Bush (1999) notes that these "Colored" middle-class marriages were taken as evidence that the middle class was more civilized than were the former slaves. Smith (1996) does note that Black middle-class males did not isolate themselves from lower-class Black females, but continued the practice of visiting and common-law unions. Curtin (1955) describes the failure of most Christian churches to attract the former slaves, who resented the churches' insistence on marriage and a ban on African-derived rituals. Thus it seems that the Christian churches did not reach the African slaves and their descendants and failed to impose on them views on the need for a stable, sanctioned marriage (Stewart, Robert, 1999).

An economic historical underpinning for the Afro-Caribbean family is favored by other authors: Afro-Caribbean males were and are forced to migrate to earn and save money so that the sex ratio in the sending and the receiving regions is unbalanced. For example, migration has been seen as a contributor to the high frequency of matrifocal families in Barbados and Antigua (Handwerker, 1992; Otterbein, 1965). In contrast, St. Vincent island male out-migration during the nineteenth century actually resulted in polygynous unions (Gearing, 1992). In Chapter 6, on Limón, Costa Rica, we take a look at family formation in the receiving country, which initially welcomed male workers and only very few females.

Ortmayer (1997) argues that the high rates of non-legal union and of illegitimacy should be explained separately from the high numbers of matrifocal families. For the former, he prefers the lack of influence of the Christian churches on the slaves and their descendants, discussed above. For the latter, he favors an economic explanation. Indeed, most matrifocal families are and were found in the poorer groups, and less so in the middle class, even among the families that descended from the slaves (Ariza and de Oliveira, 1999). Indeed, the situation of middle-class females, who could or would not work outside of the home, was very different from that of women of lower socioeconomic status who were by necessity very economically active, particularly in the emerging service industries, just like their slave ancestors had been (Ortmayer, 1997; see Chapter 1). This gave the latter the ability, the "know-how," to be self-sufficient in the absence of a partner. Given that marriages were not frequent in the poorer classes, the tie between partners was looser and more likely to break. After such a break, the women already part of the job market would be able to care economically for themselves and their children. Mohammed and Perkins (1999), however, warn us not to over-stress the importance of women's economic roles outside of the home to the detriment of their household duties. Indeed, the dichotomy of household and extra-household work perhaps is only relevant to upper- and middle-class females. Many lower-income women have small-scale businesses such as cooking or sewing, run out of their own homes.

Important also is the fact that motherhood gave a woman a high social status. Recent surveys among Afro-Caribbean females indicate that motherhood is the primary and most fundamental issue in women's lives, to which all others (career, partners) must take second place (Mohammed and Perkins, 1999). Indeed, several sources indicate that the mother/ offspring link is stronger than that between male/female partners, and that women are able to head a viable household with their children in the absence of a male partner (Abraham-van der Mark, 2003; Ariza and de Oliveira, 1999; Gearing, 1992; Henriques, 1953; Otterbein, 1965; Smith, 1996).

Many sources agree that the Afro-Caribbean mature woman is the magnet that draws her adult children to come back from overseas and who makes decisions on the household economy and manages its labor pool. Indeed, the important position of the mother and grandmother in Curaçao is evident in proverbs, songs, etc. (Abraham-van der Mark, 2003; Gonzales, 1984; Mohammed and Perkins, 1999). We should be mindful, however, that this stereotype of strong Caribbean women might not allow researchers to see the emotional and financial dependency that women do have on their partners and which might not be met. Indeed, Handwerker (1992) presents a rather different view of Afro-Barbadian and Antiguan women, who, according to him, relied on their children's fathers for support. According to him, women in these two islands did not have economic independence before 1980, when new jobs and education became available. This is not too different from what Gearing (1992) describes for St. Vincent females, who may enter relations with men to obtain support for their offspring, relations that will probably produce another child and which will make the women less attractive as a partner in the future. Gearing (1992) does note that women have traditionally worked the land to support their children, so he does not present them as being as vulnerable as Handwerker (1992) does. It is clear though that when the Caribbean family structure is discussed, the ideology of the researcher colors his/her view of the position of the woman: some see her as a self-reliant strong person who is in charge of her own matrifocal family without the need of a male partner and whose influence extends across generations, and others see her as using sex and her reproductive potential to attract males on whom she is dependent. The older she gets the more children she has and the less attractive as a partner she becomes, but ultimately she is in need of a man to support her and her children.

Equally important to Afro-Caribbean families is the strong network of female relations of the female head of household, who support her in the household and in the raising of the children (Abraham-van der Mark, 2003; Gearing, 1992; Madrigal, 1988). Indeed, among the Garifuna the care of the children and the elderly is one of the most important functions of the household, one to which a mature grandmother is likely to contribute (Gonzales, 1984).

Abraham-van der Mark (2003) notes that recently the fostering of a relative's child is no longer taken for granted, and that children are now distributed between their father's as well as their mother's relatives. This might be a recent change in the tradition of fostering children of relatives or of affinal relations.

It should be noted that the father is not necessarily an absent figure in a child's life, although father and child may never live in the same household. Indeed, men are expected to contribute to the raising of their offspring, even if these children were a result of a visiting union (Ariza and de Oliveira, 1999; Charbit, 1984; Stycos and Back, 1964). Gonzales (1984) notes that the literature sometimes portrays the father's position in the Afro-Caribbean family as being "unhealthy" for men, a result of European-family style ethnocentrism. Such portrayal of men in Caribbean families can be found in older sources (Blake, 1961; Henriques, 1953; Matthews, 1953) and also in recent publications (Handwerker, 1992; van den Berghe, 1979). As Smith (1988) mentions, there is plenty of evidence to indicate that both males and females benefit from the Afro-Caribbean family structure (Mohammed and Perkins, 1999). We agree with Coppin's (2000a) assertion that much of the negative light in which the Afro-Caribbean family has been portrayed is a result of the ideology of writers who favor a male-headed nuclear family.

Indeed, the Afro-Caribbean family has been portrayed in professional journals or books in a negative manner (van den Berghe, 1979), and been called "dysfunctional" and "abnormal," both highly ethnocentric terms (Barrow, 2001; Bush, 1999; Mohammed and Perkins, 1999). Not infrequently a reference is made to "Blacks'" unusual sexual appetite and promiscuity (Henriques, 1953; Matthews, 1953). Smith, (1988) provides a history of anthropological writings on the Afro-Caribbean family. Higman (1975), after concluding that the nuclear, not the matrifocal, family was the typical arrangement among slaves, notes that this conclusion does not mean that the "normal" family type is the nuclear. On the contrary, it is perfectly possible that in comparison with the African norms of polygyny, the nuclear family is abnormal and "disorganized." Bush (1999) argues that the matrifocal family during the slavery period was probably a result of cultural continuity with African traditions, certainly not evidence of dissolute behavior.

In conclusion, although the matrifocal family has been portrayed as the typical Afro-Caribbean family type, it might not be so. Evidence is emerging that nuclear and polygynous unions existed during and after slavery (Bush, 1999). However, recent surveys indicate that the frequency of common-law or visiting unions is very high throughout the Caribbean, that, with some degree of variation, Afro-Caribbean groups do not see marriage as the marker of the beginning of sexual behavior, and that many women move through several relationships of different types at different times of their lives, while relying on a strong group of women folk. Men are usually expected to be economically and emotionally involved in child-rearing, although they might not cohabitate with their children.

### 5.5  Family structure and fertility

Morrissey (1989) presents a review of possible causes for the low fertility found among Afro-Caribbean slaves. She notes that the alleged ability of slave women and their midwives to control fertility might have been overstated by the slavers, and that there is too little information about women's desires or lack of for a family and fertility control. However, she notes that abortion and infanticide were frequently reported by planters and other European observers. Above contraceptive measures, Morrissey (1989) favors subfecundity due to malnutrition, disease, etc., as a reason for low slave fertility. Whatever its causes, it is clear that during slavery Afro-Caribbean groups had low fecundity. Therefore, a study on the relation between Afro-Caribbean family structure and fertility should be focused on more recent periods, when women's fecundity was not compromised as it was during slavery.

In many cultures, marriage marks the beginning of sexual activity for females, and regulates females' ability to engage in coital behavior. Indeed, there is some evidence (though equivocal) to indicate that women involved in polygamous marriages have lower fertility than do those in monogamous marriages in parts of Africa (Wood, 1994). As was seen above, in Afro-Caribbean populations marriage has a very different role in women's lives, as it does not mark the beginning of sexual activity, nor does it provide the only manner in which sexual activity occurs.

But data from studies with Afro-Caribbean groups indicate that the type of partnership in which a woman is involved might affect her fertility.

Indeed, Roberts (1975) refers to the relationship between union type and fertility as one of the most fundamental components of fertility variation in the Caribbean. However, it is clear from the literature that the relation between union type and fertility has changed due to the introduction of contraception and higher levels of female education.

Before the introduction of effective contraception and female education the data overwhelmingly indicated that non-visiting unions resulted in higher fertility, with some studies indicating higher fertility of common-law unions, but most indicating higher fertility of married wives (Handwerker, 1992; Nobbe *et al.*, 1976; Quinlan, 2001). The results were most clear when visiting unions were compared with non-visiting unions (common-law and marriage as one union type). Roberts (1975) notes that the important issue is not whether common-law or married wives have the highest fertility, but that both are in a stable non-visiting union and have higher fertility than do women in visiting unions. Higher fertilities of women in non-visiting unions as opposed to visiting unions have been reported in virtually every study (Harewood, 1976; Hobcraft, 1985; Quinlan, 2001; Roberts, 1975; Roberts and Sinclair, 1978; Stycos and Back, 1964). The most likely explanation for this finding is that women in visiting unions do not have the same exposure to sexual activity as do those residing with their partners. However, just as important is the duration of the unions: women who had been in married or in common-law unions for more than 20 years have very high fertility (Roberts, 1975; Stycos and Back, 1964). Roberts (1975: 197) concludes that the high frequency of visiting unions has the effect of depressing fertility in Afro-Caribbean females.

The type of partnership a woman enters is clearly tied to her socio-economic status. Whereas women of high socioeconomic status are more likely to enter a married partnership, those of low socioeconomic status are more likely to enter a common-law relationship. More importantly, women of higher socioeconomic status are more likely to leave visiting unions that are associated with lower fertility, and enter marriage, which is associated with higher fertility (Abdulah, 1985; Castro-Martin, 2002).

By the time of the 1980s, however, the situation had changed in much of the Caribbean. By the 1980s education was more widespread and contraception was available to such an extent that once females or couples achieved their desired number of children, they would use contraception effectively (George *et al.*, 1976; Lightbourne, 1984). Therefore, even though women in married and common-law partnerships might have greater exposure to sexual activity than do women in visiting unions, they might not have more children than the latter, because the former will stop conceiving once their target number of offspring is achieved. Lightbourne (1984) found a significant difference in fertility across social class, with females with higher socioeconomic and occupational status having fewer children as a result of contraception use. And, interestingly enough, desired family size did not differ across socioeconomic groups.

In conclusion, the relation between partnership type and fertility in Afro-Caribbean groups is complex and has changed as a result of greater education and contraception availability. Before the widespread adoption of contraception, females in non-visiting partnerships (whether married or common-law) had higher fertility than did those in visiting unions. Although most of the evidence indicated that married women had higher fertility than did common-law wives, this was not always so. There was also a clear link between socioeconomic status and partnership type, as women of high socioeconomic status were more likely to be married and thus to have higher fertility. After the introduction of contraception, and the broader education of women, the situation changed: educated women are now more likely to control their fertility with contraception whereas women who spend all their reproductive careers in visiting unions might achieve higher fertility as they are likely to have a different child with each partner. The link between fertility and family type, then, is not simple; nor has it been the same for the last 100 years.


## 5.6   Fecundity: contraception and reproductive health

We will follow here Wood's (1994) definition of fecundity as the biological capacity to reproduce. In the section on family type (Section 5.5), we reviewed an important cultural component of pregnancy risk: exposure to coitus as it is mediated by family type. In this section, we focus on more biologically mediated influences on fertility. Of course, even biological causes of fertility differentials, such as disease and breast-feeding duration, are culturally mediated, a point that will be kept in mind here.


### 5.6.1   Contraception

By 1964, women's age and parity were correlated with contraception use and knowledge in Jamaica: young women with low parity were less likely to know about and use contraception. Urban women also had more access to information about contraception than did rural women (Stycos and Back, 1964). In their recent report, Westoff and Bankole (2000) state that the demand for contraception in the Caribbean is being met, with the majority of users seeking to limit instead of spacing births. Indeed, the percentage of contraception users who were limiting births in Haiti was 61% in 1977 and 65.8% in 1994–5. In Trinidad and Tobago the percentage of users was 50.7% in 1977 and 64.3% in 1987. As Micklin (1994) notes, between 1983 and 1989 there was a drop in the number of countries who considered their fertility to be too high from 11 to 9. Importantly, no Caribbean country has governmental policies against contraception, and all but two (the Bahamas and Belize) provide government support for family-planning programs.

Although the initial picture of contraception use is perhaps that it is wide and successful, this is not the case everywhere in the Caribbean. In St. Vincent for example, Gearing (1992) notes that there is a general pronatalist attitude among males and females, deeply rooted in the social and economic value of children. Gearing does note that recent reluctance on the part of relatives to foster children, as well as greater opportunity for females to migrate, might result in greater use of contraception but that had not occurred by the time of his study.

Abdulah (1985) attributes the fertility decline seen in Trinidad and Tobago beginning in the 1960s to an increasing use of contraceptives. A key variable affecting contraception use is women's age, as young women have low use because they have not achieved their desired family size, and older women use contraception more frequently up until age 35, when use decreases again as a result of lower risk of pregnancy. Use of contraception is more frequent in married and common-law wives, and is positively correlated with parity. But the most important predictor of contraception use is education: the more educated the woman, the more likely she is to use contraception (Abdulah, 1985).

In their recent study on motherhood and women's choices in Barbados, St. Lucia, and Dominica, Mohammed and Perkins (1999) note that contraceptives are widely available and that education programs are seeking to increase awareness about them. The fertility decrease seen in these three islands has been explained mostly in terms of education, which allows women to make use of contraception because it has opened to them new economic opportunities.

Handwerker (1992) does not think that contraception was responsible for the fertility drop in Barbados and Antigua. Rather, other intermediate factors were deemed necessary, before contraception was widely used: power, access to resource, education, and jobs.

In general then, most sources stress the importance of education of women in the use of contraception. Further support for this position is given by Singh and Casterline (1985), who calculated that for the entire region of the Caribbean the difference in fertility between women with no education and those with at least completed secondary schooling was two or three children. More specifically, even a few years of primary schooling results in lower fertility. Upper primary and secondary education bring substantial reductions in fertility.

### 5.6.2    *Reproductive health and fecundity*

Under this heading we are including a woman's disease load as it affects her ability to become pregnant. Our emphasis, however, will be on diseases that affect reproduction as well as on injuries caused by unsafe abortions. The frequency of fetal loss due to congenital and genetic abnormalities can be assumed to be a constant for the species, being individually rare and uncommon in the population (Wood, 1994). For that reason, we concentrate on the effect of poor reproductive health on fecundity. We take a historical view, beginning with the slavery period.

Sexually transmitted diseases such as gonorrhea, *Chlamydia*, puerperal sepsis, and genital tuberculosis can lead to pelvic inflammatory disease. Also, unsafe abortion and female genital mutilation can result in pelvic inflammatory disease, which results in partial or total blockage of the fallopian tubes by scar tissue, thus inhibiting the transport of ova by normal ciliatory movements (Mascie-Taylor, 1996; Wood, 1994). Unfortunately, the literature on sexually transmitted diseases in the contemporary Caribbean (except HIV, which was discussed in Chapter 3) is very disappointing.

The incidence of induced abortion among female slaves cannot be known: there are no reliable data (Morrissey, 1989). Unfortunately as well there are very few sources on the contemporary frequency of unsafe abortion, as reliable data are virtually non-existent for the Caribbean. Ahman and Shah (2002) report an incidence ratio of 11 unsafe abortions per 100 live births, and an incidence rate of unsafe abortions per 1000 women aged 15–49 in the Caribbean. A higher figure of 17 unsafe abortions per 100 live births is reported by www.who.int/reproductive-health/publications/MSM_97_16/MSM_97_16>chapter4.    For comparison, these figures in Central America were 20 and 19, and in South America they were 39 and 30, respectively. According to Rice (1991–2), 30% of maternal deaths are caused by unsafe abortions. She estimates that the risk of women dying from causes associated with maternity is 1 in 140 in the Caribbean. Clearly, unsafe abortion is relatively frequent in the Caribbean, and it is likely to contribute to low fecundity in some Caribbean women.

More data are available for reconstructing frequencies of sexually transmitted disease among the slaves. Evidence from paleopathology indicates that sexually transmitted disease has negatively impacted fecundity in the Caribbean since the time of slavery. In their comprehensive study of the Newton plantation in Barbados, Jacobi and colleagues (1992) conclude that syphilis contributed substantially to morbidity, mortality, and infertility in the slave population. Morrissey (1989) notes the likely contribution of gonorrhea and syphilis to the low fertility of slaves, but emphasizes tuberculosis as a more likely contributor to impaired slave fertility. She also notes that yaws could have made intercourse painful for both males and females. Also, the general poor state of health and high mortality of the slaves could have acted as a barrier to sexual behavior and shortened reproductive life span. The likely contribution of disease to infertility is also stressed by Craton (1978). In contrast, Bush (1996) notes that it is difficult to determine the actual extent of venereal disease among the slaves, as medical reports from the time give conflicting reports about it.

Prevalence rates for sexually transmitted diseases for Latin America and the Caribbean (as one single region) are found in WHO (2001), but the lack of data on sexually transmitted diseases (in comparison with data on obesity, hypertension, and diabetes) is frustrating. Many more reports are found of sexually transmitted diseases of Afro-Caribbean migrants to London (for example, DakerWhite and Barlow, 1997; Dragovic et al., 2002). But what data are available do indicate that sexually transmitted diseases are a significant problem. For example, chlamydial infections were found among 12.2% of attendees to family-planning clinics in Jamaica. Trichomoniasis was found in 3.6% of pregnant women in Barbados. Equally worrisome is that the occurrence of gonorrhea strains that are resistant to tetracycline and penicillin is very high and very widespread through the region: in Cuba 68% of the strains were resistant to penicillin and 83.5% to tetracycline (Sosa et al., 2003). Similarly high frequencies of strains resistant to either tetracycline or penicillin were found in other regions, namely 92.9% in Guyana, 44.1% in St. Vincent, and 42.24% in Trinidad (Dillon et al., 2001). Thus, although we do not have data for much of the region, the few studies we do have indicate that sexually transmitted diseases are common in the area, and that they are caused in great part by strains that are resistant to tetracycline and penicillin. For a study on the molecular evolution of gonorrhea worldwide, including Jamaica, see Turner et al. (1999).

In an interesting Trinidadian study linking rates of sexually transmitted disease and sexual behavior, Castor *et al.* (2002) showed that the risk of gonorrheal infection increased significantly with increasing numbers of sexual partners in the 6 months prior to the study. Whereas males were shown to have an average of two partners, females had an average of 1.5 partners for the same period. Thus it is likely that women in visiting unions, which are less stable, are more likely to be affected by gonorrheal infection.

The problem of low condom use for prevention of HIV transmission was discussed in Chapter 3. Here we just confirm what was discussed then; namely that condom use is low and that it is tied to power within a relationship. For example, in a recent research project which took place in Kenya, Tanzania, and Trinidad, only 19% of respondents said that they used a condom with the most recent sexual partner. Unfortunately the data were not broken down by country (Norman, 2003).

As Wood (1994) notes, fetal loss and infant death contributes to infertility, as the woman loses reproductive time on a failed pregnancy. The likelihood of experiencing non-congenital and non-genetic fetal loses increases for women with closely spaced pregnancies. Infant or early childhood death is also associated with short birth intervals (Rice, 1991–2). Bush (1999) reviews the extremely high frequency of infant and childhood mortality during slavery. She concludes that infanticide might have been rather common, given the terrible conditions under which slave mothers lived.

Roberts and Sinclair (1978) provide frequencies of miscarriages and infant mortality in Jamaica during the 1970s. They tried to answer the question of whether women intended on replacing their dead infant. The data are not conclusive either way, as a large percentage of women continue bearing children after a death, whether they stated a conscious effort of replacing or not. More recently, and unexpectedly, Brittain (1992) reports that in a study performed during the 1970s in St. Barthelemy, short birth interval was not a significant predictor of childhood death.

## 5.7    Conclusion: fertility in Afro-Caribbean groups

In this first part of the chapter we have looked at fertility in a holistic perspective, by including biological as well as cultural components of fertility variation. Fertility during slavery was exceedingly low, possibly as a result of the harsh conditions of slave women (subfecundity), or even as a result of an active protest by females of their situation, and their refusal to bear children (Bush, 1999). After emancipation, fertility increased, most likely because fecundability increased due to the more favorable life conditions. A link between better life conditions and higher fecundability has been shown before (Rosetta, 1996). However, fertility rates never rose to be as high in the Caribbean as they were in Latin America at the same time.

In contemporary Afro-Caribbean groups, the variable that emerged to be of paramount importance in fertility differences was family structure: most studies indicated that women in stable unions, whether legal or common-law, had higher fertility than did women in visiting unions. This has been reported even in recent studies. However, the introduction of contraception, and above all greater women's education, started to affect fertility. Educated women are more likely to use contraception, which appears to be reasonably well available throughout the region. Therefore, although in the past women of higher socioeconomic status tended to have higher fertility because they were more likely to be in stable unions (Stycos and Back, 1964), in the last 20–30 years women of high socioeconomic status were more likely to limit their fertility with contraception.

The data on sexually transmitted diseases are very inadequate for the contemporary Caribbean region. Therefore, it is difficult to gauge the importance of pelvic inflammatory disease on fertility, whether the inflammation is caused by an infectious disease or by unsafe abortion. The few sources on sexually transmitted diseases do indicate that these diseases are common in the general population, and even that gonorrhea is resistant to antibiotics throughout the region. Why information on sexually transmitted disease is so hard to come by, when data on other conditions such as hypertension are so easily available, is an interesting question. Data from the time of slavery do suggest that syphilis was rampant in the slave population, causing women to have had low fecundity and fertility.

It is interesting to speculate on the contribution of culture and biology to observed fertility differentials in the Caribbean. Given that women in visiting unions have less frequent exposure to sexual behavior, that they are more likely to be of low socioeconomic status and thus less likely to have good access to medical treatment for sexually transmitted disease, it is possible that both culture and disease together act in a synergistic fashion to lower their fertility and fecundity.

### 5.8   Migration in the Caribbean

The history of anthropology's interest in migration is reviewed by Brettell (2003). In the 1950s and 1960s, the emphasis of migration anthropological research was on rural to urban migration, especially to large cities in the

Third World. By the beginning of the twenty-first century, anthropologists are paying more attention to global migration as it affects the communities from which migrants come and to which they go in large numbers. As was noted in Chapter 2, the globalization of capitalist economy has affected within-country migration by encouraging young people to abandon rural areas and move to urban ones, thus affecting their likelihood of suffering from obesity, hypertension, and diabetes. But globalization has also caused millions of people to migrate outside of their own countries, making migration one of the best examples of why globalization is truly global, as opposed to just international (see Chapter 2 for a longer discussion on this process).

Perhaps no other region in the world has been so affected by migration as the Caribbean (Ho, 1999; Momsen, 1986). As was mentioned in Chapter 1, after the native Caribbean population was decimated by the European invasion, African slaves were brought across the Atlantic in great numbers. As a result of this forced migration, the genetic map of the Caribbean was totally changed from what it was before 1492. Since population genetics was covered in Chapter 4, we will consider Afro-Caribbean migration beginning with the emancipation of the slaves. We also do not review here theories on migration, which can be found in Duany (1994), Simmons and Guengant (1992), and in several chapters of the volume edited by Mobasher and Sadri (2004). Our emphasis here is the effect of migration on the demographic structure of Afro-Caribbean groups, and on their microevolutionary changes.

Although we focus on postemancipation migration, we do need to note the importance of slavery in the formation of the Afro-Caribbean culture. However many slaves were brought from Africa (see Chapter 1), millions and millions of uprooted people were forcefully put together in a most inhumane condition. The sense of alienation that came from this situation, according to Simmons and Guengant (1992), is one of the historical factors contributing to a culture of migration that is typical of Afro-Caribbean groups. A steady Caribbean out-migration is over 200 years old, and is thus an integral part of Afro-Caribbean culture. Several authors see migration as a successful strategy of moving from an area of limited opportunities to a richer one (Connell and Conway, 2000; Duany, 1994; Ho, 1999).

### 5.8.1   A history of migration in the Caribbean

A review of the literature indicates that there is not a single historical pattern of migration for the entire Caribbean region. Perhaps the only general statement that applies to all of the Caribbean is that laborers were brought as slaves or indentured workers to work on plantations when the economy required labor, and that the descendents of these laborers became an export commodity when the economy did not require their work in their place of birth (Momsen, 1986). Besides that, different islands with different sizes and different ecological conditions experienced contractions and expansions in their economy, and out- and in-migration, at different times of their history. These same expansions and contractions were experienced through the Atlantic coast of Central America, with the boom and bust of the banana industry and the building of large projects such as the Panama Canal and the Costa Rican railroad. The latter is covered in the last chapter in this volume, on the Limón Afro-Caribbean population. What is clear is that remittances from migrants to their families have been a successful economic strategy of Afro-Caribbean families, from emancipation to the present time (Itzigsohn, 1995). Connell and Conway (2000) present a comparison of migration and remittances between South Pacific and Caribbean microstates. They argue that the history of both areas is intrinsically tied to international or transnational migrations.

After emancipation (beginning in 1793 in Haiti, continuing in 1833 in the British colonies), whereas many former slaves continued working in the same plantations, in the same miserable conditions they did as slaves, others left the plantations and established peasant villages [a process Simmons and Guengant (1992) refer to as villagization]. This, however, was only possible in the islands in which land was available for this purpose. These villages were viable as long as there was seasonal local labor and a market for small-scale farming. When the sugar plantation economy fell in certain areas (Haiti, Jamaica, Barbados, St. Kitts, Nevis, and Montserrat) and grew in others (Trinidad, British Guyana, Cuba, and the Dominican Republic) during the 1860s and 1870s, migration primarily of young males became a frequent survival strategy for many Afro-Caribbean families (Gearing, 1992). This strategy, though, left great numbers of females alone in the sending islands (Ortmayer, 1997). This time is what Duany (1994) denotes the period of interterritorial migration. Interestingly, it is in this period, in the 1860s and 1870s, that indentured workers were brought to the Caribbean from India, China, and to a lesser extent Europe. These workers filled the labor void left by out-migrating plantation workers and by the concentration of former slaves in villages (Momsen, 1986; Simmons and Guengant, 1992). Some of these indentured workers formed large communities, for example, in Trinidad and Guyana. Some formed very small groups that have been largely unnoticed by anthropologists, for example in Costa Rica (Madrigal *et al.*, 2004). During the postemancipation period there was a parallel out-migration movement of European-derived families who fled the revolutionary movements of Haiti and Santo Domingo, and settled in Cuba, Venezuela, Puerto Rico, Jamaica, and Trinidad (Duany, 1994).

In the last decades of the 1800s and up until the period of the Great Depression, migration became crucial to Afro-Caribbean populations. Whereas the plantation economy declined in some islands, it grew in others, causing an important movement of people through the islands (Brittain, 1990; Ortmayer, 1997). In St. Vincent island, so many adult males migrated out that the adult population in the island was primarily female (Gearing, 1992). The same occurred in several other sending islands (Ortmayer, 1997). Crucially important during this period, however, was the tremendous movement of Afro-Caribbean men to Panama, Cuba, the Dominican Republic, Honduras, and Costa Rica to work on the Panama canal and railroad constructions, and in the expanding banana industry (Duany, 1994; Momsen, 1986; Purcell, 1993). As Plummer (1985) notes, it is well known that migrants from the former British colonies came to work in Panama, but it is less recognized that Haitian migrants did as well. It is because of these population movements that a viable community of Afro-Caribbeans was established in Costa Rica, changing the demographic and cultural profile of the country irreversibly (Purcell, 1993). Equally important from the point of view of the Afro-Caribbean families was the increased migration to the United States. For Haitians, it was Cuba that was the recipient of migrants (Plummer, 1985). During this period of heightened migration, villagization became less of a viable option for family survival, and migration became the main mode for obtaining an income for the family. During the First World War, increased demand for and production of sugar resulted in heightened migration from Haiti (Plummer, 1985). The Depression, however, brought a decrease of migration to the USA and other receiving centers (Gearing, 1992; Momsen, 1986). For example, the sugar economy was weakened in Cuba, which caused the expulsion of Haitian workers (Plummer, 1985). The mass murder of thousands of Haitian workers in the Dominican Republic is well known, and followed the sugar economy's bust. The period between the two world wars was one of decreased Caribbean out-migration (Duany, 1994; Plummer, 1985).

During the Second World War, different islands had different migratory patterns: St. Barthélemy became isolated and experienced a sharp drop in emigration. St. Thomas, which had seen a rise in US presence as a protection against the Germans, lost importance and money brought by the US once large boats that did not require frequent refueling were adopted (Brittain, 1990). For some islands the period after the Second World War brought an increased impetus for migration, particularly to the USA, Canada, and Europe (Simmons and Guengant, 1992). Thus, in Haiti, entire families migrated, actually creating a labor shortage in the sending country (Plummer, 1985). Britain, Canada, and the USA at different times opened up their borders to migrants (Duany, 1994; Momsen, 1986). The development of the tourist industry in some islands made them attractive to migrants from others, so that interisland migration became once again important (Brittain, 1990). Another economic activity that affected migration patterns after 1945 was light industry in small factories. For example, in Haiti, rural migrants came to Port-au-Prince to work in small factories which produced export items. Haitian migration to the USA continued despite punitive measures from the US government (Plummer, 1985). According to Duany (1994), between 1950 and 1980, 4 million people out-migrated from the Caribbean.

The post-1945 migration pattern differs from that of previous periods, with a shift from male-led migration to female-led migration. Female nurses are frequent migrants to the UK, in great part because the nursing curriculum is similar and there is automatic acceptance of the degree in the UK, and in some cases these laborers migrated as citizens from British colonies to Britain (Grosfoguel, 2001). Furthermore, after the Second World War, entire families migrated and settled on a permanent basis in the receiving county (Duany, 1994; Simmons and Guengant, 1992). Ho (1999) notes that most families who migrated intact were of upper- and middle-class extraction and that the lower-class worker continued to out-migrate alone.

During the 1980s and 1990s Caribbean migration continued to include migration to the USA, Canada, and Europe, to economically growing Caribbean regions, to Latin America, and to sending islands by returned migrants (Byron, 2000; Duany, 1994). A fascinating aspect of Caribbean migration since the 1980s is that many islands are both senders and receivers of migrants, so that most Caribbean regions have sizeable foreign communities. Trinidad and Tobago had a period of great economic growth during the 1970s and 1980s because of its oil industries, and thus attracted many migrants. However, after the 1980s decline in oil price, out-migration increased (Phillips, 1996). Curaçao experienced heightened out-migration of young adults in the late 1990s, especially to the Netherlands (Abraham-van der Mark, 2003). Pellegrino (2000) presents the number of emigrants as proportions of various Latin American and Caribbean countries' populations in 1990. Several Caribbean areas have very high proportions of emigrants, including Guyana (more than 25%), Belize (more than 20%), and Trinidad and Tobago (just under 15%). Momsen (1986) notes that between 1965 and 1975 one-third of Surinam's population moved to the Netherlands. Indeed, the out-migration of nurses from Trinidad and Tobago caused serious shortages of nurses in the islands during the 1980s (Phillips, 1996). Migrants usually favor receiving countries with language commonality: French-speaking Caribbean migrants migrate to France and French-speaking Canada, English-speaking migrants favor the UK and the USA, Dutch-speaking migrants from Curaçao favor the Netherlands, etc. (Momsen, 1986). The long colonial history between the migrants and the receiving countries is also emphasized by Abraham-van der Mark (2003), Giraud (1999), Grosfoguel (2001), and Phillips (1996).

   Although migrants are part of a global expanding capitalist system, such expansion is asymmetrical, benefiting mostly the migrant-receiving countries. Indeed, the permanent out-migration of professionals from the Caribbean to the USA, Canada, or Europe benefits much more the receiving rather than the donor country (Duany, 1994). The Caribbean region's main resource is cheap labor to be used within or without the Caribbean, according to expansions and contractions of the global economy (Byron, 2000; Grosfoguel, 2001). Ho (1999) notes that the global economic situation since the 1980s that has encouraged Caribbean out-migration has only increased poverty and unemployment in the region.


### 5.8.2   *Migration, the family, and fertility*

As Connell and Conway (2000) note, migration decisions are shaped within a family context, one which contains the expectation of remittances. The fact that the modal gender of migrants has changed from male to female reflects an understanding of the economic context in the receiving countries, from the banana plantations and railroad and canal constructions in Central America, to housemaid work in Canada, the USA, and Europe. Indeed, families of migrants operate on a world stage, making decisions that will benefit the entire family, not the individual, let alone the sending country's gross national product (Connell and Conway, 2000).

   Momsen (1986) reviews the effect on the rural household of male-led migration before female-led migration became more frequent. She notes that frequently the female head of the family was the grandmother or the mother, who farmed for subsistence as opposed to cash. In situations in which most of the adult population in the sending island was female, polygamous unions or high numbers of females without partners resulted. In either situation, fertility must have been lowered, given that polygamy appears to result in low fertility (Wood, 1994), and that women had few opportunities to become pregnant (Gearing, 1992). When females became better able to gain employment overseas than were males and female-led migration became more frequent, males were still expected to contribute to the upkeep of the children. This new situation caused many couples to break up, and in some cases accentuated the matrifocality of Caribbean households in the receiving countries, as migrant mothers brought their sisters and mothers to help with the children. Clearly, if unions fail to continue after migration, fertility is also negatively affected. Ho (1999) notes that Caribbean transnational families rest upon a strong web of women folk. Of course, if a young mother needs to leave her offspring behind, she suffers from the separation from her children, which is considered such an important bond in the Caribbean.

Whether female- or male-led, migration is ultimately tied to lower fertility in the Caribbean. Not unlike visiting unions, transnational male–female unions are unstable, whereas matrifocal and mother–offspring links remain strong. The reduced fertility of females with low socioeconomic status, whether they migrate or stay in the sending communities without a male partner, would have a similar effect on the population structure of Afro-Caribbean populations to the reduced fertility of visiting unions, which was mentioned in Section 5.5. If females of higher socioeconomic status have historically higher fertility (in the absence of contraception) because they more frequently enter married unions, and also because they or their spouse do not migrate – or if they do, they migrate together – then the end result is that these females make a greater genetic contribution to the population. Thus the population structure of Afro-Caribbean groups has been affected in a similar manner by the mating patterns and by the migration of its members. In terms of the microevolution of these populations, if Afro-Caribbean females of higher socioeconomic status are more likely to descend from European–African matings, as seems to be the case, then the contribution of European-derived genes to future generations is greater than that of African-derived genes.

For centuries, the Caribbean family has responded to economic growth and contractions, sending its members to wherever labor is needed. The matrifocal family has remained strong and able to adapt itself to changing conditions. As Ho (1999: 38) so aptly puts it, "Clearly, the matrifocal relations described above are not the problem but the *solution* to the problem of the economic support of women and children under the capitalist mode of production in the Caribbean" [italics in original].

## 5.9   The demographic transition model in the Caribbean

As a whole, the Caribbean never had the high fertility rates seen in Latin America. As was discussed previously, both migration and family structure contributed to comparatively low fertility. Demographic data from the 1950s through 2050 on the Caribbean can be found at CEPAL (2003).

In 1998, Serow and Cowart presented demographic data for the present, 2025, and 2050. Although in 1998 the total fertility rate in the Caribbean (the number of births a woman would have over her reproductive lifetime if current age-specific patterns of childbearing remain constant) varied, it was on the whole low: from 4.3 in Belize and 3.9 in Grenada to 1.8 in Barbados and 1.7 in Antigua and Barbuda. There is as much variation in the life expectancy at birth, from more than 74 years for men and 80 years for women in Dominica to 58 and 64 years respectively in Guyana. By the year 2050, male and female life expectancy will exceed 75 and 80 years everywhere except in Guyana. The projections presented by Serow and Cowart (1998) indicate that there will be a trend towards population aging throughout the Caribbean. The growth of the elderly population is expected to be much higher (125%) than the overall rate of population growth (80%). As a result, the number of individuals who are old or young (dependent) will rise from 69 to 75 dependents per 100 active people. The change is significant because when the Caribbean had 69 dependents per 100 active people, 80% of these dependents were children and 20% were old. When the ratio changes to 75 dependents per 100 active people, 60% of the dependents will be elderly and 40% will be children. Therefore, the Caribbean is experiencing a trend towards population aging, which will alter its population pyramid. Where it differs radically from Latin America is that most of its islands did not have very high rates of fertility to begin with.

After reviewing the arguments that have been proposed against the applicability of the demographic transition theory (which were discussed earlier in this chapter), Oeschsli and Kirk (1975) conclude that the theory does apply to the Caribbean and Latin American regions. They note that data show that declines in mortality occur at a very early stage in the transition, earlier than was the case in the European countries. Declines in birth rates are seen later, after the decline in mortality has stabilized. Natality declines are usually observed after a certain level of development has been reached. In Jamaica, natality rates fell after mortality declined, as predicted by the demographic transition model (Agyei, 1978). In Barbados, a decline in fertility between two subsequent generations was reported by George and collaborators (1976).

However, data from various islands indicate that the demographic transition model might not apply to the entire region in a homogeneous fashion, if it applies at all to some islands. For example, a study in St. Barthélemy from 1800 through 1967 reports that, after mortality had decreased, fertility did not. On the contrary, fertility remained fairly high, after the time frame in which the demographic transition model would have predicted that it would decrease. Brittain (1990) argues that migration needs to be entered into the equation, as parents might maintain relatively high fertility as an "insurance" against loss of offspring not to mortality but to migration. Similarly, in the 1960s the population of Bimini had achieved stability. However, this was not due to a classic transition as predicted by the theory, but to still-high childhood mortality and high out-migration, counterbalanced by high fertility (Halberstein, 1980).

In conclusion, it is clear that the entire region of the Caribbean is on its way through the demographic transition. However, not all islands have experienced this change in the same manner. A key component to the demographic variation seen in the area is the importance of out-migration as a means of decreasing population pressure. Thus even in the presence of lower mortality, the expected decline in fertility does not always take place, as parents might wish to have a large family as an insurance against migration, not against childhood mortality. When the demographic transition is to be studied, the variation in fertility due to the family structure of the Caribbean should also be considered. Thus when mortality started declining in the area, not all females had high fertility. Rather, high fertility before the introduction of Western contraception was found mostly in females of upper socioeconomic status, who tended to enter stable unions, and whose partners did not out-migrate – or if they did, they did so with their wives. Although the demographic transition model remains a powerful tool to understand the demographic evolution of human populations, it is challenged by a number of exceptions in the Caribbean.

### 5.10   Conclusion: migration and the demographic transition model in Afro-Caribbean groups

Perhaps no other region in the world has been so affected by massive migration movements as the Caribbean. Thus it is to be expected that, through migration, gene flow has been a strong evolutionary force in the microevolution of Afro-Caribbean groups.

After the collapse of the native population, millions of African slaves were forcefully brought to the Caribbean, and a culture of migration was born in the midst of the slaves. After emancipation, important numbers of former slaves migrated out of the plantations and concentrated in small villages, which later lost importance to the job openings in Honduras, Costa Rica, and Panama during the late 1800s. The massive male migration to these regions left many females alone in the sending regions. At the same time, and to alleviate the labor shortage caused by these migrant movements, indentured servants were brought from China and India, servants who also forever changed the demographic profile of several Caribbean areas. During the first half of the 1900s, different regions of the Caribbean experienced economic contractions and expansions, and thus became senders and receivers of male migrants respectively. In the second part of the 1900s, female or entire-family migration became more frequent.

A demographic review of Afro-Caribbean groups shows that migration must be considered when we look at fertility and at the demographic transition of these populations. The effect of migration on fertility is similar to the effect of visiting unions on fertility; that is, migration separates males and females and reduces the risk of pregnancy. Given that visiting unions are more frequently found in lower socioeconomic groups, and given that migrants of low socioeconomic status migrate without spouses, the end result of visiting unions and out-migration is to depress the fertility of females of low socioeconomic status.

Afro-Caribbean families have faced economic changes and forced separations successfully. Not only have these groups been able to survive brutal conditions, but they have been able to maintain strong kinship ties over large geographical regions. Christine Ho is perhaps the clearest exponent of the position that matrifocal families are the solution to the problem of poverty of these populations. Afro-Caribbeans have successfully adjusted to economic changes and have been able to sustain both the old and the young for many generations. Attempts to explain the matrifocal family as a social pathology are fueled by narrow, ethnocentric views of what families should be (van den Berghe, 1979). A holistic approach to demography allows us to see that among Afro-Caribbean groups fertility, migration, and family structure should be considered together.

# 6 The Afro-Caribbean population in Limón, Costa Rica

This chapter is the culmination of the entire book, as it will present a microevolutionary history of the Afro-Caribbean population in Limón, Costa Rica. We will start with an historical overview, tying the initial and subsequent migrations which formed this group with the contractions and expansions of the Caribbean economy that were reviewed in Chapter 5. Then we will discuss some of the cultural-anthropological and linguistic work on the group, although this will be by necessity a short section, as this book is about human biology, not cultural anthropology. We will then discuss work on obesity, hypertension, and diabetes in the region, as well as on infectious diseases, and put Limón in the wider Caribbean epidemiologic context. Data are limited for both chronic and infectious diseases unfortunately: in Costa Rica data are collected not according to ethnic group but only to geography. Thus if we work with data from the Limón region we might be looking at data of the Afro-Caribbean and the Hispano-Limonense groups combined. However, a few research projects have focused on the African-derived population, and these will be very helpful. In contrast with epidemiology studies, there are plenty of demographic projects which focus exclusively on the Afro-Limonense population, projects that look at the family structure and other demographic aspects of interest. There have also been more data published on the population genetics of the Afro-Limonense group than on any other Costa Rican group. Thus the demographic and population genetics part of the chapter will be more extensive than those on epidemiology.

## 6.1 A history of African-derived groups in Costa Rica

Although the population of interest to us resides in the Atlantic coast of Costa Rica (see Figure 6.1) we should say a few words about the first arrival of African slaves to the country, which occurred in the early stages of Spanish exploration, and whose descendants' history and current ethnic perception are very different from those of the Afro-Limonenses (Herzfeld, 2002). African slaves were initially brought during the early

Figure 6.1. A map of Costa Rica.

1500s as members of exploration teams, who focused their efforts in the north–Central Pacific areas of the country, specifically Guanacaste and Puntarenas (Blutstein, 1970; Olien, 1980). Pescatello (1975) notes that the initial role of Africans in the colonial expansion of Spain was one of support in the military establishment of Spanish troops. In 1611 there were 200 people of African ancestry in Costa Rica (Melendez, 1981).

The African area of origin of the slaves brought to Costa Rica is difficult to ascertain (Melendez, 1981). Some documents about colonial slaves do mention the origin or the ethnic group of these individuals. Blutstein (1970) and Melendez (1981) indicate that colonial slaves could have originated from Togo, Angola, Guinea, Guinea-Bissau, Niger, Congo, Senegal, and Sudan. According to Rawley (1981), the source of African slaves for the Spanish Empire changed through the centuries. Whereas most slaves before 1615 originated from Upper Guinea, most originated from Angola thereafter. The differences in ethnic origin of the early slaves did not contribute to the preservation of any of their languages, and to this day there are no remnants of the language spoken by them among their descendents in Guanacaste and Puntarenas (Herzfeld, 2002).

As in all Latin American countries, the Costa Rican Amerindian population suffered tremendously from the European invasion, and was reduced in numbers dramatically: thousands of Indians were given, in
*encomiendas*, as slaves to Spanish colonists who had power over their life
and death (Putnam, 2002). But in contrast with areas such as Colombia,
Perú, and México, there was not a demand for a large population of
African slaves, as there were no major natural resources to exploit in
Costa Rica, which became one of the poorest and least important regions
of the Spanish Empire. A new generation of Costa Rican historians
(Cáceres, 2000; Lobo-Wiehoff and Meléndez-Obando, 1997) argues that
the history of Costa Rica has been presented in a rosy way which under-
emphasized both the plight of the Amerindians as well as the large
number of African slaves during colonial times and their contribution to
the country. There are close to 2000 documents of legal transactions of
slaves in Costa Rica, although there was a viable illegal trade through the
colony occurring in the Atlantic coast, where the English pirates and their
allies the Zambo Mosquitos sold African slaves with an unknown frequency. The Zambo Mosquitos were "Mosquito" Indians (a corruption
of the word Miskito) who had intermarried with run-away or ship-
wrecked African slaves and who were allied with the English (see Azofeifa
*et al.*, 1998, for a recent population genetics study on present-day Miskito
Indians in Nicaragua).

Throughout the colonial period, the Costa Rican population experienced a high level of intermarriage among its various groups (Spanish,
Indian, African), which resulted in a significant number of "mixed"
individuals (Gudmundson, 1977; Lobo-Wiehoff and Meléndez-Obando,
1997; Putnam, 2002). The so-called mulattoes were individuals of partial
African ancestry, who were usually granted their freedom by their slave
owners (Melendez, 1981). Many of them lived in separate neighborhoods
in the larger urban areas. For example Cartago (then the capital of Costa
Rica) had a separate neighborhood created in 1650 called *La Puebla de los
Pardos,* in which people of African ancestry lived. Other urban centers
also had an important number of slaves and their descendants, such as *La
Villa Nueva de la Boca del Monte* (later San José, Costa Rica's capital; see
Figure 6.1). These urban slaves performed all the tasks associated with the
household, though many were sent to work at their slavers' cacao plantations in Matina close to the Atlantic coast of Limón, or to the cattle farms
in the northern plains of Costa Rica (Putnam, 2002). Of course, the
female slave faced the same problems and challenges faced by all female
slaves in the entire Caribbean: in addition to being the main household
worker, contributing to the cooking, washing, sawing, etc, she was exploited

as a prostitute to the benefit of the slaver and faced sexual harassment from her slaver. The importance of the African slaves in the history of Costa Rica has been emphasized in recent years, with the work of Lobo-Wiehoff and Meléndez-Obando (1997) showing that most Costa Rican families (mine included), who have always considered themselves to be "White", descend from at least one of these African slaves.

However, during colonial times the largest concentration of people of African ancestry was found in the rural north and central Pacific provinces of Guanacaste and Puntarenas, where the Spanish conquistadors had invaded the country. According to Olien (1980), in 1801 there were 8929 people of African ancestry in the country, which amounted to 17% of the entire colony of Costa Rica.

After achieving independence from Spain, the Federal Republic of Central America abolished slavery in 1823. This republic was a short-lived country of which all Central American countries were part (Luján, 1962–63). In Costa Rica, although 17% of the population was considered to be of African ancestry, fewer than 100 individuals were slaves at the time of the emancipation (Luján, 1962–3; Melendez, 1981; Olien, 1980). Thus by the time of the abolition of slavery, the majority of the Costa Rican population of African ancestry had been incorporated into the general population (Herzfeld, 2002).

Presently, the descendants of those early African slaves in Guanacaste and Puntarenas are not considered by the rest of the population as "Black." Instead, they are colloquially referred to as "*cholos,*" in reference to their relatively dark skin color, but are clearly differentiated from descendents of the second migration of people of African ancestry who came to Costa Rica at the end of the 1800s and who are the subject of this chapter. In Guanacaste and Puntarenas there are some signs of the African culture which these early slaves brought, such as in some musical instruments. Sadly, their language has disappeared, as was mentioned above.

## 6.2   A history of the Afro-Limonense population

Figure 6.1 shows a map of Costa Rica with the main cities only. The province of Limón is on the Atlantic coast and it extends from the northern border with Nicaragua to the southern border with Panamá. Puerto Limón is the capital city of the province. In 1997 30% of the province's population was urban and 70% was rural. Not withstanding this distribution, Puerto Limón is a major urban center in Costa Rica,

Figure 6.2. A typical house in Puerto Limón. Note that all photographs in this chapter were taken by the author or by another member of her research team.

with a population of 178 769 (out of a total of 3 464 170 in the country) in 1997 (JAPDEVA, 1999). Figure 6.2 shows a typical wooden house in Puerto Limón, which shows architectural affinities with housing styles in the English-speaking Caribbean, rather than with the traditional adobe-based housing style of the rest of Costa Rica. Figure 6.3 shows a beach in the outskirts of Puerto Limón. (Note that all photographs in this chapter were taken by the author or by another member of her research team.)

### 6.2.1 A short history of Limón I: 1500s–1870

The Limón province was inhabited by several Amerindian groups from the Caribbean – the Nahua – and the South American cultural area (Bryce-Laporte, 1962). The earliest encounter between Europeans and the Indians of the region apparently took place in September of 1502. During his last voyage to the New World, Christopher Columbus contacted the Indians living in present-day Puerto Limón, called Cariay by its inhabitants. Columbus mentioned that both men and women wore cotton clothing, and that they painted their faces and bodies. He was also impressed by the gold ornaments the natives wore and he assumed that

Figure 6.3. A beach in the outskirts of Puerto Limón.

Cariay had great quantities of the metal. Thus he named this place Costa Rica, which means rich coast (Bryce-Laporte, 1962; Granados and Estrada, 1967; Mennerick 1964; Olien, 1968). Granados and Estrada (1967) review the arguments for and against the designation of Cariay as Limón by several historians. The main arguments for such designation are, first, that the description of the harbor where Columbus arrived resembles Limón. He mentioned a small island in front of the beach similar to the Uvita Island located in Limón. Second, Columbus described two ceremonial objects, namely a head-portrait figurine and a big flat stone where dead bodies were positioned. Both objects are frequently found in archaeological sites throughout the Limón province, but they are absent in other areas of Central America (Granados and Estrada, 1967). Whether this encounter did or did not take place in Limón will probably never be known for sure.

During the 1600s the Costa Rican Atlantic coast was explored occasionally by the Spaniards, and some settlements were founded usually without success (Chavez, 1982). By the late sixteenth and early seventeenth centuries the Spanish occasionally raided Indian villages on the Atlantic coast for slaves, demanding tribute from the Indians. This policy resulted in violent rebellions of the Talamanca Indians, who were the last ones subjugated by the Spanish. Throughout the seventeenth century there were constant confrontations between the Talamanca and the

Spanish. One of the last Indian revolts resulted in the execution of the celebrated chief, or *cacique*, Pablo Presbere (Chavez, 1982; Granados and Estrada, 1967; Purcell, 1993).

By the end of the 1600s some wealthy inhabitants of the central highland started to cultivate cacao in the valley of Matina, close to the Atlantic coast (Chavez, 1982). The owners of the plantations maintained their residence in Cartago, which was then the capital of Costa Rica, while their crops were attended by Indian and African slaves (Lobo-Wiehoff and Meléndez-Obando, 1997; Purcell, 1993; Stewart, Rigoberto, 1999). However, the cacao plantations could not develop successfully because of the constant raids of English pirates and Zambo Mosquito groups from Nicaragua (Bryce-Laporte, 1962; Mennerick, 1964; Olien, 1980). The Zambo Mosquitoes constantly attacked the settlements on the Atlantic coast, demanding tribute and capturing Indian slaves. Granados and Estrada (1967) suggest that these raids were an extremely important factor in the population decline of the Costa Rican native Atlantic populations. They also note that the armed confrontations between the English pirates and the Spanish province reflected the political situation in Europe, where the Spanish and British Empires were competing politically and economically. The best known pirate attack occurred in 1666, when 700 men, lead by Mansfield and Morgan, marched inland for 70 miles until they were repelled by the Spanish (Mennerick, 1964). The hostilities of the Zambo Mosquitoes and the British pirates ended with a treaty signed in 1850 between the USA and the British Government. In this treaty the British-backed groups promised not to attack any settlements in Central America. This treaty foreshadows the rising influence of the USA in the area (Granados and Estrada, 1967).

From about 1820 through 1870 the Atlantic coast did not receive much attention from the Spanish Imperial or the young Costa Rican Government. However, by 1840 a road was built to Matina. Granados and Estrada (1967) note that its construction was extremely difficult due to the disease encountered by the workers in the lowlands. The health problems in the area were so pronounced that a government official had recommended in 1830 to close down Matina because of its "pestilent and mortal climate for man and beasts" (translated from Granados and Estrada, 1967).

### 6.2.2   *A short history of Limón II: 1870 – present*

Throughout the 1800s, coffee, by then the main export commodity of Costa Rica, was shipped to the (mostly) European market through the

Pacific coast port of Puntarenas and then had to be taken around South America until it reached its destination. Although inefficient and costly, this route was the only one available to coffee growers. The development of an Atlantic-coast port was extremely important to the economic development of the country. The Costa Rican president signed two contracts with two US companies in the 1860s for the construction of a railroad to Limón but neither contract was fulfilled. In 1871 the Costa Rican Government signed another contract with Mr. Henry Meiggs Keith, from the USA, who was able to construct little over 4 miles of track, after which he ran out of funds. At that point (1873) Keith's brother or nephew (depending on the source), Minor C. Keith, took over the direction of the project (Casey-Gaspar, 1979; Chomsky, 1996; Echeverri-Gent, 1992; Koch, 1975, 1977; Melendez, 1981; Mennerick, 1964). In 1884, the Soto–Keith contract was signed, stipulating that Keith was to finish the track (Casey-Gaspar, 1979; Stewart, 1964). In exchange he had the right to commercially exploit it for 99 years. After that period those rights would return to the State. Keith also was awarded 800 000 acres of land for agricultural development on the Atlantic coast. Mennerick (1964) observes that the contract was harshly criticized in Costa Rica because it allowed a monopoly on the transportation of agricultural exports to the Atlantic. In 1972 the contract was declared invalid by the Costa Rican Government and the railroad was nationalized (Chavez *et al.*, 1987; Casey-Gaspar, 1979). Independently from the construction of the railroad, the Costa Rican Government made several attempts to settle the Atlantic with European-born immigrants, but these attempts failed (Chomsky, 1996).

One of the main problems encountered by Keith during the railroad construction was a shortage of labor. In 1883 Costa Rica had only 182 073 inhabitants and unskilled laborers would not work in the Atlantic area for fear of malaria (Fernandez-Esquivel and Mendez-Ruiz, 1973; Mennerick, 1964). In 1873, the government ordered the return of Costa Rican workers from the lowlands due to the illnesses they were suffering (Melendez, 1981). As a result the Government authorized Keith to bring foreign labor to finish the construction (Fernandez-Esquivel and Mendez-Ruiz, 1973), and lifted a ban on the immigration of Chinese and Black people (Hutchinson-Miller, 2002). It seems that some of the earliest workers brought by Keith were US citizens who were victims of a US system of convict-leasing, and who experienced exceedingly high mortality (Chomsky, 1996). Melendez (1981) reviews extensively the series of migrations of laborers to Limón. He indicates that the first workers came from about 1871 to 1873, and from diverse Caribbean areas such as

Panamá, Honduras, Curaçao, Belize, Cartagena, Aruba, Surinam, and Jamaica (Echeverri-Gent, 1992). At that point a Frenchman named Lesseps was engaged in the construction of the Panamá Canal and Keith was not able to obtain sufficient laborers because Lesseps offered better wages. Thus Keith decided to import Chinese workers at a lower wage. In 1873, 653 Chinese arrived in Costa Rica, and their descendants have since remained a numerically important ethnic group in Limón (Melendez, 1981). Putnam (2002) reviews the abuses and discriminatory practices to which the Chinese workers were subjected by both Keith and the Costa Rican Government.

When the Panamá project was stopped in 1887, 762 Italians arrived in Limón and were joined in 1888 by 1000 Italian, German, Swedish, and Jamaican laborers (Melendez, 1981). By 1889 there were 4 200 men working on the railroad, most of whom were foreign laborers (Mennerick, 1964). An important aspect of this labor migration was its constant fluidity. For example, the Italians revolted against their abysmal working conditions and either moved to other areas of Costa Rica (which dark-skinned people were legally prohibited from doing) or left the country entirely. Moreover, many Afro-Caribbean workers moved from Limón to Panamá and back, depending on the availability of jobs and the salary. Indeed, most of the men who were brought to work on the railroad or in the banana plantations had no intention of making Limón their permanent home (Purcell and Sawyers, 1993). The constant in- and out-migration in Limón of Afro-Caribbean peoples was and continues to be aided by strong kinship ties among Jamaica, Limón, Bocas del Toro in Panamá, and Bluefields and San Juan del Norte in Nicaragua (Putnam, 2002). Viales-Hurtado (1998) notes that the ebb and flow of Jamaican workers to and from Costa Rica can be tied directly with the ups and down of the world economy in general and the banana prices in particular.

By far the largest migration of foreign workers to Limón was that of Jamaicans. This group permanently changed the ethnic composition and culture of Costa Rica (Fernandez-Esquivel and Mendez-Ruiz, 1973; Harpelle, 1993). The exact number of Jamaican migrants is unknown, but it may have been as high as 4000 by 1890 (Fernandez-Esquivel and Mendez-Ruiz, 1973). Although Jamaicans were the largest group of migrants, there were migrants from almost everywhere in the world: Europe, the entire Caribbean area, Central America, México, Russia, Sweden, Tunisia, the USA, Syria, China, and East India to name a few. The East Indians settled to the south of Puerto Limón in Westfalia, and are currently being researched by Madrigal, Otárola, and collaborators (Kenney and Madrigal, 2004; Madrigal et al., 2004).

The great number of Jamaican migrants who came to Costa Rica was a consequence of the extreme economic depression of Jamaica during the 1800s. Bryce-Laporte (1962) suggests that the economic situation of the Black Jamaican was worse in the second part of the nineteenth century that at the time of slavery. Jamaica had suffered a series of droughts, hurricanes, and epidemics that forced many unskilled laborers to seek jobs overseas, first in Panamá and later in Costa Rica (Bryce-Laporte, 1962; Duncan, 1981; Melendez, 1981). Keith and the Costa Rican Government both enticed Jamaican workers with high salaries and the possibility of claiming a piece of land of their own. These former slaves or their offspring were drawn by the possibility of obtaining and owning a piece of land, which was out of their reach in Jamaica (Chomsky, 1996). However, these migrants always hoped to return to Jamaica, after having saved some money. Duncan (1981) emphasizes the strong anti-Costa Rican sentiment of the Jamaicans who considered themselves members of the British Empire (Stewart, Rigoberto, 1999). Duncan (1981) suggests that Keith took advantage of the pro-British feelings among the Jamaicans to avoid paying them: Keith made his workers believe that he was British and reinforced the idea that they were working for the Empire. Although the Jamaicans continued to work without pay, sometimes for months, they did revolt against Keith at least once (Melendez, 1981).

However, many Jamaican workers did not return to the island because the project suffered serious economic setbacks as early as 1874 and Keith failed to pay them. For that reason the Government allowed the allocation of free land to the Jamaicans for cultivation (Melendez, 1981). These plots of land were located along the railroad, which resulted in the present-day population dispersion in Limón: throughout the province settlements are located along the railroad (Chavez, 1982). The construction of the Atlantic railroad was officially completed in 1890 after a tremendous loss of life due to disease, undernutrition, and accidents. Mennerick (1964) estimated that approximately 20 000 men died during its construction, and that 4000 men died in only the first 25 miles of the railroad (Chomsky, 1996; Echeverri-Gent, 1992). Infrequently mentioned victims of the construction of the Atlantic railroad were the American Indians who still lived in the Atlantic region, and who were pushed to the highlands, first by the railroad construction and then by the banana agricultural expansion (Chomsky, 1996).

But the Jamaican workers were not alone. Hutchinson-Miller (2002) has engaged in the difficult task of reconstructing the history of early female Jamaican migrants in Limón, a difficult task because women were usually uncounted in records. These women accompanied the male workers, but subsequently became engaged in economic activities associated with the United Fruit Company. Women, however, were not employed in the agricultural work, as had been the case in the Caribbean sugar plantations (Putnam, 2002). Hutchinson-Miller (2002) notes that an early letter (1877) to the Governor of Limón complains of imprisonment of a woman (among seven other plaintiffs), showing that women were not spared the awful treatment given to Jamaican males. Putnam (2002) notes the existence of two documents, one that shows that an Afro-Limonense woman sued to evict a man from her property, and one which describes a social gathering in which champagne was drank to celebrate the arrival of a woman and her daughter in Limón. Interestingly, this latter gathering occurred at a time in which the railroad construction was at a standstill because of lack of funds, which shows that not all Afro-Limonenses were indigent and at the mercy of the railroad company. But women are virtually non-existent in the historical documents of the 1800s and even 1900s on the Afro-Limonense population. Based on her interviews of elderly women in Puerto Limón and on research on other Caribbean regions, Hutchinson-Miller (2002) suggests that women contributed greatly to the preservation of the Jamaican culture in Limón. She notes that women were likely responsible for the preservation of major cultural traits such as religion, cooking, medicine, and Black consciousness. In addition, women certainly contributed greatly to the household economy through the nearly endless list of occupations in which they could engage, such as sewing, laundry, cooking, etc. An obvious economic activity in which women engaged was prostitution, which is very likely to have been rather well paid. In addition, Afro-Limonense women were likely to have been in charge of petty commerce, as they were in the rest of the Caribbean, relying heavily on kinship and affinal ties. There is evidence of some women being the owners of property, but this was probably rare (Putnam, 2002). Purcell (1993) notes that women of higher socioeconomic status would tend to be educated and thus be nurses or teachers. If they had lighter skin, they would certainly be more desirable. Thus once a viable community of Jamaicans with enough single women was established, a woman's education and skin color were her main assets. By the early 1900s the sex ratio had become more equal as a result of the larger number of wives who came from Jamaica and the birth of girls in Costa Rica (Viales-Hurtado, 1998). By the 1920s about 25% of women were educated and were working outside of the economic sphere, whether as teachers, seamstresses, etc. At the same time, girl children were expected to be economically active by helping with the household tasks, although these tasks were not considered to be economically important.

In the late 1870s Keith started to plant bananas in his plots and shipped the first harvest to New Orleans in 1878. He rapidly expanded the cultivation of the crop (Duncan, 1981; Casey-Gaspar, 1979; Harpelle, 1993; see Stouse, 1970, for a history of agricultural production and land use in the Limón province). In 1899, Keith and the Boston Fruit Company founded the United Fruit Company, which in the following years purchased land in other Central American and Caribbean countries. Once the United Fruit Company and its subsidiaries controlled most of the banana production, the entire transportation system to get the fruit to the port, and its international marketing, a true enclave was established. Chavez (1982) indicates that this enclave depended entirely on foreign capital for the production, transportation, and marketing of the product. The company paid a minuscule amount of its revenue to the Government in the form of taxes. With the expansion of the banana production additional labor force was needed, resulting in another important migration of Jamaican laborers. By 1927, and as a result of the banana boom, there were 17 245 Jamaicans living in Limón (Mennerick, 1964).

But Keith was not the only person growing bananas: there is evidence of large and small Costa Rican *hacendados* or even independent Jamaican workers who started raising banana, and who had conflicts with Keith because the latter would not transport their fruit to the markets (Chomsky, 1996). Although Costa Rican workers still feared going to the Atlantic zone because of malaria, some national workers did migrate to Limón, beginning the in-migration of Hispano-Costa Ricans to Limón. This labor movement resulted in great part from the depression of coffee prices in the world market, and from a change in land tenure that resulted in larger holdings in fewer hands and displaced workers (Chavez, 1982; Harpelle, 1993). In total there were about 70 000 workers in banana-related jobs and the main employer was the United Fruit Company (Fernandez-Esquivel and Mendez-Ruiz, 1973).

The work conditions in the banana plantations were nothing short of dismal, although they were particularly bad for those who had to clear the virgin forest for the bananas to be planted: these people had to sleep in the middle of the forest with no protection from the elements, insects, and animals until they were relieved by other workers (Chomsky, 1996; Echeverri-Gent, 1992).The United Fruit Company unfairly used the Jamaican workers' foreign status to its advantage when the workers complained of their working conditions: individuals who objected to their working and living conditions were threatened with deportation (Purcell, 1993). The company also instituted a policy of separation of workers by ethnicity, as the Hispano-Limonenses worked and lived separately from the Afro-Limonenses, contributing to a growth of racism from both sides and resulting in a divided work force. Not only were Jamaicans separated from Costa Ricans, but migrants from other areas of the Caribbean lived separately from the Jamaicans. Of course, the Anglo-USA elite lived in "the zone," an area restricted to all but Anglo-USA dwellers and their domestic workers (Purcell and Sawyers, 1993).

During the 1930s the situation in the province changed radically. Firstly, because of the irrational use of land, the soil was exhausted and the banana production diminished considerably. More importantly, during the first part of the decade the crop was attacked by two banana diseases, one named "Panamá" and the other Sigatoka. The United Fruit Company could not overcome these problems and decided to close down its production, thus firing the great majority of the working population in the province (Casey-Gaspar, 1979; Chavez, 1982; Mennerick, 1964). At the same time the company negotiated a new contract with the Government and continued to grow bananas on the Pacific coast. Fernandez-Esquivel and Mendez-Ruiz (1973) review the political struggle that took place when the United Fruit Company requested to move to the Pacific coast. It should be noted that the new contract stipulated that the company would not contract the services of people of color in the Pacific coast and that only one politician (Manuel Mora, longtime head of the communist party) protested this part of the contract (Harpelle, 1993, 2000; Putnam, 2002).

When the company abandoned Limón the province was left in a profound economic depression. The Costa Rican workers either followed the United Fruit Company or looked for work in other areas. However, many of these Costa Rican workers were in Limón because they had been displaced by falling coffee prices and an increase in the establishment of large landholdings in the rest of the country (Purcell, 1993). They did not necessarily have an open job market to which they could go, so there was obviously the potential for ethnic conflict between the Costa Rican and Jamaican disenfranchised workers.

But for the Jamaicans the situation was much worse. Firstly, they had no money to return to their homeland as they had planned. Secondly, they were not Costa Ricans and could not seek employment outside of those jobs stipulated by the initial contract between the United Fruit Company and the Government (Mennerick, 1964). They were simply prohibited from leaving the Atlantic zone of Costa Rica, even if they had been born in Costa Rica (Duncan, 1981; Putnam, 2002). Bryce-Laporte (1962) notes that some Jamaicans were able to migrate to Panamá. Thus in 1950 the Afro population of Limón had decreased by 23.9% of the 1927 population size (Fernandez-Esquivel and Mendez-Ruiz, 1973; Harpelle, 1993). By this time, there was a sizeable number of Afro-Limonense women who had come to get married to the Jamaican workers. When the economy crashed and many of the males having left, these women stayed in Limón, raising their families, following the long-time established practice of transnational families described in Chapter 5 (Putnam, 2002). The remaining workers turned to subsistence farming in the abandoned farms. In such a depressed condition, the Costa Rican workers were in direct competition with the Jamaicans, and the former and the local officials complained to the national Government about the presence of foreign labor in the province, which was the only area in which they could legally be (Casey-Gaspar, 1979). In the following years more stringent laws were passed prohibiting the hiring of foreigners in Costa Rica except in the Atlantic coast (Fernandez-Esquivel and Mendez-Ruiz, 1973), and protests for their presence in Limón were staged in San José (Harpelle, 1993). This situation of economic depression was ameliorated for a few years in about 1946 because of the increase in cacao prices which prompted the population to raise this crop. When the cacao prices dropped the population was again in a state of economic depression (Bryce-Laporte, 1962; Mennerick, 1964).

Part of the reason for the obvious resentment between the Jamaican and the Costa Rican workers is that during the 1920s and 1930s many of the former were employed in managerial, higher positions because of their ability to speak English, whereas the Costa Rican workers were relegated to the lowest positions (Purcell, 1993; Purcell and Sawyers, 1993; Putnam, 2002). Moreover, Jamaican workers were usually paid better than were Costa Rican workers and had overt disdain for the Hispano-Costa Ricans, whom they referred to as *Paña* (short for *España*, the Spanish for Spain), and whom they accused of being dirty, drunken, disorderly, etc. It is obvious that the Jamaican workers felt no kinship with Costa Rica; for example, when the Company abandoned banana production in Limón, many of the Jamaican workers attempted to register their Costa Rican-born children as British citizens (Echeverri-Gent, 1992; Purcell, 1993; see Purcell, 1987, for an in-depth examination of the shifting nature of ethnic relations among the Hispano-Limonenses, Afro-Limonenses, and Anglo-USA group in Limón). This situation created great resentment on the part of the Costa Ricans and exacerbated the racism that was growing in the province and the nation. Both Hispano- and Afro-Limonenses crossed each other's picket lines, and this division of the working class only benefited the Company (Harpelle, 2000; Purcell and Sawyers, 1993). As Purcell (1993) notes, the importation of Jamaican workers was seen by the country at large as a necessary inconvenience, but later as a problem which caused competition for jobs. The Jamaican workers were unfairly perceived as a threat by the rest of the country, which by the beginning of the 1900s had already convinced itself of its racial European homogeneity, overlooking the fact that the colonial African slaves had contributed greatly to the formation of the nation (Putnam, 2002). Many prominent Costa Rican writers and politicians, such as Rodrigo Facio and Carlos Monge Alfaro (after whom the University of Costa Rica campus and its library are named, respectively), wrote against the incorporation of the Jamaican workers into "White" Costa Rica. Putnam (2002) notes that in the first part of the twentieth century, the rise in racism in Costa Rica is paralleled by the rise of "scientific" racism's prestige worldwide. The only organization in Costa Rica that tried to support the Afro-Limonenses before 1948 was the communist party, which tried to unite all workers against the United Fruit Company (Harpelle, 1993, 2000).

After the United Fruit Company abandoned the banana plantations and left large areas fallow, many enterprising unemployed Jamaicans were able to produce the fruit (though not of top quality) in the diseased soil with labor-intensive techniques that allowed them to make a living out of their lands. Thus many of the Jamaican migrants were able to fulfill their aspiration of cultivating their own piece of land, and contributed to the economy of the Limón province for many years. This contribution has been frequently overlooked by historians of Limón (Chomsky, 1996). But the fact that many former banana-plantation workers had a piece of land to call their own engendered more resentment among the Hispano-Costa Ricans who were moving to Limón. Harpelle (1993) notes that during the 1930s and 1940s the racial divisions between the USA Company elite and the Jamaican workers were substituted with racial divisions between the Hispano-Costa Ricans and the Jamaicans. These divisions were obvious from separate seating arrangements in movie theaters, separate swimming areas, and even lack of access to the Limón park by Afro-Limonense children (Harpelle, 1993; Putnam, 2002).

We should note that the environmental devastation that the banana production has caused in this and other regions of Costa Rica (and, of course, the rest of Central America) is enormous. Not only has the environment suffered because of irrational use and overuse of pesticides and herbicides, but these chemicals have severely affected the lives of untold numbers of workers, many of whom have been left infertile (Ramírez-Mayorga and Cvenca-Berger, 2002). At the same time, the Costa Rican Government has consistently supported the international banana companies to the detriment of the Costa Rican workers and the environment.

For example, the Government did not interfere when recently a company (BANDECO) fired hundreds of workers and re-hired them at a lower salary and with fewer benefits (Trejos, 2004).

In 1948 the new National Constitution signaled the beginning of the incorporation of Afro-Limonenses to the country. This constitution legally recognized the once-Jamaicans as Costa Rican citizens and incorporated laws against racial discrimination (Fernandez-Esquivel and Mendez-Ruiz, 1973). Harpelle (1993) rightly notes that the incorporation of the once-Jamaicans into the country was a clever political move by José Figueres, the politician who promoted their incorporation, who saw in the former Jamaicans a large electoral pool which could support him in the following elections. Not all Jamaican workers opted for citizenship, the process of naturalization being more onerous for female applicants than for male applicants. Although currently many Afro-Limonenses look positively at the 1948 events because they allowed them to adopt Costa Rican citizenship, the change was actually negative for many: they were now under the control of the Spanish-speaking government of a country to which they did not feel particularly close and from which they did not receive much affection, they had to deal in Spanish under a new legal system, and because of the insecurity of the moment, many ended up selling their property to Hispano-Costa Ricans, so that they lost their prized property (Purcell, 1993). Moreover, those who sought naturalization were sometimes ostracized by those who did not, without obtaining the benefits of equal access to jobs, education, and other economic opportunities because of racism and the lack of opportunities in Limón. Several prominent Afro-Limonenses supported by a few Hispano-Costa Rican politicians worked on the formation of organizations for the protection of Afro-Costa Ricans, and urged the people in Limón who still had not opted for naturalization to go through the process as the only means to protect their rights (Harpelle, 1993). According to Purcell and Sawyers (1993) this was one of two attempts by Afro-Costa Ricans at ethnic mobilization, the second one occurring in the 1970s. Both attempts were spearheaded by the prominent Afro-Limonense leaders supported by sympathetic Hispano-Costa Rican supporters. Unfortunately, both attempts failed because of racial discrimination and cultural domination. Racism is alive and well in Costa Rica, and it continues to hurt not only Afro-Limonenses, but the entire Costa Rican population.

Nonetheless, starting in 1948 there was a great influx of Afro-Limonenses to the cities located in the Central Valley in search of better jobs and education. Since 1960 a number of public institutions were created to develop the Atlantic area and to provide jobs for the unskilled workers of the former plantations (Chavez, 1982). Since Costa Rica does not use "racial" labels in its censuses it is difficult to know what the current numbers of the different ethnic groups are. Herzfeld (2002) reports that the population of Puerto Limón consists of about 60% Hispano-Costa Ricans, 35% Afro-Costa Ricans, and 5% Chinese, Indians, and Indo-Costa Ricans. For the entire country the proportion of Afro-Caribbean descent is about 2%. The cholos of Guanacaste and Puntarenas are not included in this figure.

Notwithstanding governmental efforts to promote growth in the province, Limón is still underdeveloped in comparison with the rest of the country, although it is the province that brings the most wealth to it (Harpelle, 1993). In many of its health measures, Limón is rather underdeveloped, whereas the rest of Costa Rica enjoys very high standards of health, including a life expectancy comparable to that of industrialized countries. For example, in 1996 the infant death rate for the entire country was 11.83 per 1000, whereas for Limón it was 15. In 1995, the crude death rate for the country was 4.4 per 1000, but it was 5.52 for the Central Limón county, where Puerto Limón is located. At the same time the crude birth rate for the entire country in 1995 was 24.8 but it was 29.94 in the Central Limón county, and as high as 33.02 in the rural county of Guacimo (these data were taken from the Costa Rican Ministry of Health website, www.netsalud.sa.cr/index.htm). A project by a Governmental agency in 1999 noted that Limón is exceedingly poor and that it suffers from high unemployment and several social ills, such as violence against women and children (JAPDEVA, 1999). In his call for a declaration of autonomy of Limón from the Costa Rican State, Rigoberto Stewart (1999) cites the legal-institutional setting and racism as the main causes for the underdevelopment of Limón.

Not only is Limón an underdeveloped province within the Costa Rican system, but its Afro-Limonense population remains alienated, impoverished, and to some extent obscure and forgotten in the history books of the country (Echeverri-Gent, 1992; Purcell, 1993). Herzfeld (1995) notes that the organizations which represent the Afro-Limonenses are few and stand for sections of the community, not the ethnic group as a whole and therefore are not efficient advocates for the community. Herzfeld (1995) also notes that the 1991 earthquake did a lot more than destroy the coastal settlement of the Valle de la Estrella and demolish buildings in Puerto Limón; it left a defeatist attitude among the Limonenses. In a recent study on social exclusion in Costa Rica, El Salvador, and Guatemala, the entire Limón province was ranked very low in terms of not only poverty but social ills.

McIlwaine (1997) looks at poverty of the Afro-Limonenses, considering gender and non-economic measures of poverty. She notes that after the former Jamaicans were granted citizenship, the ethnic group transitioned from being a majority (in Limón) to being a minority in a wider national job market, in which they were much more vulnerable. McIlwaine(1997) argues that this vulnerability can be explained in part by the fact that Afro-Limonenses face a horizontal and vertical "glass ceiling" in Costa Rica, which denies them work flexibility and choices. Interestingly, both Afro-Limonense males and females in her survey in Limón fared better in terms of job prestige and salary than did her Hispanic subjects. Thus, it could be argued that the Afro-Limonenses are doing very well for a minority. However, the fact that they have been "boxed" into certain occupations so that lateral job transfers are rare and the fact that they do not move up to the highest positions translates into a sense of vulnerability which has resulted in high international migration. The box in which (particularly male) Afro-Limonenses have been placed is that of public-sector jobs. Unfortunately, with the post-1980s neo-liberal policies put into place following the International Monetary Fund's restrictions on loans to Costa Rica, it is precisely these jobs that have been cut, affecting disproportionately the Afro-Limonenses, who have few additional options (McIlwaine, 1997).

### 6.3   The culture of Afro-Limonenses

Given its history of migration and resulting tremendous ethnic diversity, Limón boasts several ethnic groups (Chinese, Amerindian, and East Indian), each with its own culture. In this book of course we are interested in the culture of the Afro-Limonense group, and the reader is referred to Duncan (1981) for a more detailed description than follows. If it is put in a historical perspective, the culture of Afro-Limonenses should be seen as an Afro-British Jamaican culture which integrated itself with a Costa Rican one, resulting in a unique invention (Herzfeld, 2002; Lefever, 1992). As a result, the culture of Afro-Limonenses is sharply different from that of the rest of the country. Bryce-Laporte (1962) points out that the Afro-Limonenses belong to the Caribbean cultural area rather that to the Latin American one. And Purcell (1993:13) proposes that the Caribbean culture is ". . .part African, part European, and wholly Caribbean." As is the culture of any immigrant group, the culture of Afro-Caribbean populations is one of duality, of belonging and not belonging.

Crucially important are two cultural values (Purcell, 1993), those of reputation (a lower-class response to colonial dependence) and respectability (the culture of conformity which comes by embracing the colonial elite values). Cultural duality, conformity, and respectability are all juggled by the immigrant as s/he tries to do the best s/he can in a context in which her/his skin color and culture are a liability. Sometimes conformity and respectability are taken to an extreme in which the one who is exploited ends up denigrating him/herself, as we saw in Chapter 1, where we discussed the importance the slaves themselves attached to skin color. According to Purcell (1993), ambition to "make it" in Costa Rica is aided by the false ideology of a pluralistic and open democracy, a myth which if adopted by the victims of the racism might be perpetrated by them. As a result of their desire for self-improvement in the wider Costa Rican population, Afro-Limonenses measure prestige both by occupation and by education. In the Afro-Limonense culture, greater respect is afforded to individuals who seek to educate themselves than to those who engage in commercial ventures (Purcell, 1993). Thus they see education as an obvious means of achieving a better position (and of bettering oneself morally), although the educational system does very little to validate their existence and importance as an ethnic group.

This section reviews some cultural aspects of Afro-Limonenses based on the following sources: Bryce-Laporte (1962) extensively examined the culture of a rural area in Limón several decades ago, Herzfeld (2002) describes life in Limón in the 1970s and in 2000, and Purcell (1993) provides an outstanding ethnography of rural and urban Afro-Limonenses based on his fieldwork during the late 1970s. In addition, I performed field work in Puerto Limón and adjacent areas in 1987 and in 2003 (Madrigal, 1988, 2003). The general conclusion after reading these sources, which span several decades, is how rapidly Limón has changed and become part of the global capitalist economy. For example, when Bryce-Laporte (1962) did his fieldwork there was no television in Limón; in 2003 television, video games, boom boxes, etc. were everywhere (L. Madrigal, unpublished work). Bryce-Laporte also reported differences in clothing between Afro- and Hispano-Limonenses, whereas Herzfeld (2002) reports none in the decade of the 1970s. Herzfeld (2002) herself comments that in the late 1970s she noted that drugs were not a problem in Limón, whereas more recently they have become a serious problem. Indeed, Puerto Limón is a large city with large-city problems such as prostitution, drug trafficking, and urban poverty (L. Madrigal, unpublished work). Thus this description of Afro-Caribbean culture is only an approximation to an ever-changing target.

The food of the Afro-Limonenses differs from that of most Costa Ricans in its reliance on coconut products (Bryce-Laporte, 1962). Although Duncan (1981) indicates that the use of tubercles is a unique trait of the Black Limonense diet, Bozzoli de Wille (1986) notes that the Indians of southern Limón utilized these foodstuffs. Both ethnic groups consume *yucca, ñampí,* and *ñame.* The dish considered the typical Limón food is rice and beans, which differs from the Costa Rican *gallo pinto* in the use of coconut milk in its preparation. Other typically Limonense foodstuffs are *pan Bon*, sweet bread, and *patí,* a pastry filled with spicy chopped meat (Hutchinson-Miller, 2002). Duncan (1981) notes that rice and beans was not traditionally the everyday dish that it is now, but that it used to be a special dinner, as beans were expensive. On the other hand Afro-Limonenses have traditionally complemented their tuber-based diet with hunting of small animals, such as *tepesquintle* and iguana, or with fishing. Duncan (1981) proposes that the traditional Afro-Limonense diet was healthy and that few people were undernourished. This of course was not the case in the banana plantations, but might have been the case for families who raised their own bananas and were in charge of their own diet. Duncan (1981) also emphasizes the importance of herbal teas as a medicinal complement to the diet, whether to cure or to prevent illnesses.

According to Duncan (1981) the two most important forms of dance in Limón are the quadrille and the calypso. Although Bryce-Laporte reported in 1962 that the quadrille had disappeared, Duncan (1981) indicated that it is still danced among certain groups. This is a dance derived from the European sixteenth century contra dances. Calypso is a popular dance and it is spreading to the wider national population. This musical form originated from the Caribbean (Duncan, 1981). Finally, reggae is becoming increasingly popular in Limón and in the entire country. This musical form is related to the Rastafarian Black social movement, and has a political connotation.

Afro-Limonenses have traditionally belonged to Protestant churches whereas most of Costa Rica's inhabitants are Catholic (Bryce-Laporte, 1962; Mennerick, 1964). The most common Protestant denominations are the Anglican, Baptist, and Methodist Churches (Duncan, 1981). More recently there has been an increase in the missionary activity of Mormons and Jehovah's Witnesses (Headley and Sandino, 1983). Historically, the presence of the Protestant churches preceded by many years the establishment of the Catholic Church in Limón. Indeed, the first Catholic churches were established not by Hispano-Costa Ricans but by Afro-Caribbean workers from French colonies, where the slaves and their descendents were Catholic. Purcell (1993) sees the role of the Protestant churches in Limón as deeply embedded in the entire life experience of the community, including the social and political arenas. Obviously the Protestant work ethic, which emphasized prosperity, was very akin to the desires for improving in the Costa Rican society. Socioeconomic divisions were obvious within the churches, both in the Sunday clothes and in the sitting arrangements, as some pews were occupied by the same families across generations; the closer to the altar, the higher the social position of the family. The Protestant churches were also a means of acquiring education. Before 1948, there were numerous private schools which followed the British curriculum and taught in English (Viales-Hurtado, 1998). In addition, Sunday school was attended, and provided an additional medium for self improvement. In contrast, the present-day public schools do nothing to support a sense of pride in being Afro-Limonense. Duncan (1981) is right to question the curriculum taught at school in Costa Rica in general and Limón in particular, a curriculum which overlooks all contributions from Limón and which openly works against the preservation of the Limonense creole (Purcell and Sawyers, 1993).

According to Duncan (1981), an important feature of all Limonenses which is absent in much of the country is tolerance for religious differences, as there are many more Protestant churches in Limón than there are in the rest of the country. Perhaps the fact that Catholic Hispano-Costa Ricans arrived after the Afro-Costa Ricans, when the latter had already set up various churches, or simply the fact that there are many more people who belong to different churches, account for this tolerant view in Limón.

Two traditional Jamaican spiritual practices (obeah and Pocomía) existed throughout the first part of the twentieth century but one has apparently faded. The Obeah man is said to have supernatural powers that may be used for good or evil actions, although Herzfeld (2002) describes obeah more as a set of beliefs for healing. Chomsky (1996) notes that during the construction of the railroad and in the banana plantations Jamaican healers were active, trying to alleviate the appalling health of the workers. In 1981 Duncan reported that the Obeah man was still present in the community. During the course of Madrigal's (1988) field work several informants, including well-educated hospital workers, made reference to the Obeah man. Herzfeld (2002) also concurs on the fact that the Obeah man is alive and well in present-day Limón.

Pocomía has been described as the Limonense version of voodoo, and its rituals have apparently disappeared from Limón. Most information about it is based on hearsay and no anthropological study of it has been performed (Duncan, 1981). According to folklore in a Pocomía ceremony a white boy is kidnapped, sacrificed, and eaten. Duncan (1981) stressed that this idea stems from the ignorance and fear of a different culture. He adds that during a Pocomía ritual there was dancing and singing and the possession of the participants by spirits. Mennerick (1964) mentions that sometime before 1950 a Pocomía ritual took place in which a white boy was kidnapped, killed, and eaten.

Lodges have had an important function among Black Limonenses. More than a religious organization, lodges are fraternities which provide their members with respectability (Duncan, 1981; Herzfeld, 2002; Mennerick, 1964). According to Purcell (1993), respectability and prestige or lack thereof is enforced by gossip, an effective mechanism for maintaining individuals within acceptable codes of behavior. I also noted that gossip was everywhere and that it frequently concerned male–female unions, whether visiting, common law, or married.

One of the most conspicuous cultural traits of the Black population in Limón is its creole, one of three languages spoken in Limón, with Spanish and Standard English being the others. Limonense creole is known to its speakers by the affectionate name /mekaytelyuw/ from Jamaican creole, in which "make I tell you . . ." means "let me tell you. . ." (Herzfeld, 1995). The Standard English of previous generations was that of Jamaica, with a British, not an American, slant. However, with the fading influence of British culture and the rising influence of the US, Standard English is becoming American while losing its British pronunciation and vocabulary. During the days of the United Fruit Company, all official business was carried out in English, so this was the language of prestige and social advancement, and was one of the reasons why Jamaicans were favored over Costa Ricans by the Company. English, not Creole, was the language used at church, read in books, and taught at private schools (Herzfeld, 2002). However, after the Company left Limón, and the province opened up to the influx of Hispano-Costa Ricans and government agencies, the language for conducting professional and legal transactions became Spanish. For the younger generations, Spanish is necessary for moving up in the social scale, for achieving a university education, and for obtaining a job.

But through these several decades of transition from dominance of English to a dominance of Spanish, the Limonense creole has been the language spoken at home. The unique language of Limón descends from Jamaican creole but has evolved on its own, being closer to Standard English in Puerto Limón (because the Company had its offices there) and being more true to creole in the rural areas, where all speakers were

Jamaican. Of course, since Spanish became the dominant language, Limonense creole has adopted much from Costa Rican Spanish recently. For example, Afro-Limonenses use the quintessential Costa Rican expression *diáy* while conversing in English almost as much as do Hispano-Limonenses while conversing in Spanish (L. Madrigal, unpublished work). At this point Limonense creole is being threatened not only by Spanish but also by American English. Spanish is necessary for conducting any legal or administrative business and for interacting with the rest of society. Standard English is becoming more and more important for entering into the rising tourism industry and is ever present in movies, music, etc. (Purcell, 1993). Still, for most Afro-Limonenses creole is alive and well. Although the younger generations are completely fluent in Spanish their mother tongue is still Limonense creole (Duncan, 1981). Herzfeld (2002), however, expresses concern that some young parents might not be using creole with their children in favor of Spanish, because one of the parents is Hispano-Costa Rican and does not understand it, or because they want to make sure that the children learn Spanish "to get ahead", or simply because they find it easier to use Spanish at home, after having used it all day at work. Herzfeld (1995) notes that many Limonenses, even Afro-Limonenses, look down on Limonense creole, calling it a "dialect" or a "patois" (derogatory terms in this context), even claiming that it has no grammar. Many Hispano-Limonenses are also fluent in the Limón creole (Bryce-Laporte, 1962). In a 1980s survey in Puerto Limón it was determined that 8.7% of Afro-Limonenses speak only Spanish, 18.4% speak only English/creole, and 72.8% speak both languages (Headley and Sandino, 1983). Concerning the Hispanic population 86.4% speak only Spanish, 13.2% speak both languages, and 0.4% speak only English/creole (Headley and Sandino, 1983). Purcell (1993) prefers to see the use of creole as in constant flux, where the first generation and the rural Afro-Limonenses speak mostly creole and the third generation, the more educated, the English teachers, speak Standard English. My own experiences in the field agree with Purcell's proposal that there is a continuum of linguistic use: I, a Hispano-Costa Rican, approached Afro-Limonenses in my American-acquired English (replete with a Spanish accent), and they endeavored to respond in a standard-as-possible English. It was obvious that the English they used with me was very different from the creole they used among themselves, demonstrating great linguistic flexibility. The most important "take-home" message from these linguistic adventures was the fact that Afro-Limonenses deeply appreciated a Hispano-Costa Rican approaching them in English and not in Spanish, validating their culture and language.

### 6.4    Demography of the Afro-Limonense population

This section reviews work on demographic variables such as mortality, fertility, migration, and mating patterns in Limón. In these variables too the province differs from the remainder of the country, beginning with the population pyramid. In the 1980s, while in Costa Rica the average sex distribution was 49.6% males and 50.4% females, in Limón it was 52.3% males and 47.7% females (Chavez, 1982). The most likely reason for this difference is the high immigration rate of male laborers who are attracted by the shipping industry and temporary agricultural jobs (Casey-Gaspar, 1979).

### 6.4.1    *Migration*

Migration to and from Limón is reminiscent of what we see in the rest of the Afro-Caribbean area: the well-educated Limonenses leave the province seeking better jobs in the central valley in general and in San José in particular. There has also been a continuous migration of Afro-Limonenses to the USA, which has occurred in three waves. The first took place when the Company abandoned the province, and it consisted mostly of single males. The second one occurred in the 1950s and 1960s, and consisted mostly of educated females, particularly nurses. In the 1980s most migrants were males, who took jobs in the USA cruise industries. These migrants, whether permanent, short or long term, send remittances home and contribute to the economic well-being of their families in Limón, as is done in much of the Caribbean and as was discussed in Chapter 5 (Chavez, 1982; Mennerick, 1964). McIlwaine (1997) notes that money is often saved to pay for the education of daughters, perpetuating the tradition of well-educated women among the Afro-Limonenses, a tradition that has allowed them to have better-paying jobs than the Hispano-Limonenses.

Many unskilled workers from other areas of Costa Rica migrate to Limón because of job openings in the shipping and agricultural industry. Panamanian and Nicaraguan workers also migrate to Limón, particularly from Bocas del Toro and from Bluefields, keeping these three Afro-Atlantic-Central American population centers linked. Since the province borders both countries many unskilled laborers enter the country illegally (Chavez, 1982). In a survey performed in the 1980s it was determined that 53% of Puerto Limón's inhabitants were born in other areas of the country or in other countries (Headley and Sandino, 1983).

### 6.4.2   Mortality

Throughout its history the Limón province has suffered higher mortality rates than those of the rest of the country (Casey-Gaspar, 1979). Although mortality in Limón has decreased dramatically since 1970 it is still well above the national average. For example, in 1995 the infant mortality rate in the Limón province was 15.0 per 1000 live births, much higher than the average for the entire country, which was 11.83 per 1000 live births. Clearly the poverty in the province results in an increased mortality of its inhabitants. This greater mortality contrasts sharply with the marked decline in death rates for the entire country during the 1970s. During those years life expectancy rose from 65 to 72 years (Rosero-Bixby, 1985). Currently the Costa Rican life expectancy is 78 or 77 years (depending on the source), which is closer to the life expectancy of the industrialized countries than to those of other Central American countries (www.nationmaster.com/graph-T;   www.unicef.org/infobycountry/costarica_statistics.html;   www.who.int/whr/2004/annex/country/cri/en). Notwithstanding these enormous gains in health for Costa Rica, mortality in Limón remains very high.

### 6.4.3   Family structure

The family structure of Afro-Limonenses has not been the same throughout the history of this group. Indeed, Viales-Hurtado (1998) notes that initially, when most of the Jamaican migrants came alone without a partner, most families were declared to consist of one single member. Later, with the increase in female migration and the establishment of small family farms in the countryside or with increased urbanization, the family of the Afro-Limonense became similar to that of the rest of the Afro-Caribbean and therefore different from that of the remainder of the national population: the Afro-Limonense family is characterized by a high instability of male–female unions and a relatively low frequency of marriages. Thus whereas in the 1980s the national average of couples living in common-law unions was 4.6% of all unions it was 12.2% in Limón (Chavez, 1982). Not only are common-law unions more frequent in Limón, these unions are also more unstable than marriages. Sanchez (1970) reports in her survey that in Puerto Limón 2.75% of separated women had been involved in common-law unions and 2.05% of these had been previously married.

Afro-Limonense families are frequently consanguineous households which include members of the extended family. Headley and Sandino (1983) report that in their survey of Puerto Limón families 5.6% of the

Afro households included relatives outside the nuclear family, whereas only 3.4% of Hispanic households were extended. Within the mother's family the strongest ties are found among the females, which results in a powerful support group of women. Several of the households surveyed by Madrigal (1988), for example, were composed of the grandmother, her middle-aged daughters, and their daughters of reproductive age and younger children of both sexes. Thus the Afro-Limonense family structure closely resembles previously described domestic units in the wider Afro-Caribbean region, which were discussed in Chapter 5.

Purcell (1993) looks at the Afro-Limonense family structure in a historical perspective. He begins by describing the skewed sex ratio during the first decades of the Jamaican migration, a ratio which was later alleviated. He then notes that males were usually separated from their partners, as the former would be working at the plantations and the latter in the towns. Such separation, as well as the imbalance in the sex ratio, resulted in the tremendously successful business of prostitution in Limón. It also made child-rearing exceedingly difficult, with little access to healthcare and education, particularly in the rural areas. And it put the weight of raising the family on the shoulders of the women.

In the late 1970s when Purcell (1993) did his research, urban–rural and class differences emerged in the household composition of his subjects. Many of these differences could be explained by migration. Purcell noted that household size was positively correlated with wealth, as better-off households were larger, and that this was particularly marked in urban households. Households of upper socioeconomic status were more likely to consist of several generations and to foster children of relatives. Many of these children, close relatives or not of the household head, end up in such large homes because their mothers migrated either to study or to work or because they have recently established a new union with a man who is not the father of the child. Putnam (2002) agrees that child-fostering is very common in Limón, as it is in the wider Afro-Caribbean area, and adds that it even crossed country boundaries. For example, she notes an example of a girl who was being fostered in Jamaica but was brought by her foster parents to Costa Rica, where she stayed permanently. If a woman in Limón had a trade such as a bakery or a shop, she would frequently bring a child from Jamaica to help her in her venture or to watch over her children. This openness of households to minding the children of relatives might be threatened as class distinctions emerge among Afro-Limonenses, but has served up to now to blur such differences (Purcell, 1993). As we saw in Chapter 5, recent surveys have shown that there is evidence of a de-emphasis on child sponsoring in some Afro-Caribbean populations.

In her research on household composition and employment, McIlwaine (1997) notes the marked difference in the household composition of Afro- and Hispano-Limonenses. As is the case in other Afro-Caribbean communities, Afro-Limonense females head many more households (36.9%) than do Hispano-Limonense females (19.4%). At the same time, paid employment in professional settings is much more common among Afro females, even if they live with a partner. In contrast, Hispanic females tend to validate themselves more often in terms of their domestic spheres, and to depend on their partners much more for economic support. As we have seen in other Afro-Caribbean groups, Afro-Limonense females are not without support but rely on the strong network of female folk for child-minding, while they are pursuing their careers.

### 6.4.4    Fertility

The fertility ratio before 1950 in Limón was lower than in the remainder of the country mostly because of the high sex ratio of the province (Casey-Gaspar, 1979). After 1950 the fertility ratio increased and surpassed the national average. As Herzfeld (2002) notes, the governmental contraceptive campaigns, which have been successful in the rest of the country, have not been so in Limón. In 1995 there were 24.8 births per 1000 inhabitants in Costa Rica. In Limón the rate was 29.4, much higher that the national average. Casey-Gaspar (1979) notes that although fertility has not decreased in Limón the actual ratio of children to women remained below the national average because of the higher neonatal mortality in the province.

An important fertility determinant is the age of the women at the beginning of their reproductive careers. Sanchez (1970) reports in her survey that out of the 15–19-year-old female cohort only 34.4% remained single. Thus 65.6% of these female were already married or in a common-law or a visiting union, or their unions had already terminated. Clearly, females in Puerto Limón engage in sexual unions early in their lives. Bermúdez-Méndez *et al.* (1982) found that 46% of their teenage sample were already in a union by the time they got pregnant, and that of those who were not in a union at the time, almost 20% entered a union as a result of the pregnancy. However, many of these early unions are unsuccessful, as one out of six interviewees terminated that union by the time of the interview. Bermúdez-Méndez *et al.* (1982) also note that the teenagers who did not become pregnant were of higher socioeconomic status than those who did and were likely to be economically supported by their father and to have a professional mother. A recent survey by JAPDEVA (1999) shows that 34% of teenagers in Puerto Limón became pregnant, this being the highest rate for the country. All of these studies indicate that in the Afro-Limonense community reproductive behavior begins early in life, that it is not tied to marriage, and that the higher the socio-economic status of the adolescent's family the less likely she is to become pregnant.

Sanchez (1970) examined the influence of the mother's education and religious affiliation on fertility among women in Puerto Limón. She reports that there is a strong negative correlation between education and fertility and that Catholic women have more children that do Protestant women. However, this difference was not statistically significant. In her survey Sanchez (1970) found that 58% of all subjects did not use any form of contraception but found that contraception use was related to a woman's education: educated women were more likely to use contraception.

Sanchez (1970) also examined the relationship between union type (common-law compared with married) and fertility and reports that women who are or were in a married union as opposed to a common-law union have lower fertility. On the other hand, a contributor to higher fertility is the length of union: the younger the woman is at the beginning of the union, and the longer the union lasts, the higher the fertility of the woman. The lower fertility of married women is comparable with what was observed in the 1980s in other Afro-Caribbean groups among highly educated females who used contraception, among whom the earlier association of marriage with higher fertility had been reversed. We do not have data to establish whether the same occurred in Limón; that is, whether married unions had higher fertility before the introduction of contraception and widespread female education. Sanchez (1970) also found a negative correlation between fertility and prestige of a woman's or her partner's occupation: the higher the prestige of the occupation the lower the woman's fertility. Thus the lower fertility seen among Afro-Limonenses who were in non-visiting unions occurred fairly early in Puerto Limón, in the 1970s. In contrast, as we reported in Chapter 5, such a transition occurred in most of the Caribbean in the 1980s. But evidently the availability of contraception is not homogenous in the country, as more recently Glaser (1999) reports that in Cahuita, a rural town of Limón, there was little use of contraception. Indeed, Glaser (1999) reports that women in consensual unions state that they would be very likely to have another child should they enter another consensual union, as a means of cementing such a union. But Glaser does not state whether such desire actually results in higher fertility of women with

Table 6.1. *Reproductive variables of 103 Afro-Limonense females aged 50 years or older*

| Variable | Mean | Standard deviation | Minimum | Maximum |
|---|---|---|---|---|
| Age at time of interview (years) | 64 | 9.12 | 50 | 90 |
| Age at menarche (years) | 14.17 | 1.88 | 10 | 20 |
| Age at first pregnancy (years) | 19.42 | 4.11 | 13 | 42 |
| Total number of pregnancies | 6.85 | 4.53 | 0 | 17 |
| Live births | 6.22 | 4.29 | 0 | 17 |
| Completed family size | 5.03 | 3.72 | 0 | 15 |

*Source:* Madrigal (1991).

successive unions. Indeed, given the fast pace of modernization in the Limón province it would not be surprising to observe opposite correlations between fertility and union type, depending on the socioeconomic situation surrounding women, and whether they are in a rural or an urban setting.

In 1987 Madrigal (1988) interviewed 103 Afro-Limonense females who were 50 years of age or older with an interest in understanding the reproductive history of a sample from first- and second-generation Jamaican migrants to Limón. None of these women used biomedical contraception (and none of them said that they used any form of contraception). The reliability of the data was tested and all of the variables presented below were found to be reliable (Madrigal, 1988, 1991). The data are shown in Table 6.1.

The age at marriage is not included in Table 6.1 because only 26% of the females were married before their first pregnancy, showing that marriage in this community, as in other Afro-Caribbean ones, does not mark the beginning of reproduction. These data show an interesting "snapshot" of the reproductive career of women who were born around the late 1930s: these women had a rather late age at menarche, as would be expected of women who did not go through the process of early maturation associated with recent globalization. When the sample was divided into those who were older than the mean age at the time of the interview (64 years) and those who were younger, the older subjects had a mean menarcheal age of 14.74 years and the younger subjects of 13.65 years. At the same time, the mean age at first pregnancy shows that half of the sample had its first pregnancy before age 20, indicating an early start of reproduction. It should be noted that the correlation between age at menarche and age at first pregnancy is not significant ($r = 0.08$, $P = 0.44$), indicating that women who started menstruating early did not become pregnant any earlier than those who had their menarche late. Although the total number of pregnancies and live births is rather high, the completed family size reflects the high infant and child mortality of the Limón province when these women were young mothers.

### 6.4.5    *Interethnic mating*

A potentially important evolutionary force in the change of gene frequencies in a population is gene flow. In Chapter 3 we discussed population genetics studies including the Afro-Limonense population. We concluded that the genetic make-up of Afro-Caribbean groups was varied, with some populations having a large component of Amerindian and European admixture, and others having very little. In this continuum, the Afro-Limonenses were one of the groups with the smallest percentage of European and Amerindian genes. However, although all of the subjects in that sample were at least 40 years of age, most were 50 years at the time of the data collection (1987). Madrigal *et al.* (2001a) speculated that the situation should change within a few years, as evidence of gene flow between Hispano- and Afro-Limonenses was great at the time of Madrigal's fieldwork (1988).

Historically of course this was not always the case. Before the Hispanic migration to Limón started, gene flow must have been limited to members of the Jamaican community and the prostitutes in Puerto Limón, although perhaps some of the USA elite did engage in relations with the few Jamaican women. As we have already mentioned, when the Hispano-Costa Ricans started coming to Limón, the two communities remained very isolated from each other, with separate seating areas in the movie theaters, etc. But that separation has been eroding slowly beginning in the 1950s, and the two communities are becoming more and more integrated (Purcell, 1993). Most authors speak of the very frequent exchange of mates between the Afro-Costa Rican and the Hispano-Costa Rican communities in Limón, particularly in Puerto Limón. This increased gene flow was already taking place in the late 1970s when Purcell (1987) did his work: of the 217 households that he sampled, 6.5% were "mixed," with 45.2% of respondents expressing positive feelings about interethnic unions. In 1987 when I did my research I did not take a survey, as did Purcell, but my impression was that interethnic unions were exceedingly frequent in Limón. Even more recently, Herzfeld (2002) speaks of interethnic matings as being so common in the year 2000 as to be a potential threat to the preservation of the Limonense creole.

In conclusion, a demographic overview of the Afro-Limonense population finds strong similarities with other Afro-Caribbean groups. Unfortunately Limón is probably the most underdeveloped area of Costa Rica and as such has mortality indices that are unusually high for the country. However, this does not mean that the Afro-Limonenses have the highest mortality indices, as it is the Amerindian groups in the southern part of the province that have the poorest health status, thus driving the indices up for the entire province. Nevertheless, mortality rates are still very high for the Afro-Limonense population, and are one reason for the recent call by Rigoberto Stewart (1999) to declare Limón an autochthonous region. The migration pattern of the Afro-Limonense population also mirrors that seen in the rest of the Caribbean: We see transnational migration uniting Limón with Bocas del Toro in Panamá, Bluefields and San Juán del Norte in Nicaragua, and various areas in Jamaica. Moreover, there is plenty of evidence for migration of the best-educated Afro-Limonenses to the urban centers in Costa Rica or even in the USA, resulting in families that extend over wide geographical areas.

The family structure of the Afro-Limonense population is also characterized by the same features that we see in other Afro-Caribbean areas: a disassociation between marriage and sexual behavior, unstable male–female unions, strong female-folk networks, and households headed by females with several generations and with sponsored children. Perhaps where the Afro-Limonense population departs from the rest of the Caribbean is in its high rate of gene flow with another ethnic group, namely the Hispano-Limonenses.

## 6.5   Epidemiology of the Afro-Limonense population: infectious diseases

Throughout its history, the most feared health hazard of the Limón province has been malaria. The importance of malaria in the history of Costa Rica has received attention from several workers, some of whom think it alone is responsible for the present-day distribution of ethnic groups in Costa Rica (Adams, 1996). Mennerick (1964) indicates that malarial infestation is one of the most important factors responsible for the underdevelopment of the Limón province. The disease slowed colonization and agricultural development of the vast lowlands, and it was one of the most common causes of death during the construction of the Atlantic coast railroad from 1871 through 1890. Casey-Gaspar (1979) notes that malaria was the most frequent cause of death in the province since establishment of the United Fruit Company's enclave.

Chomsky (1996) offers an excellent account of the role of malaria during the construction of the railroad and in the banana plantations, but he presents a view that de-emphasizes the role of malaria as the number-one killer. According to him, although malaria was such a deadly disease it was not the major killer in these enterprises: the main causes of death were the abysmal working conditions and the diet of the workers, which rendered them weak and unable to fight off infection. Moreover, tuberculosis and pneumonia both killed more workers than did malaria. Evidence of nutritional deficiencies is everywhere, in the form of night blindness, scurvy, pellagra, and beriberi. There is also abundant evidence that the workers had heavy loads of intestinal parasites which compromised their nutritional status as well. But these nutritional problems did not receive the attention which they merited, because such attention would have required a second look at the conditions of the workers. The same goes for the horrible accidents that occurred while the railroad was being constructed or the land cleared: the company emphasized malaria single-handedly. Chomsky (1996) proposes that the Company's focus on malaria was due to the fact that its American-elite workers were more affected by it than by tuberculosis or pneumonia and, of course, they were not affected at all by undernutrition or poor working conditions. Tuberculosis, as we saw in Chapter 3, is a disease of poverty and poor living conditions broadly defined, and the conditions of the workers in Limón can be described as poor at best. Pneumonia was such a serious problem given the dampness of the environment, and the living conditions, which forced the workers to go to sleep with wet clothes, a practice about which the Company complained, but which it did not seek to alleviate. Instead the Company focused on malaria, forcing the workers to take prophylactic doses of quinine which made the workers sick and did not alleviate the main issues that caused such high morbidity and mortality. For example, whereas the company's US elite slept in screened houses, workers were exposed to mosquitoes through the entire day. As Chomsky (1996: 114) so well puts it, the United Fruit Company emphasized ". . . treating the disease rather then patient, and the patient rather than the underlying social causes of disease." Moreover, the Company consistently blamed the workers for their poor health, with one official stating that there was no reason for an intelligent person to get malaria. Nonetheless, there is abundant evidence of the abysmal environmental conditions which contributed to malaria endemicity in the early to mid 1900s. There are accounts and governmental documents which show that drainage was inadequate in both urban and rural areas, and that the entire region did not have adequate sewage disposal or a clean water supply, and a document from the late 1920s states that malaria had taken over the entire city of Puerto Limón (Chomsky, 1996).

Although malaria might not have been the number-one killer during the railroad construction, it is of interest to us as the selective agent which helped keep abnormal hemoglobin frequencies so high among the Afro-Limonense population. Thus here we discuss the evolution of malaria in Costa Rica. In 1939, Kum and Ruiz carried out a malarial survey across the entire country. At the time, the Atlantic and Pacific coasts were areas of endemicity, and *P. falciparum*, *P. vivax*, and *P. malariae* were present, and the most common vector was *A. albimanus* (Faust, 1941; Kum and Ruiz, 1939; Watson and Hewitt, 1941). Most of the country has never been affected by malaria in an endemic fashion because of its high altitude.

Kum and Ruiz (1939) palpated 9126 children in the entire country for splenomegaly, and obtained blood films for 3981 of the subjects. Since 74.2% of the children with *P. falciparum* infection had enlarged spleens, the rate of splenomegaly fell short of the actual rate of parasitation. Although some splenomegaly cases had no peripheral blood parasites, Kum and Ruiz (1939) stress that as the size of the spleen increased so did the percentage of positive blood films. In Limón, 11.9% of the 1550 children palpated had an enlarged spleen, and 21 of the 28 localities sampled were infested with *P. falciparum*. Kum and Ruiz's survey (1939) demonstrates that *P. falciparum* was endemic in Limón in 1939.

The evolution of malaria cases in Costa Rica from 1939 through 1985 has been described by Madrigal (1988, 1989). In 1946, the number of malarial deaths was nearly the same as it was in 1939. In 1939 the number of malarial deaths in the country was 843 (11% of all deaths), whereas in 1946 it had decreased to 802, after a steady increase through 1945 (Rosero-Bixby, 1985). The number of malarial cases in the country decreased from 1947 (12 749) to 1964 (1210), increased from 1965 (2563) to 1967 (4418), and then steadily decreased to 110 cases in 1982 (see Madrigal [1988, 1989] for a complete list of the WHO and PAHO publications used for this summary). There was an increase in the number of cases in 1983 (245) through 1985 (734), with several serious outbreaks reported in Limón in 1983 as a result of the USA-backed *contra* guerrilla war against the democratically elected *Sandinista* government. Presently, the Costa Rican Ministry of Health periodically sprays houses with insecticides and carries out epidemiologic surveys throughout the province (Rosero-Bixby, 1985; Tropical Disease Program, 1986). Costa Rica is one of three countries with the highest annual blood-examination rate in the

Americas, and most of its cases are of *P. vivax*, a milder form of malaria (Malaria Action Programme, 1987). However, the country has not achieved a malaria-free status. For example, PAHO (1996) reports an annual parasite index of 4.09 (for a comparison, the index was 5.75 in Guatemala and 0.34 in Panamá); most of these cases were due to *P. vivax*, although some were due to *P. falciparum* and mixed infections. This index was down from that of 1992, when it was 7.9. Interestingly, since the 1980s most of the cases are found in the Limón Atlantic coast in the northern regions, coinciding with the population movements caused by the Nicaraguan war, with changes in the banana industry, and with deforestation. Although there had been no malaria deaths in 20 years in Costa Rica, two deaths due to *P. falciparum* occurred in 1996 (www.paho. org/english/sha/prflcor.htm).

More important in the twenty-first century, however, is the dramatic rise in dengue cases in Limón, a disease associated with poor drainage. As recently as 2003, I observed that stagnant waters, swampy areas, and poor sewage drainage were everywhere in Puerto Limón (Madrigal, 2003). Rigoberto Stewart (1999) confirms that currently malaria is not the problem, but that dengue is. According to the PAHO (www.paho.org/english/sha/prflcor.htm) in 1993 there was a dengue outbreak with 4612 cases, with 13 929 cases in 1994 and 5135 in 1995, the latter year reporting the first case of hemorrhagic fever. In 1996 there were two deaths due to dengue. Although the epidemic started with serotype 1, serotype 3 is now the most frequent form.

AIDS has been on the rise in Costa Rica, and as in the USA it was initially associated with gay men and hemophilic patients. The disease is now becoming more of a heterosexual one (www.worldhealthcare.net). Since the first cases were reported in 1990, there have been 1156 AIDS cases and 621 deaths in the country (www.paho.org/english/sha/prflcor. htm). Downe (1997) speculates that half of cases in Costa Rica are unrecorded, and that the disease is spreading at an alarming rate. Although the government has been very active in the promotion of condoms, these efforts have been less than effective in the Limón province, as we saw in Chapter 3. In addition, there are certain beach-side towns to the south of Puerto Limón in which sex tourism is booming. As early as 1987, when I conducted my first fieldwork, the word was that European, USA and Costa Rican Hispanic women were coming to these places looking for sex with the local Afro-Limonense males. Although I have not seen any studies in support of these allegations, sex tourism involving males and females is an expected outcome of an economy of dependence, where the commodity sold is tourism. Of course, given the fluidity of male–female relations in the Afro-Limonense population, it should be expected that sexually transmitted diseases pose a major problem to the community. Downe (1997) has written the only paper we could find on Costa Rican prostitutes' views of the risk of AIDS contagion. According to her, prostitutes (in San José, not in Limón) do not separate the risk of AIDS infection from the risk of being violently attacked by their clients. In other words, for these women AIDS and other diseases which are sexually transmitted are not a clinical, infectious disease, but part of a broad risk complex which includes disease, drug abuse, and – always – physical violence. Downe (1997) sees Costa Rica's anti-AIDS campaigns as irrelevant for her subjects, who do not see AIDS transmission in the same manner as the Government.

Unfortunately, hard data on sexually transmitted diseases are simply very difficult to find for Costa Rica. According to the PAHO (www.paho. org/english/sha/prflcor.htm) the cases of gonorrhea and syphilis have decreased dramatically, the former from 433.8 per 100 000 in 1982 to 68.6 in 1995, the latter from 99.8 per 100 000 in 1982 to 44.7 in 1995. Congenital syphilis, however, has persisted, with close to 100 annual cases reported.

An infectious disease that does not figure prominently in the other Afro-Caribbean countries described in Chapter 3 but which is very important in Limón is filarasis or elephantiasis. Indeed, Puerto Limón is the only focus of the disease in the entire Central American region, and one of the few seen in the tropical Americas (PAHO, 2000). The disease is caused by a nematode (*Wuchereira bancrofti*), which lives in the lymph nodes, and whose microfilaria are found in blood smears of the patients. The pathogen is transmitted by a nocturnal mosquito vector (*Culex quinquefasciatus*).

Filariasis has been a problem in Puerto Limón for many decades (Butts, 1948), where it was found in 1.8–2.7% of a large sample in eight scattered areas, but not in 13 rural communities, where it was only found in 0.1% of the sample. The disease affects disproportionately individuals who are between 10 and 19 and over 40 years of age. Most importantly, it was found in a significantly higher frequency in Afro-Limonense than in Hispano-Limonense subjects. (Anonymous, 1983; PAHO, 2000, 2002; Paniagua *et al.*, 1983; Weinstok-Wolfowicz *et al.*, 1977, 1979). Further research showed that the disease was concentrated in two neighborhoods of Puerto Limón (with a higher concentration of Afro-Limonenses than Hispano-Limonenses), which prompted a strong response from the Government to control sewage disposal and limit standing water, ideal environments for the vector. As a result of these controls and an aggressive therapeutic campaign, the disease has been successfully controlled (Garcés and Paniagua, 2003).

Besides malaria, other infectious diseases have had a resurgence in Costa Rica, beginning in the 1980s: there were epidemics of measles and rubella, and several cholera cases. Equally troublesome is the re-emergence of tuberculosis whose incidence in 1992 was 11.4 per 100 000 and in 1996 19.0 per 100 000. In 1994 80 tuberculosis deaths were reported, being 25% of all deaths from communicable diseases. Unfortunately, no data are available for the Limón province or for the Afro-Limonenses population (www.paho.org/english/sha/prflcor.htm).

In conclusion, the history of the province is tightly linked to the history of malaria, a disease which has still not been eradicated. More recently, infectious ills which have not been problems for the rest of Costa Rica for at least a generation still plague the Limón province; diarrhea and intestinal parasites still occur in Limón because of inadequate sewage disposal and lack of clean water. No doubt the increase in poverty which has followed the neoliberal policies since the 1980s has contributed to the increase in these easily solvable conditions, conditions which Costa Rica has been famous for eradicating.

### 6.6    Epidemiology of the Afro-Limonense population: obesity, diabetes, and hypertension

There are very few sources that list the prevalence rates of obesity, diabetes, and hypertension among Afro-Limonenses. Given that survey data collected by the Ministry of Health do not include ethnicity, we have very little to rely upon. However, we expect to find that the higher the degree of urbanization and the greater the exposure to a non-traditional lifestyle, the higher the prevalence rates of these three diseases should be. During the last 20 years, the Costa Rican population pyramid has changed because the population is getting older, with a decrease in natality and an increase in life expectancy. As expected, the national data indicate a rise in cardiovascular disease. In a 1996 national survey 16.3% of girls and 13.6% of boys were overweight (www.paho.org/english/sha/prflcor.htm). Furthermore, evidence is mounting for a decrease in physical activity and an increased adoption of fast foods (Rondero, 2004). Moreover, the PAHO estimates that 15% of the population is hypertensive, and diabetes has now become the ninth leading cause of death, causing 258 deaths in 1994. Cardiovascular disease was the leading cause of death in the country, with a mortality rate of 12.5 per 10 000 in 1994 (www.paho.org/english/sha/prflcor.htm). During 1997–9 cardiovascular diseases and tumors were responsible for approximately half of deaths

Figure 6.4. Taking a blood-pressure measurement.

in the country. Although there is evidence that the clinical management of type-II diabetes has improved and that life expectancy of such patients has been extended, there has been an increase in the mortality rate due to this disease as a result of its higher frequency. Of interest to us is Rondero's (2004) observation that in Limón and Puntarenas there is an elevated mortality rate due to infectious diseases – not surprising, given the socioeconomic and health conditions in Limón – together with high mortality due to cardiovascular diseases among females in Limón.

We have been unable to locate any research project which has specifically looked at obesity, hypertension, and diabetes among Afro-Limonenses besides our own from 2003, in which we did not do any diabetes tests. The work of Madrigal *et al.* (2004) was a pilot study which focused on the frequencies of hypertension and obesity in a small sample from Puerto Limón and another one taken from the Indo-Limonense Culí group south of Puerto Limón in Westfalia. Our sample was not randomly obtained from Puerto Limón but was collected at the Fisherman's Cooperative and, as a result, most of our subjects were males. Figure 6.4 shows the author, her assistant, and a subject before a blood-pressure reading was taken in the latter. Figure 6.5 shows a member of the research team taking the anthropometric measurements of a subject, and Figure 6.6 shows the view in front of our research station, specifically the fishing boats used by the members of the cooperative. Our results were already discussed in Chapter 2, so we will not repeat

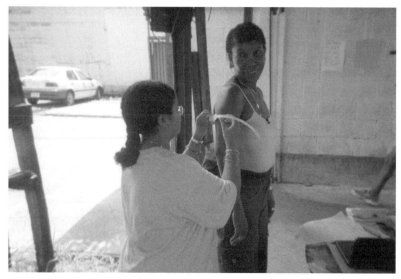

Figure 6.5. Taking anthropometric measurements.

Figure 6.6. The view from our research station.

the numerical data here, but we report here that we found an exceedingly low frequency of hypertension (in the presence of a sizable rate of obesity). Our results argue strongly against the so-called "slavery hypothesis," which proposes that the African slaves went through natural selection in the middle passage, a selection which predisposes them to high rates of hypertension. Our results instead strongly support the proposition that hypertension is a condition found in certain environmental conditions, namely those of industrialized or globalized societies, and that it is particularly associated with stressful life conditions. Perhaps the best way to describe the environment of our subjects is that it is a semi-urban area where people still walk on a daily basis and eat and drink their traditional foods and drinks, and the social network has not been changed too much, as the area has not been fully engulfed by the globalized capitalist market.

### 6.7   Population genetics of the Afro-Limonense population

In Costa Rica, population genetics research of abnormal hemoglobins has focused on both the Pacific (Guanacaste and north Puntarenas) and Atlantic (the province of Limón) coasts. The emphasis on these two regions clearly mirrors the distribution of populations of African ancestry in Costa Rica: Guanacaste and Puntarenas had a large population of colonial African slaves and Limón is where the descendants of Jamaican workers are geographically concentrated. Moreover, these two regions of the country have been endemic malarial areas until recently. In this chapter we limit ourselves to work on the Atlantic region of Limón (the frequency of Hb S in Guanacaste and Puntarenas is between 7 and 8%; Sáenz, 1985).

   The work of Germán Sáenz and collaborators on abnormal hemoglobins in Costa Rica is noteworthy (Chavez *et al.*, 1987; Elizondo *et al.*, 1979; Sáenz, 1985; Sáenz *et al.*, 1971, 1974a, 1974b, 1976, 1977, 1981a, 1981b, 1984). In an early large-scale survey at the national level Rivera (1967) reports that abnormal hemoglobins (Hb S and Hb C) were found mostly in Guanacaste, Puntarenas, and Limón. In Limón specifically, the frequency of Hb S has been reported as ranging from 20% (Rivera, 1967) to 8.2% (Sáenz *et al.*, 1971) and 6.0% (Sáenz *et al.*, 1984).

   In 1987 I collected blood samples in door-to-door surveys in Puerto Limón and surrounding neighborhoods and at the Limón hospital in order to determine the frequency of abnormal hemoglobins in the region. The genotypes of two carriers were known before the samples were taken. Otherwise, sampling for the research had no known bias. Table 6.2 summarizes the incidence of various hemoglobin genotypes identified in the Limonense sample which consists of 137 females. The following genotypes were obtained: 108 AA, 1 SS, 22 AS, 2 SC, 3 AC, and 1 SF. The Hb SF individual was diagnosed as having hereditary persistence of fetal hemoglobin (HPFH). According to Sáenz (1985), Hb F had been

Table 6.2. *Gene frequencies, and observed and expected hemoglobin genotypes in a sample from Limón (including and excluding the two known carriers)*

Including the two known carriers

| Genotypes | AA $p^2$ | AS $2pq$ | SS $q^2$ | SC $2qr$ | AC $2pr$ | SF $2qs$ | Total |
|---|---|---|---|---|---|---|---|
| Observed genotype | 108 | 22 | 1 | 2 | 3 | 1 | 137 |
| | 78.9% | 16% | 0.73% | 1.45% | 2.19% | 0.73% | 100% |
| Expected genotype | 106.2 | 24 | 1.5 | 0.5 | 4.6 | 0.2 | |
| Gene frequency | $p = 0.88$ | $q = 0.099$ | $r = 0.018$ | $s = 0.003$ | | | 1.0 |
| | $\chi = 8.62$, 5 df, $P > 0.05$ | | | | | | |

Excluding the two known carriers

| Genotypes | AA $p^2$ | AS $2pq$ | SS $q^2$ | SC $2qr$ | AC $2pr$ | SF $2qs$ | Total |
|---|---|---|---|---|---|---|---|
| Observed genotype | 108 | 20 | 1 | 2 | 3 | 1 | 135 |
| | 80% | 5% | 0.75% | 1.5% | 2% | 0.75% | 100% |
| Expected genotype | 107.1 | 22.1 | 1.20 | 0.50 | 4. | 0.1 | |
| Gene frequency | $p = 0.89$ | $q = 0.09$ | $r = 0.017$ | $s = 0.003$ | 1.0 | | |
| | $\chi = 13.09$, 5 df, $P <$ 0.025 | | | | | | |

*Note:*
df, degrees of freedom.
*Source:* Madrigal (1989).

previously sampled in Limón. A $\chi$ test of the expected and observed genotypic frequencies including the two known carriers indicates that the observed frequencies are at equilibrium ($\chi = 8.62$, 5 degrees of freedom [df], $P > 0.05$). However, when the two known carriers were excluded, the $\chi$ achieved significance ($\chi = 13.09$, 5 df, $P < 0.025$), perhaps indicating that at the time of the survey the frequency of Hb S was decreasing as a result of a relaxed malarial selective pressure (20 heterozygotes were observed whereas 22 were expected).

In addition, the G6PD phenotypes in a larger sample consisting of 141 females and 72 males were determined (the phenotype could not be determined in some females whose hemoglobin was established successfully). Given that G6PD is an $\chi$-linked trait, its deficiency is usually reported for males and females separately. In the Limón sample four males were found to be $A^-$ and one $B^-$, whereas six females were $A^-$ and four $B^-$ (Madrigal *et al.*, 1990).

The results of this research indicate that there is much heterogeneity in the Afro-Limonense population, as it contains several abnormal hemoglobins besides Hb S in addition to G6PD deficiency; not only the A$^-$ type, which is more common in Africa, but also B$^-$, which is more common in Europe. Such high genetic variation confirms previous work by Sáenz and collaborators who have reported in the past various thalassemic mutations (Sáenz *et al.*, 1974a, 1976, 1977, 1984) as well as G6PD deficiency (Chavez *et al.*, 1987; Sáenz *et al.*, 1984) and other abnormal hemoglobins (Sáenz *et al.*, 1981a, 1984). Clearly the Afro-Limonense population has been under the selective pressure of malaria and as a result has maintained high frequencies of abnormal hemoglobins and other erythrocyte abnormalities which are associated with the disease. As of the present, we should start seeing a decrease in the frequencies of these polymorphisms as a result of the relaxation of selective pressure, assuming that the disease does not keep on increasing in frequency.

A recent paper looks at the frequency of Hb S haplotypes (see Chapter 4) among Hb S carriers in Costa Rica. Rodriguez-Romero *et al.* (1998) report that in Limón the Benin haplotype predominates at a frequency of 73%, whereas in Guanacaste and Puntarenas the Benin haplotype's frequency is not as high (although it is still the most frequent), and the Bantu type has a higher frequency. This difference in haplotype frequencies suggests that the source of the slaves brought to Guanacaste/Puntarenas by the early Spanish conquistadors and by the English to Jamaica was different. Rodriguez-Romero *et al.* (1998) note that such a difference in haplotypes explains the wide range in clinical manifestation of Hb SS sickle cell anemia, which has been shown to vary within communities such as those of Limón (Sáenz, 1985), a fact that I observed in my fieldwork.

In addition to my research with hemoglobins and G6PD deficiency, I also performed population genetics research with the Afro-Limonense group to determine how gene flow with the Hispano-Limonense group (which was discussed above) had affected the genetic make-up of the Afro-Limonenses. The microevolution of the Afro-Limonense population was researched by focusing on admixture estimates (that is, what proportion of the groups' genetic make-up has African, European, and Amerindian ancestry) and by computing the Fst values based on the variance of allele frequencies with respect to their expectations generated by the admixture model (see Chapter 5 for a review of evolutionary forces). These Fst values pinpoint the importance of genetic drift in the populations' evolutionary history. The gene frequencies of both Hispano- and Afro-Limonenses are displayed in Table 6.3. The data for both ethnic groups are shown because both ethnic groups are affecting each

Table 6.3. *G6PD phenotypes in the Afro-Limónense sample*

| Phenotype | Males | Females |
|---|---|---|
| B$^+$ | 54 | 109 |
| A$^+$ | 13 | 9 |
| B$^-$ | 1 | 4 |
| A$^-$ | 4 | 6 |
| A$^+$B$^+$ | – | 12 |
| A$^+$B$^-$ | – | 1 |

*Source:* Madrigal *et al.* (1990).

other's evolution. The differences in sample sizes were caused by loss of specimens during shipping to the USA.

Madrigal *et al.* (2001b) discuss the methodology for the computation of the gene frequencies and test whether these systems are under equilibrium. A system-by-system analysis of the data (Table 6.4) reveals that the systems for which Africans and Europeans have rather different frequencies are those for which the Hispano- and the Afro-Limonense samples differ. Conversely, systems for which African and European populations have similar frequencies are not significantly different between the Limón groups (all European and African frequencies referred to below were taken from Roychoudhury and Nei, 1988). Thus the Limón groups differed for group-specific component (GC1, $\chi_c = 49.37$, df = 9, $P < 0.001$), with the Afro group having high frequencies of the 1F allele (1F = 0.68) similar in range to those in Africa (0.68–0.841 in sub-Saharan Africa), and the Hispanic group having frequencies of the 1S allele (1S = 0.48), similar to those of French (1S = 0.47) and Basque (1S = 0.548) samples. Indeed, when the Limón frequencies were compared to those shown by Crawford *et al.* (1984) in their Figure 6.1, the Afro-Limonense group fell within the African, not the hybrid cluster, and the Hispano-Limonense group fell in between the Amerindian and European clusters. The Limón groups also differed significantly for the Properdin factor B(BF) system ($\chi_c = 35.66$, df = 6, $P < 0.001$), with the Afro group having intermediate frequencies of the S allele (S = 0.42), similar to those observed in African groups (ranging from 0.393 through 0.282 in sub-Saharan Africa), and the Hispanic group having high frequencies of the S allele (S = 0.75), similar to that reported in Spain (S = 0.65). The groups also differ for the Hb system ($\chi_c = 20.79$, df = 5, $P < 0.001$), with the Afro group having about 12% abnormal hemoglobins, similar to the frequencies observed in sub-Saharan Africa (close to 10–15%), and the Hispanic group having less

Table 6.4. *Gene frequencies for the Afro- (AL) and Hispano- (HL) Limonense samples*

| System | Phenotype | AL phenotypic frequency | HL phenotypic frequency | Alleles present | Allele frequency in AL | Allele frequency in HL |
|---|---|---|---|---|---|---|
| GC1 | 1 1 | 1 | 0 | 1 | 0.01 | 0 |
| | 2 2 | 2 | 2 | 2 | 0.095 | 0.188 |
| | 1F 1F | 49 | 10 | 1F | 0.68 | 0.33 |
| | 1S 1S | 1 | 24 | 1A1 | 0.03 | 0 |
| | 2 1F | 8 | 15 | 1C10 | 0.015 | 0 |
| | 2 1S | 7 | 8 | 1S | 0.17 | 0.482 |
| | 1F 1S | 23 | 13 | | | |
| | 1F 1A1 | 4 | 0 | | | |
| | 1F 1C10 | 3 | 0 | | | |
| | 1S 1A1 | 2 | 0 | | | |
| | Total | 100 | 72 | | | |
| BF | F F | 33 | 4 | F | 0.5423 | 0.219 |
| | F S | 56 | 23 | S | 0.4197 | 0.753 |
| | S S | 20 | 42 | F1 | 0.0338 | 0.021 |
| | F F1 | 6 | 1 | S07 | 0.0042 | 0.007 |
| | F1 F1 | 0 | 0 | | | |
| | F07 | 0 | | | | |
| | S07 S07 | 1 | | | | |
| | S F1 | 2 | 2 | | | |
| | S S07 | 0 | 1 | | | |
| | F1 S07 | 0 | | | | |
| | Total | 118 | 73 | | | |
| PGM1 | 1+ 1+ | 92 | 32 | 1+ | 0.6305 | 0.527 |
| | 1+ 1– | 49 | 25 | 1– | 0.1903 | 0.232 |
| | 1– 1– | 10 | 6 | 2+ | 0.1305 | 0.143 |
| | 1+ 2+ | 38 | 19 | 2– | 0.0487 | 0.098 |
| | 2+ 2+ | 4 | 2 | | | |
| | 1+ 2– | 13 | 10 | | | |

Table 6.4. (*cont.*)

| System | Phenotype | AL phenotypic frequency | HL phenotypic frequency | Alleles present | Allele frequency in AL | Allele frequency in HL |
|---|---|---|---|---|---|---|
| | 1– 2+ | 10 | 7 | | | |
| | 2– 2– | 0 | 1 | | | |
| | 1– 2– | 7 | 8 | | | |
| | 2+ 2– | 3 | 2 | | | |
| | Total | 226 | 112 | | | |
| ACP | A A | 13 | 11 | A | 0.2234 | 0.281 |
| | A B | 67 | 40 | B | 0.7697 | 0.706 |
| | B B | 132 | 60 | C | 0.0023 | 0.013 |
| | A C | 0 | 2 | R | 0.0023 | |
| | B C | 1 | 1 | A′ | 0.0023 | |
| | R R | 1 | 0 | | | |
| | B A′ | 1 | 0 | | | |
| | Total | 215 | 114 | | | |
| Hb | A A | 185 | 124 | A | 0.8797 | 0.988 |
| | A S | 43 | 2 | S | 0.1054 | 0.008 |
| | S S | 2 | 0 | C | 0.0126 | 0.004 |
| | A C | 4 | 1 | F | 0.0023 | |
| | S C | 2 | 0 | | | |
| | S F | 1 | 0 | | | |
| | Total | 237 | 127 | | | |
| Plasminogen | 1 1 | 67 | 48 | 1 | 0.7743 | 0.783 |
| | 1 2 | 36 | 20 | 2 | 0.2035 | 0.197 |
| | 2 2 | 5 | 5 | 3 | 0.0089 | 0.007 |
| | 1 B | 1 | 0 | B | 0.0044 | 0 |
| | 1 D | 2 | 0 | D | 0.0089 | 0 |
| | 1 E | 0 | 2 | E | 0 | 0.013 |
| | 1 3 | 2 | 1 | | | |
| | Total | 113 | 76 | | | |

*Note:*
GC1, group-specific component; BF, properdin factor B; PGM1, phosphoglucomutase1; ACP, acid phosphatase.

Table 6.5. *Admixture estimates for the Hispano- and Afro-Limonense samples*

| Ancestral population | Admixture estimate | S.E. of admixture |
|---|---|---|
| Hispani-Limonense sample | | |
| European | 0.5866 | 0.069 |
| Amerindian | 0.3383 | 0.0653 |
| African | 0.0751 | 0.0434 |
| Afro-Limonense sample | | |
| European | 0.1047 | 0.1482 |
| Amerindian | 0.1357 | 0.1437 |
| African | 0.7595 | 0.1266 |

*Note:*
Hispano-Limonense / Means square error = 0.009, $R^2$ = 0.991, Fst = 0.00558.
*Source:* Madrigal *et al.* (2001a).

than 1% abnormal hemoglobins. Although the frequencies of G6PD (both sexes, $\chi_c$ = 21.338, df = 13, $P$ > 0.5) were not significantly different, the corrected $\chi$ value does approach significance, as a result of the very low frequency of the $A^+$ and $A^-$ alleles in the Hispanic group, similar to the Spanish frequencies (the frequency of $A^+$ and $A^-$ in Spain approaches 0). The two Limón groups did not differ for plasminogen ($\chi_c$ = 1.83, df = 6, 0.1 > $P$ > 0.05), a system for which Europeans and Africans have high frequencies of 1 and intermediate frequences of 2. The phosphoglucomutase 1(PGM1) frequencies ($\chi_c$ = 5.24, df = 9, $P$ > 0.05) do not differ between the groups either, reflecting the similarly high 1+ frequency found in European and African groups. Finally, the Limón groups do not differ for acid phosphatase (ACP; $\chi_c$ = 3.57, df = 6, $P$ > 0.05), reflecting the high B frequency found in Europe and Africa. The genetic data are shown in Table 6.4.

These admixture estimates based on the genetic data in Table 6.4 are shown in Table 6.5. These admixture estimates for the Hispanic population indicate a not-too-different contribution of the Amerindian and European parental populations to the formation of this gene pool. This contradicts the popular notion that "White" Costa Ricans are "mostly Europeans," a notion that has been challenged by historians, as noted above. Indeed, the European component for the Hispanic group is less than 60% (M1 = 0.5866), with 34% deriving from the Amerindian (M2 = 0.3383) and 7% from the African (M3 = 0.0751) parental groups. The admixture estimates for the Afro-Limonense group indicate that it derives mostly from the African parental population (M3 = 0.7595), with very similar contributions from the European (M1 = 0.1047) and the Amerindian (M2 = 0.1357) parental groups. The Fst value of the Afro group (Fst = 0.05137) is higher than that of the Hispanic group (Fst = 0.00558), and indicates a greater importance of genetic drift in the evolution of the Afro-Limonense group. As proposed by Long (1991), the admixture estimates can be evaluated by the proportion of variance of allele frequencies explained by the admixture model. For both groups, the $R^2$ value is very high, indicating that the model is satisfactory ($R^2$ = 0.9467 for the Afro-Limonense group and $R^2$ = 0.991 for the Hispanic group). The high standard errors of the admixture estimates probably reflect the relatively small number of loci used for the calculations.

To summarize, the admixture estimates reveal a sizable contribution of the Amerindian and a small contribution of the African parental populations to the Hispanic group. These results contradict the popular notion that Costa Ricans are "mostly European," and suggest a low level of gene flow from the Afro-Limonense group into the Hispanic one. The genetic data also indicate that the Afro-Limonense sample is overwhelmingly of African origin and has received few genes from the Hispanic group. When compared to a table showing admixture estimates of 14 Afro-Latin American samples, the Afro-Limonense group is second in African ancestry to only one sample (Sans, 2000).

The Fst values demonstrate clearly the differential importance of genetic drift in the evolution of these two groups. Given that the Fst value is computed from the variance of allele frequencies with respect to their expectations from the admixture model, it is to be expected that the Fst value of the Afro group (Fst = 0.05137) is higher than that of the Hispanic group (Fst = 0.00558). Since Fst measures the "reduction in heterozygosity of a subpopulation due to random genetic drift" (Hartl, 1988), a higher Fst value indicates that genetic drift has been more important in the evolution of the Afro-Limonense breeding population. The Fst value of the Afro-Limonense probably reflects the group's historically small size and its relative isolation from the Costa Rican population at large. This Fst value may also reflect genetic drift in the form of a founder effect, since the Afro-Limonense group is a sample taken from a Jamaican group, which was itself a sample taken from Africa. That the $R^2$ value is lower for the Afro-Limonenses also supports the notion that they have experienced more genetic drift.

Since Madrigal (1988), Herzfeld (2002), and Purcell (1993) observed frequent interethnic unions during their fieldwork in the 1980s, 2000, and 1970s, respectively, we were surprised that the two groups, when plotted along the scaled $R$ matrix eigenvectors, did not cluster with each other (see Figure 4.4). The plot shown in Chapter 4 clearly clustered the Afro-Limonense group with other Afro-Caribbean groups and the Hispanic-Limonense group with the St. Vincent Black Caribs. This apparent discrepancy (both groups do not cluster, yet they engaged in gene flow) can be resolved by noting that the people whose blood samples were obtained by Madrigal (1988) were at least in their 40s, and that most of them were in their 50s, 60s, and 70s. In contrast, the people whom Madrigal (1988), Herzfeld (2002), and Purcell (1993 and personal communication) observed in frequent interethnic unions were in their teens and 20s. Thus it is likely that the subjects whose blood samples and surnames were analyzed here were not the offspring of the liberal interethnic mating observed by Madrigal and Purcell. Rather, it appears that they were the offspring of mostly within-ethnic mating.

Two recent projects using the Y chromosome do indicate the presence of substantial European admixture into the Afro-Limonense gene pool, although the ages of the subjects are not specified. Presence of typically European haplotypes in the Y chromosome gene pool of Afro-Caribbeans indicates that there has been enough gene flow from European males into the Afro-Limonense group to provide frequent European-derived haplotypes to the Afro-ethnic group (Gusmão *et al.*, 2003; Jimenez-Arce, 2000). Of course, we are unable to determine whether this gene flow took place early in the history of Limón and came from the USA managerial elite class, when there were few Jamaican women, or if it is the result of recent Hispano-Costa Rican gene flow. If the subjects of these two projects are young enough, they might be the result of what Madrigal *et al.* (2001a) predicted, namely that although there were differences in the genetic make-up of her Afro- and Hispano-Limonense subjects, within a few years these differences would blur as a result of the frequent gene flow between the two ethnic groups.

In conclusion, population genetics research in the Afro-Limonense population allows us to reconstruct the microevolutionary history of this group; the data indicate that the origin of African-derived populations from Costa Rica varies, reflecting the differences in the slave origins through the centuries. The data also indicate that malaria must have exerted a strong selective force on the population, as the frequencies of abnormal hemoglobins and other erythrocyte abnormalities are very high in the population. Fst values indicate that genetic drift was much more important in the evolution of Afro-Limonenses than it was, for example, for the Hispano-Limonenses. Data collected in the late 1980s from people who were born around the 1930s indicate that, genetically speaking, Afro- and Hispano-Limonenses do not cluster but are significantly different for those systems in which African and European populations differ. However, the younger generations, which were seen by Purcell (1993), Madrigal (1988), and Herzfeld (2002) to engage in liberal interethnic unions, are likely to produce a rather different progeny, one whose genetic boundaries are less marked. Gene flow is more likely to become more important, whereas genetic drift is likely to lose its importance as the Afro-Limonense group becomes less isolated.

### 6.8    Conclusion

The history of the Afro-Limonense population in many ways mirrors that of the rest of the Afro-Caribbean groups which have been the focus of this book. Perhaps the constant theme through this book is that of constant fluidity: change in the populations which peopled an area, change in their genetic make-up, and change in their demography and epidemiology.

The native populations of the Caribbean islands and of the Atlantic coast of Costa Rica were decimated, more quickly and effectively in the former, and less so in the latter, where there are still Amerindian communities. In the Caribbean islands, plantation economies developed on the shoulders of the millions of African slaves brought by the European powers. In Costa Rica, just like in Panamá and Honduras, large construction projects and banana plantations developed by foreign capital rested on the backs of the descendants of the African slaves. The picture shown in the cover of this book encapsulates the nature of Limón in the 1800s: it shows anonymous workers of African descent loading banana bunches in railroad carts. The carts are labeled *Northern Rail Way of Costa Rica*, indicating that business was handled in English. Perched on top of the train are two managers or overseers, probably from the USA, one of whom is even sporting a tie. Bananas and railroad, Jamaican workers and US managers: all in a foreign land, engaged in an enterprise which exploited the former and enriched the latter. Books have been and will continue to be written about the effects of this enterprise on Costa Rica.

The history of Afro-Caribbean groups is marked from the beginning by constant population movements: from Africa to the islands, after emancipation from one island to the next, from the islands to Central America, and from the entire Caribbean area to Europe, Canada, and the USA. The Afro-Limonense population was established as a result of migration, and it has experienced waves of migration through its history, aided by strong kinship ties with the populations of Bocas del Toro, Bluefields, and

Jamaica in particular. Migration has affected the genetic make-up, the epidemiology, and the culture (particularly the family structure) of Afro-Caribbean groups. In Limón, just like in the rest of the Caribbean, we see international families which are held together by a strong group of women folk and who mind each other's children, and a reduced emphasis on male –female unions, when compared with the rest of the country.

Like other Afro-Caribbean groups, the Afro-Limonenses have suffered through generations of poor health, due to their poor living conditions, diet, and exposure to pathogens. Although malaria might not have been the largest killer in the construction of the railroad or in the banana plantations, it did select for high frequencies of abnormal hemoglobins and other erythrocytic abnormalities in the community. During the late 1800s and early 1900s, perhaps the biggest infectious disease killers were pneumonia and tuberculosis, aided by extremely poor diet, exposure to the elements and a heavy intestinal parasite load. Unlike other Afro-Caribbean populations, the population of Limón suffered from elephantiasis, though it seems that recent governmental efforts have nearly eradicated this disease. Like other Afro-Caribbean populations, the Limón group is seeing rising rates of tuberculosis, AIDS, and dengue. But never has the Limón province achieved the health status of the rest of Costa Rica. Its demographic and epidemiological profile stand in contrast with the rest of the country, whose profile is virtually that of an industrialized country. In addition to the Afro-derived populations, the Amerindian groups are also terribly disadvantaged in comparison with the rest of the country; both of these minorities suffer from basic ills such as diarrheal diseases due to lack of clean water and poor sewage disposal.

Although only one pilot study on obesity and hypertension of the Afro-Limonense group could be found in the literature, the Afro-Limonenses did not seem to be suffering from the rising hypertension rates seen in other Afro-Caribbean communities, even in the presence of moderate obesity. These results argued strongly against the so-called slavery hypothesis, which has been attacked from many other perspectives previously. The fact that the Limonense sample had frequencies of hypertension similar to those of rural African samples strongly argues against a genetically deterministic reason for the explosive hypertension rates seen in the US-African-derived groups. However, our prediction is that in a matter of a few years cardiovascular diseases will become a serious problem for Afro-Limonenses, as they become subsumed in the globalized capitalist economy.

The fact that hypertension in populations of African ancestry in the New World is tied to specific sociocultural, psychological, economic, and discriminatory situations is one more argument against making epidemiological statements about "Black people" in general. Another one is the genetic studies of New World populations of African ancestry, which showed that almost every one had a different evolutionary path which resulted in a different genetic make-up. This is particularly true if Afro-South American populations are considered, as many experienced high levels of gene flow with Amerindian groups, whereas others experienced genetic drift as a result of their small size. In the Caribbean, some African-derived groups experienced very large amounts of gene flow with Amerindian groups, specifically the Black Caribs of Central America. In contrast, there is less evidence for an Amerindian component in island Afro-Caribbean groups, where the Amerindian population rapidly became extinct. Within this map of gene frequencies stand the Afro-Limonenses, with whom I worked in the late 1980s, who were born when little if any gene flow occurred with the Hispano-Limonenses, and who genetically speaking are rather different from the latter, incorporating basically equivalent percentages of Amerindian and European admixture. But change is a constant feature of Afro-Caribbean populations, and by all accounts the Afro- and the Hispano-Limonenses are beginning to exchange genes more and more across ethnic lines. Thus it is very likely that the genetic make up of the two groups has changed as a result of such gene flow. Our study did indicate that genetic drift had been important in the evolution of the Afro-Limonense population, which is not surprising, as our sample was taken from a population that had a very small effective size as a result of its isolation, and which itself was a sample from that of Jamaica.

Although the first African slaves were brought to the Caribbean hundreds of years before the writing of this book, the descendents of those slaves who live in Limón still suffer from inequalities in health, income, life expectancy, job availability, and life conditions in general. The African slaves worked in deplorable conditions in the plantations. Their newly emancipated descendents did not fare much better. Their descendents who migrated to Costa Rica suffered abysmal conditions and a sense of separation and alienation. And their present-day descendents, Costa Ricans with all the rights of Costa Rican citizens, have still not realized the bounty promised to them in the late 1940s, when they became citizens. In a land that for many generations was not their own, they have created a lively and viable culture, with its own language, music, and ideology. They continue to struggle to achieve what is due to all citizens and to keep their precious culture. A sense of non-permanence, of change, is palpable in the streets of Puerto Limón.

# References

Abdulah, N. (ed.). 1985. *Trinidad and Tobago 1985. A Demographic Analysis*. UNFPA project no. TRI/84/PO2. Greater Georgetown, Guyana: CARICOM Secretariat.

Abe-Sandes, K., Silva, W.A., and Zago, M.A. 2004. Heterogeneity of the Y chromosome in Afro-Brazilian populations. *Human Biology*. **76**: 77–86.

Abraham-van der Mark, E. 2003. Continuity and change in the Afro-Caribbean family in Curaçao in the twentieth century. *Community, Work and Family*. **6**: 77–88.

Adams, D.P. 1996. Malaria, labor, and population distribution in Costa Rica: a biohistorical perspective. *Journal of Interdisciplinary History*. **27**: 75–85.

Agarwal, A., Guindo, A., Cissoko, Y., Taylor, J.G., Coulibaly, D., Kone, A., et al. 2000. Hemoglobin C associated with protection from severe malaria in the Dogon of Mali, a West African population with a low prevalence of hemoglobin S. *Blood*. **96**: 2358–63.

Agyei, W.K.A. 1978. Modernization and the theory of demographic transition in the developing countries: the case of Jamaica. *Social and Economic Studies*. **27**: 44–68.

Agyeman, C. and Bhopal, R. 2003. Is the blood pressure of people from African origin adults in the UK higher or lower than that in European origin white people? A review of cross-sectional data. *Journal of Human Hypertension*. **17**: 523–34.

Ahman, E. and Shah, I. 2002. Unsafe abortion: worldwide estimates for 2000. *Reproductive Health Matters*. **10**: 13–17.

Ahrén, B. and Corrigan, C.B. 1984. Prevalence of diabetes mellitus in North-Western Tanzania. *Diabetologia*. **26**: 333–6.

Aikawa, M. and Miller, L.H. 1983. Structural alteration of the erythrocyte membrane during malarial parasite invasion and intraerythrocytic development. In *Malaria and the Red Cell. Ciba Foundation Symposium*, vol. 94, eds. D. Evered and J. Whelan. London: Pitman, pp. 45–63.

Akinboboye, O., Idris, O., Akinboboye, O., and Akinkugbe, O. 2003. Trends in coronary artery disease and associated risk factors in sub-Saharan Africans. *Journal of Human Hypertension*. **17**: 381–7.

Akinkugbe, O.O. 1985. World epidemiology of hypertension in Blacks. In *Hypertension in Blacks: Epidemiology, Pathophysiology and Treatment*, eds. W.D. Hall, E. Saunders and N.E.B. Shulman. Chicago: Year Book Medical Publishers, pp. 3–16.

Ala, L., Gill, G., Gugel, R., and Cuevas, L. 2004. Evidence for affluence-related hypertension in urban Brazil. *Journal of Human Hypertension.* **18**: 775–9.

Allen, J.S. and Cheer, S.M. 1996. The non-thrifty genotype. *Current Anthropology.* **37**: 831–42.

Alleyne, G. and Sealey, K.A. 1992. *Whither Caribbean Health.* A West Indian Commission occasional paper, no. 5. Barbados: West Indian Commission.

Allison, A.C. 1954. The distribution of the sickle-cell trait in East Africa and elsewhere, and its apparent relationship to the incidence of subtertian malaria. *Transactions of the Royal Society of Tropical Medicine and Hygiene.* **48**: 312–18.

1956. The sickle-cell and haemoglobin C genes in some African populations. *Annals of Human Genetics.* **21**: 67–89.

1956/57. Population genetics of abnormal human haemoglobins. *Acta Genetica.* **6**: 430–43.

1960. Glucose-6-phosphate dehydrogenase deficiency in red blood cells of East Africans. *Nature.* **186**: 531–2.

1975. Abnormal haemoglobin and erythrocyte enzyme-deficiency traits. In *Human Variation and Natural Selection, Symposia of the Society for the Study of Human Biology*, vol. XIII, ed. D.F. Roberts. London: Taylor and Francis, pp. 101–22.

Allison, A.C. and Eugui, E.M. 1983. The role of cell-mediated immune responses in resistance to malaria, with special reference to oxidant stress. *Annual Review of Immunology.* **1**: 361–92.

Anderson, J.W. and Akanji, A.O. 1994. The reversibility of obesity, diabetes, hyperlipidemia, and coronary heart disease. In *Western Diseases: their Dietary Prevention and Reversibility*, eds. N.J. Temple and D.P. Burkitt. Totowa, NJ: Humana Press, pp. 317–48.

Anderson, M.R., Moscou, S., Fulchon, C., and Neuspiel D.R. 2001. Special article: the role of race in the clinical presentation. *Family Medicine.* **33**: 430–5.

Anonymous. 1983. Prevalence study of bancroftian filiariasis in Puerto Limón, Costa Rica. *Epidemiological Bulletin.* **4**: 13–14.

Antipatis, V.J. and Gill, T.P. 2001. Obesity as a global problem. In *International Textbook of Obesity*, ed. P. Björntorp. New York: John Wiley and Sons, pp. 3–21.

Antonarakis, S.E., Boehm, C.D., Serjeant, G.R., Theisen, C.E., Dover, G.J., and Kazazian, H.J. 1984. Origin of the beta-s-globin gene in blacks - the contribution of recurrent mutation or gene conversion or both. *Proceedings of the National Academy of Sciences of the United States of America. Biological Sciences.* **81**: 853–6.

Ariza, M. and de Oliveira, O. 1999. Escenarios contrastantes: patrones de formacion familiar en el Caribe y Europa Occidental. *Estudios Sociologicos.* **17**: 815–36.

Armelagos, G.J., Barnes, K.C., and Lin J. 1996. Disease in human evolution: the re-emergence of infectious disease in the third epidemiological transition. *Anthropological Notes.* **18**: 1–7.

Ashley-Koch, A., Yang, Q., and Olney, R.S. 2000. Sickle hemoglobin (Hb S) allele and sickle cell disease: A huge review. *American Journal of Epidemiology.* **151**: 839–45.

Azofeifa, J., Ruiz, E., and Barrantes, R. 1998. Genetic variation and racial admixture in the Miskito of the southern Mosquito Shore, Nicaragua. *Revista de Biologia Tropical.* **46**: 157–65.

Bah, M.A. 1993. Legitimate trade, diplomacy, and the slave trade. In *African Studies. A Survey of Africa and the African Diaspora.* ed. M. Azevedo. Durham, NC: Carolina Academic Press, pp. 65–85.

Bailey, J., Blankson, J.N., Wind-Rotolo, M., and Siliciano, R.F. 2004. Mechanisms of HIV-1 escape from immune responses and antiretroviral drugs. *Current Opinion in Immunology.* **16**: 470–6.

Bandelt, H.J., Alves-Silva, J., Guimaraes, P.E.M., Santos, M.S., Brehm, A., Pereira, L., *et al.* 2001. Phylogeography of the human mitochondrial haplogroup L3e: a snapshot of African prehistory and Atlantic slave trade. *Annals of Human Genetics.* **65**: 549–63.

Barker, D.J.P. 2001. Type 2 diabetes: the thrifty phenotype. Preface. *British Medical Bulletin.* **60**: 1–3.

Barker, D.J.P., Gardner, M.J., and Power, C. 1982. Incidence of diabetes amongst people aged 18–50 years in nine British towns: a collaborative study. *Diabetologia.* **22**: 421–5.

Barker, D.J.P., Shiell, A.W., and Barker, M.E. 2000. Growth in utero and blood pressure levels in the next generation. *Journal of Hypertension.* **18**: 843–6.

Barker, D.J.P., Shiell, A.W., and Law, C.M. 2001. Growth in utero and blood pressure levels in the next generation. Reply. *Journal of Hypertension.* **19**(1): 163–4.

Barrow, C. 2001. Contesting the rhetoric of "black family breakdown" from Barbados. *Journal of Comparative Family Studies.* **32**: 419–41.

Baschetti, R. 1998. Diabetes epidemic in newly westernized populations: is it due to thrifty genes or to genetically unknown foods? *Journal of the Royal Society of Medicine.* **91**: 622–5.

Bastos, F.I., Strathdee, S.A., Derrico, M., and Pina, M.D.F. 1999. Drug use and the spread of HIV/AIDS in South America and the Caribbean. *Drugs: Education, Prevention and Policy.* **6**: 29–49.

Basu, A.M. 1995. *Anthropological Demography in the Understanding of Child Mortality: the Underinvestment Framework and some Misapplications.* Working Paper no. 95.01. Ithaca, NY: Cornell University, Population and Development Program, Working Papers Series.

Basu, A.M. and Aaby, P. (eds.). 1998. *The Methods and Uses of Anthropological Demography.* New York: Oxford University Press.

Beaglehole, R. and Bonita, R. 2004. *Public Health at the Crossroads. Achievements and Prospects*, 2nd edn. Cambridge: Cambridge University Press.

Bean, R.N. 1975. *The British Trans-Atlantic Slave Trade. 1650–1775.* Dissertations in American Economic History. New York: Arno Press.

Beauvais, P. and Beauvais, B. 1986. Drepanocytose et paludisme. *Archive Francaise de Pediatrie.* **43**: 179–282.

Beaver, S.E. 1975. *Demographic Transition Theory Reinterpreted: an Application to Recent Natality Trend in Latin America.* Lexington, MA: Lexington Books.

Beckles, H. McD. 2002. Crop over fetes and festivals in Caribbean slavery. In *In the Shadow of the Plantation. Caribbean History and Legacy. In Honour of Professor Emeritus Woodville K. Marshall,* ed. A.O. Thompson. Kingston: Ian Randle Publishers, pp. 246–63.

Beiser, M., Collomb, H., Ravel, J.L., and Nafziger, C.J. 1976. Systemic blood-pressure studies among the Serer of Senegal. *Journal of Chronic Diseases.* **29**: 371–80.

Bermúdez-Méndez, V., Raabe-Cercone, C., and Ortiz-Malavassi, L. 1982. *Embarazo entre las adolescentes. Sultados de una encuesta realizada en la ciudad de Limón.* San José, Costa Rica: Asociación Demografica Costarricense.

Bertrand, E., Serie, F., Kone, I., *et al.* 1976. Study of prevalence and of certain epidemiological aspects of arterial hypertension in Ivory Coast. *Bulletin of the World Health Organization.* **54**: 449–54.

Betrán, A.P., de Onís, M., Lauer, J.A., and Villar, J. 2001. Ecological study of effect of breast feeding on infant mortality in Latin America. *British Medical Journal.* **323**: 303–6.

Bezruchka, S. and Mercer, M.A. 2004. The lethal divide: how economic inequality affects health. In *Sickness and Wealth. The Corporate Assault on Global Health,* eds. M. Fort, M.A. Mercer, and O. Gish. Cambridge, MA: South End Press, pp. 9–20.

Blackburn, H. 2003. Commentary: the slavery hypothesis of hypertension among African-Americans. *Epidemiology.* **14**: 118–19.

Blake, J. 1961. *Family Structure in Jamaica. The Social Context of Reproduction.* New York: The Free Press of Glencoe.

Blakey, M.L. 2001. Bioarchaeology of the African Diaspora in the Americas: its origins and scope. *Annual Reviews of Anthropology.* **30**: 387–422.

Blutstein, H. (ed.). 1970. *Area Handbook for Costa Rica.* Washington, D.C.: US Government Printing Office.

Boaz, N.T. 2002. *Evolving Health. The Origins of Illness and How the Modern World is Making us Sick.* New York: John Wiley and Sons.

Boonpucknavig, S. and Udomsangpetch, R. 1983. Immunological aspects in Plasmodium falciparum infection. *Journal of Clinical and Laboratory Immunology.* **13**: 133–6.

Bortolini, M.C., Zago, M.A., Salzano, F.M., *et al.* 1997a. Evolutionary and anthropological implications of mitochondrial DNA variation in African Brazilian populations. *Human Biology.* **69**: 141–59.

Bortolini, M.C., Salzano, F.M., Zago, M.A., DaSilva, W.A., and Weimer, T.D. 1997b. Genetic variability in two Brazilian ethnic groups: a comparison of mitochondrial and protein data. *American Journal of Physical Anthropology.* **103**: 147–56.

Bortolini, M.C., da Silva, W.A., Weimer, T.D., Zago, M.A., de Guerra, D.C., Schneider, M.P., *et al.* 1998. Protein and hypervariable tandem repeat diversity in eight African-derived South American populations: inferred relationships do not coincide. *Human Biology.* **70**: 443–61.

Bortolini, M.C., da Silva, W.A., de Guerra, D.C., *et al.* 1999. African-derived South American populations: a history of symmetrical and asymmetrical matings according to sex revealed by bi- and uni-parental genetic markers. *American Journal of Human Biology.* **11**: 551–63.

Bortolini, M.C., da Silva, W.A., Zago, M.A., *et al.* 2004. The phylogeography of mitochondrial DNA haplogroup L3g in Africa and the Atlantic slave trade. *American Journal of Human Genetics.* **75**: 522–4.

Bowman, J.E. 1990. The malaria hypothesis. In *Genetic Variation and Disorders in Peoples of African Origin*, eds. J.E. Bowman and R.F. Murray. The Johns Hopkins Series in Contemporary Medicine and Public Health. London: Johns Hopkins University Press, pp. 229–43.

Bowman, J.E. and Murray, R.F. (eds.). 1990. *Genetic Variation and Disorders in Peoples of African Origin.* The Johns Hopkins Series in Contemporary Medicine and Public Health. London: Johns Hopkins University Press.

Bozzoli de Wille, M.E. 1986. *El indígena Costarricense y su ambiente natural.* San José, Costa Rica: Editorial Porvenir.

Bravi, C.M., Sans, M., Bailliet, G., *et al.* 1997. Characterization of mitochondrial DNA and Y-chromosome haplotypes in a Uruguayan population of African ancestry. *Human Biology.* **69**: 641–52.

Brettell, C. 2003. *Anthropology and Migration. Essays on Transnationalism, Ethnicity, and Identity.* Walnut Creek, CA: Altamira Press.

Breuer, W.V. 1985. How the malaria parasite invades its host cell, the erythrocyte. *International Review of Cytology. Survey Of Cell Biology.* **96**: 191–238.

Brittain, A.W. 1990. Migration and the demographic transition: a West Indian example. *Social and Economic Studies.* **39**: 39–64.

1992. Birth spacing and child mortality in a Caribbean population. *Human Biology.* **64**: 223–41.

Brondolo, E., Rieppi, R., Kelly, K.P., and Gerin, W. 2003. Perceived racism and blood pressure: a review of the literature and conceptual and methodological critique. *Annals of Behavioral Medicine.* **25**: 55–65.

Bryce-Laporte, R.S. 1962. *Social Relations and Cultural Persistence (Change) among Jamaicans in a Rural Area of Costa Rica.* Ph.D. Dissertation, University of Puerto Rico.

Buckheit, R.W. 2004. Understanding HIV resistance, fitness, replication capacity and compensation: targeting viral fitness as a therapeutic strategy. *Expert Opinion on Investigational Drugs.* **13**: 933–58.

Burns, M.D., Morrison, J.A., Khoury, P.R., and Glueck, C.J. 1980. Blood-pressure studies in black and white inner-city and suburban adolescents. *Preventive Medicine.* **9**: 41–50.

Burton, F. 1995. *The Multimedia Guide to the Non-Human Primates*, Print version. Scarborough, Ontario: Prentice Hall Canada.

Buse, K., Drager, N., Fustukian, S., and Lee, K. 2002. Globalization and health policy: trends and opportunities. In *Health Policy in a Globalizing World*, eds. K. Lee, K. Buse, and S. Futukian. Cambridge: Cambridge University Press, pp. 251–80.

Bush, B. 1996. Hard labor, women, childbirth, and resistance in British Caribbean slave societies. In *More than Chattel. Black Women and Slavery in the Americas*, eds. D.B. Gaspar and D.C. Hine. Bloomington, IN: Indiana University Press, pp. 193–217.

     1999. *Slave Women in Caribbean Society. 1650–1838*. Kingston: Ian Randle Publishers; Bloomington, IN: Indiana University Press; Oxford: James Currey.

Butcher, G.A. 1998. Plasmodium vivax as a cause of malnutrition. *Transactions of the Royal Society of Tropical Medicine and Hygiene.* **92**: 123.

Butts, D.C.A. 1948. La infeccion filarica en Costa Rica. *Revista Medica de Costa Rica y Centroamerica.* **15**: 103–8.

Byron, M. 2000. Return migration to the Eastern Caribbean: comparative experiences and policy implications. *Social and Economic Studies.* **49**: 155–87.

Cáceres, C. and Stall, R. 2003. Commentary: the human immunodeficiency virus-AIDS epidemic among men who have sex with men in Latin America and the Caribbean: it is time to bridge the gap. *International Journal of Epidemiology.* **32**: 740–3.

Cáceres, R. 2000. *Negros, mulatos, esclavos y libertos en la Costa Rica del siglo XVII*, publicación no. 518. Mexico, DF: Instituto Panamericano de Geografía e Historia.

Camara, B. 1999. An overview of the AIDS/HIV/STD situation in the Caribbean. In *The Caribbean AIDS Epidemic*, eds. G. Howe and A. Cobley. Kingston: University of the West Indies Press, pp. 1–21.

Campbell, V. 1988. *Caribbean Foodways*. Kingston: Caribbean Food and Nutrition Institute, Pan American Health Organization.

Campione-Piccardo, J., Ruben, M., Vaughan, H., and Morris-Galsgow, V. 2003. Dengue viruses in the Caribbean. Twenty years of dengue virus isolates from the Caribbean Epidemiology Centre. *West Indian Medical Journal.* **52**: 191–8.

Carme, B., Sobesky, M., Biard, M.H., Cotellon, P., Aznar, C., and Fontanella, J. M. 2003. Non-specific alert system for dengue epidemic outbreaks in areas of endemic malaria. A hospital-based evaluation in Cayenne (French Guiana). *Epidemiology and Infection.* **130**: 93–100.

Carrington, C.V.F., Kondeatis, E., Ramdath, D.D., Norman, P.J., Vaughan, R. W., and Stephens, H.A.F. 2002. A comparison of HLA-DR and -DQ allele and haplotype frequencies in Trinidadian populations of African, South Asian, and mixed ancestry. *Human Immunology.* **63**: 1045–54.

Casey-Gaspar, J. 1979. *Limón: 1880–1940. Un estudio de la industria bananera en Costa Rica*. San José, Costa Rica: Editorial Costa Rica.

Castor D., Jolly, P.E., Furlonge, C., *et al.* 2002. Determinants of gonorrhoea infection among STD clinic attenders in Trinidad - II: sexual behavioural factors. *International Journal of STD & AIDS.* **13**: 46–51.

Castro, A. and Singer, M. 2004. *Unhealthy Health Policy. A Critical Anthropological Examination.* Lanham, MD: Altamira Press.

Castro-Martin, T. 2002. Consensual unions in Latin America: persistence of a dual nuptiality system. *Journal of Comparative Family Studies.* **33**: 35–55.

Cateau, H. 2002. The new "Negro" business: hiring in the British West Indies 1750–1810. In *In the Shadow of the Plantation. Caribbean History and Legacy. In Honour of Professor Emeritus Woodville K. Marshall*, ed. A.O. Thompson. Kingston: Ian Randle Publishers, pp. 100–20.

CEPAL (Comisión económica para América Latina y el Caribe). 2003. *Boletín demográfico. América Latina y el Caribe: el envejecimiento de la población.* Santiago, Chile: Centro Latinoamericano y Caribeño de Demografía. División de Población.

Charbit, Y. 1984. *Caribbean Family Structure: Past Research and Recent Evidence from the WFS on Matrifocality.* WFS Scientific Reports no. 65. Voorburg, The Netherlands: International Statistical Institute.

Charmot-Bensimon, D. 1999. Les genes de globins humaines: que nous apprend leur polymorphism? *Bulletin de la Societe de Pathologie Exotique.* **92**: 242–8.

Chaufan, C. 2004. Sugar blues: a social anatomy of the diabetes epidemic in the United States. In *Unhealthy Health Policy. A Critical Anthropological Examination*, eds. A. Castro and M. Singer. Lanham, MD: Altamira Press, pp. 257–74.

Chavez, M., Quintana, E., Sáenz, G.F., *et al.* 1987. Ictericia neonatal y deficiencia de la glucosa-6-fosfato deshidrogenasa eritrocítica. Experiencia en Costa Rica. *Sangre.* **32**: 428–35.

Chavez, R. 1982. *Los recursos fisicos de la zona Atlantica de Costa Rica.* San José, Costa Rica: Instituto de Investigaciones Sociales, Facultad de Ciencias Sociales, Universidad de Costa Rica.

Chomsky, A. 1996. *West Indian Workers and the United Fruit Company in Costa Rica, 1870–1940.* Baton Rouge, LA: Louisiana State University Press.

Clark, M. 2004. *Understanding Diabetes.* Chichester: John Wiley and Sons.

Clegg, J.B. and Weatherall, D.J. 1999. Thalassemia and malaria: new insights into an old problem. *Proceedings of the Association of American Physicians.* **111**: 278–82.

Cockburn, A. 1963. *The Evolution and Eradication of Infectious Diseases.* Baltimore, MD: Johns Hopkins University Press.

Cohen, S. 1977. Mechanisms of malarial immunity. *Transactions of the Royal Society of Tropical Medicine and Hygiene.* **71**: 283–6.

Cohen, S. and Butcher, G.A. 1972. Immunological response to Plasmodium. *American Journal of Tropical Medicine and Hygiene.* **21**: 713–21.

Collier, A.A. and de la Parra, D.A. 1952. Sickle-cell trait in Surinam Creoles. *Documenta de Medicina Geographica et Tropica.* **4**: 223–5.

Colombo, B. and Felicetti, L. 1985. Admission of Hb S heterozygotes to a general hospital is relatively reduced in malarial areas. *Journal of Medical Genetics.* **22**: 291–2.

Comuzzie, A.G., Williams, J.T., Martin, L.J., and Blangero, J. 2001. Searching for genes underlying normal variation in human adiposity. *Journal of Molecular Medicine.* **79**: 57–70.

Connell, J. and Conway, D. 2000. Migration and remittances in island microstates: a comparative perspective on the South Pacific and the Caribbean. *International Journal of Urban and Regional Research.* **24**: 52–78.

Conner, R.P. and Sparks, D.H. 2004. *Queering Creole Spiritual Traditions. Lesbian, Gay, Bisexual and Transgender Participation in African-Inspired Traditions in the Americas.* New York: Harrington Park Press.

Conniff, M.L. 1995. Afro-West Indians on the Central American isthmus: the case of Panama. In *Salvern and Beyond. The African Impact on Latin America and the Caribbean,* ed. D.J. Davis. Jaguar Books on Latin America. no. 5. Wilmington, DE: Scholarly Resources, pp. 147–72.

Cook, N.D. 1998. *Born to Die. Disease and New World conquest, 1492–1650. New Approaches to the Americas.* Cambridge: Cambridge University Press.

2002. Sickness, starvation and death in early Hispaniola. *Journal of Interdisciplinary History.* **32**: 349–86.

Cooke, G.S. and Hill, A.V.S. 2001. Genetics of susceptibility to human infectious disease. *Nature Reviews Genetics.* **2**: 967–77.

Cooper, R. and Rotimi, C. 1994. Hypertension in populations of West African origin: is there a genetic predisposition? *Journal of Hypertension.* **12**: 215–27.

Cooper, R., Rotimi, C., Ataman, S., *et al.* 1997a. The prevalence of hypertension in seven populations of West African origin. *American Journal of Public Health.* **87**: 160–8.

Cooper, R.S., Rotimi, C.N., Kaufman, J.S., *et al.* 1997b. Prevalence of NIDDM among populations of the African diaspora. *Diabetes Care.* **20**: 343–8.

Coppin, A. 2000a. Insights into the work and family lives of Afro-Caribbean men. *Reviews of Black Political Economy.* **27**: 65–86.

2000b. Does type of conjugal union matter in the labor market? Evidence from a Caribbean economy. *Reviews of Black Political Economy.* **28**: 7–27.

Corruccini, R.S., Handler, J.S., Mutaw, R., and Lange, F.W. 1982. Osteology of a slave burial population from Barbados, West Indies. *American Journal of Physical Anthropology.* **59**: 443–59.

Corruccini, R.S., Handler, J.S., and Jacobi, K.P. 1985. Chronological distribution of enamel hypoplasia and weaning in a Caribbean slave population. *Human Biology.* **57**: 699–711.

Corruccini, R.S., Jacobi, K.P., Handler, J.S., and Aufderheide A.C. 1987. Implications of tooth root hypercementosis in a Barbados slave skeletal collection. *American Journal of Physical Anthropology.* **74**: 179–84.

Corruccini, R.S., Brandon, E.M., and Handler, J.S. 1989. Inferring fertility from relative mortality in historically controlled cemetery remains from Barbados. *American Antiquity.* **54**: 609–14.

Costagliola, D., Delaunay, C., Moutet, J.P., *et al.* 1991. The prevalence of diabetes mellitus in the adult population of Guadeloupe as estimated by history or fasting hyperglycemia. *Diabetes Research and Clinical Practice.* **12**: 209–16.

Courtaud, P., Delpuech, A., and Romon, T. 1999. Archaeological investigations at colonial cemeteries on Guadelope: African slave sites or not? In *African Sites Archaeology in the Caribbean,* ed. J.B. Haviser. Princeton: Markus Wiener Publishers; Kingston: Ian Randle Publishers, pp. 277–90.

Craton, M. 1978. *Searching for the Invisible Man. Slaves and Plantation Life in Jamaica*. Cambridge, MA: Harvard University Press.

1993. What and who to whom and what: the significance of slave resistance. In *Cultivation and Culture. Labor and the Shaping of Slave Life in the Americas*, eds. I. Berlin and P.D. Morgan. Charlottesville, VA: University Press of Virginia, pp. 259–82.

1996. A recipe for the perfect Calalu: island and regional identities in the British West Indies. The 1991 Elsa Goveia memorial lecture. In *Inside Slavery. Process and Legacy in the Caribbean Experience*, ed. H. McD. Beckles. Jamaica: Canoe Press, The University of West Indies, pp. 119–40.

Crawford, M.H. 1983. The anthropological genetics of the Black Caribs (Garifuna) of Central America and the Caribbean. *Yearbook of Physical Anthropology*. **26**: 161–92.

1984. Problems and hypotheses: an introduction. In *Black Caribs, a Case Study in Biocultural Adaptation*, ed. M. Crawford. New York: Plenum Press, pp. 1–9.

1998. *The Origins of Native Americans. Evidence from Anthropological Genetics*. Cambridge: Cambridge University Press..

Crawford, M.H., Gonzalez, N.L., Schanfield M.S., *et al.* 1981. The Black Caribs (Garifuna) of Livingston, Guatemala: genetic markers and admixture estimates. *Human Biology*. **53**: 87–103.

Crawford, M.H., Dykes, D., Skradsky, K., and Polesky, H. 1984. Blood group, serum protein, and red cell enzyme polymorphisms, and admixture among the Black Caribs and Creoles of Central America and the Caribbean. In *Black Caribs. A Case Study in Biocultural Adaptation. Current Developments in Anthropological Genetics*. vol. 3, ed. M.H. Crawford. New York: Plenum Press, pp. 303–33.

Cruickshank, J.K., Jackson, S.H.D., Beevers, D.G., *et al.* 1985. Similarity of blood-pressure in blacks, whites and Asians in England: the Birmingham factory study. *Journal of Hypertension*. **3**: 365–71.

Cruickshank, J.K., Mbanya, J.C., Wilks, R., *et al.* 2001a. Hypertension in four African-origin populations: current 'Rule of Halves', quality of blood pressure control and attributable risk of cardiovascular disease. *Journal of Hypertension*. **19**: 41–6.

2001b. Sick genes, sick individuals or sick populations with chronic disease? The emergence of diabetes and high blood pressure in African-origin populations. *International Journal of Epidemiology*. **30**: 111–17.

Currat, M., Trabuchet, G., Rees, D., *et al.* 2002. Molecular analysis of the beta-globin gene cluster in the niokholo mandenka population reveals a recent origin of the beta(S) Senegal mutation. *American Journal of Human Genetics*. **70**: 207–23.

Curtin, P.D. 1955. *Two Jamaicas. The Role of Ideas in a Tropical Colony. 1830–1865*. Cambridge, MA: Harvard University Press.

1968. Epidemiology and the slave trade. *Political Science Quarterly*. **83**: 190–216.

1969. *The Atlantic Slave Trade. A Census*. Madison, WI: University of Wisconsin Press.

1988. African health at home and abroad. In *The African Exchange. Toward a Biology History of Black People*, ed. K.F. Kiple. Durham, NC: Duke University Press, pp. 110–139.

1992. The slavery hypothesis for hypertension among African Americans: the historical evidence. *American Journal of Public Health*. **82**: 1681–6.

da Fonseca, B.A.L., Nunes, S., and Fonseca, S. 2002. Dengue virus infections. *Current Opinion in Pediatrics*. **14**: 67–71.

DakerWhite, G. and Barlow, D. 1997. Heterosexual gonorrhoea at St. Thomas' – I: patient characteristics and implications for targeted STD and HIV prevention strategies. *International Journal of STD & AIDS*. **8**: 32–5.

da Silva, W.A., Bortolini, M.A., Meyer, D., *et al.* 1999. Genetic diversity of two African and sixteen South American populations determined on the basis of six hypervariable loci. *American Journal of Physical Anthropology*. **109**: 425–37.

da Veiga, P. and Carreira, A. 1979. Portuguese participation in the slave trade: opposing forces, trends of opinion with Portuguese society, effects on Portugal's socioeconomic development. In *The General History of Africa: Studies and Documents, 2*. Paris: United Nations Educational, Scientific and Cultural Organization, pp. 119–49.

Davis, P. and Fort, M. 2004. The battle against global AIDS. In *Sickness and Wealth. The Corporate Assault on Global Health*, eds. M. Fort, M.A. Mercer, and O. Gish. Cambridge, MA: South End Press, pp. 145–57.

Davis-Floyd, R. 2004. Home birth emergencies in the United States: the trouble with transport. In *Unhealthy Health Policy. A Critical Anthropological Examination*. Lanham, MD: Altamira Press, pp. 329–50.

Deans, J.A. and Cohen, S. 1983. Immunology of malaria. *Annual Review of Microbiology*. **37**: 25–49.

Delaporte, F. 1991. *The History of Yellow Fever: an Essay on the Birth of Tropical Medicine*. Cambridge, MA: MIT Press.

del Giudice, E.M., Santoro, N., Cirillo, G., *et al.* 2004. Molecular screening of the ghrelin gene in Italian obese children: the Leu72Met variant is associated with an earlier onset of obesity. *International Journal of Obesity*. **28**(3): 447–50.

DeSantis, L. 1997. Infectious/communicable diseases in the Caribbean. *Journal of Caribbean Studies. Special Issue: Health and Disease in the Caribbean*. **12**: 23–56.

Diamond, J. 1991. The saltshaker's curse. *Natural History*. **100**: 20–6.

Dillon, J.A.R., Li, H., Sealy, J, Ruben, M., the Caribbean GASP network, and Prabhakar, P. 2001. Antimicrobial susceptibility of Neisseria gonorrhoeae isolates from three Caribbean countries: Trinidad, Guyana and St. Vincent. *Sexually Transmitted Diseases*. **28**: 508–14.

Dimsdale, J. 2000. Stalked by the past: the influence of ethnicity on health. *Psychosomatic Medicine*. **62**: 161–70.

2001. No more "slavery hypothesis" yarns. *Psychosomatic Medicine*. **63**: 324–5.

Donaldson, L. 1991. *Fertility Transition*. Cambridge, MA: Basil Blackwell.

Donohoue, P.A., Tao, Y.X., Collins, M., *et al.* 2003. Deletion of codons 88–92 of the melanocortin-4 receptor gene: a novel deleterious mutation in an obese female. *Journal of Clinical Endocrinology and Metabolism*. **88**: 5841–5.

Downe, P.J. 1997. Constructing a complex of contagion: the perceptions of AIDS among working prostitutes in Costa Rica. *Social Science & Medicine.* **44**: 1575–83.

Downs, W.G. 1991. History of yellow fever in Trinidad. In *Studies on the Natural History of Yellow Fever in Trinidad,* ed. E.S. Tikasingh. Monograph Series 1. Port of Spain: CAREC, pp. 2–4.

Dragovic, B., Greaves, K., Vashisht, A., *et al.* 2002. Chlamydial co-infection among patients with gonorrhoea. *International Journal of STD & AIDS.* **13**: 261–3.

Drescher, S. 1985. Paradigms tossed: capitalism and the political sources of abolition. In *British Capitalism and Caribbean Slavery: the Legacy of Eric Williams,* eds. B.L. Solow and S.L. Engerman. Cambridge: Cambridge University Press, pp. 191–208.

Dressler, W.W. 1983. Blood pressure, relative weight, and psychosocial resources. *Psychosomatic Medicine.* **45**: 527–36.

1984a. Hypertension and culture change in the Caribbean. In *Health Care in the Caribbean and Central America, Studies in Third World Societies,* ed. F. McGlynn. Publication number 30, Department of Anthropology. Williamsburg, VA: College of William and Mary, pp. 69–93.

1984b. Hypertension and perceived stress: a St. Lucian example. *Ethos.* **12**: 265–83.

1990. Education, lifestyle and arterial blood pressure. *Journal of Psychosomatic Research.* **34**: 515–23.

1995. Modeling biocultural interactions: examples from studies of stress and cardiovascular disease. *Yearbook of Physical Anthropology.* **38**: 27–56.

1996. Hypertension in the African American community: social, cultural and psychological factors. *Seminars in Nephrology.* **16**: 71–82.

Dressler, W.W. and Bindon, J.R. 1997. Social status, social context and arterial blood pressure. *American Journal of Physical Anthropology.* **102**: 55–66.

2000. The health consequences of cultural consonance: cultural dimensions of lifestyle, social support, and arterial blood pressure in an African American community. *American Anthropologist.* **102**: 244–60.

Dressler, W.W., dos Santos, J.E., and Viteri, F.E. 1986. Blood pressure, ethnicity and psychosocial resources. *Psychosomatic Medicine.* **48**: 509–19.

Dressler, W.W., dos Santos, J.E., Gallagher, P.H. and Viteri, F.E. 1987. Arterial blood pressure and modernization in Brazil. *American Anthropologist. New Series.* **89**: 398–409.

Dressler, W.W., Grell, G.A.C., Gallagher, P.H., and Viteri, F.E. 1988. Blood pressure and social class in a Jamaican community. *American Journal of Public Health.* **78**: 714–16.

Dressler, W.W., Grell, G.A.C., and Viteri, F.E. 1995. Intracultural diversity and the sociocultural correlates of blood pressure: a Jamaican example. *Medical Anthropology Quarterly.* **9**: 291–313.

Dressler, W.W., Bindon, J.R., and Neggers, J.H. 1998. Culture, socioeconomic status, and coronary heart disease risk factors in an African American community. *Journal of Behavioral Medicine.* **21**: 527–44.

Dressler, W.W., Balieiro, M.M., and dos Santos, J.E. 1999. Culture, skin color and arterial blood pressure in Brazil. *American Journal of Human Biology.* **11**: 49–59.

Duany, J. 1994. Beyond the safety valve: recent trends in Caribbean migration. *Social and Economic Studies.* **43**: 95–122.

Duncan, Q. 1981. El negro antillano: inmigracion y presencia. In *El negro en Costa Rica*, 8th edn., eds. C. Melendez and Q. Duncan. San José, Costa Rica: Editorial Costa Rica, pp. 99–147.

Dunn, R.S. 1987. "Dreadful idlers" in the cane fields: the slave labor pattern on a Jamaican sugar estate, 1762–1831. *Journal of Interdisciplinary History.* **17**: 795–822.

1993. Sugar production and slave women in Jamaica. In *Cultivation and Culture. Labor and the Shaping of Slave Life in the Americas*, eds. I. Berlin and P.D. Morgan. Charlottesville, VA: University Press of Virginia, pp. 49–72.

Dyke, B. and Morrill, W.T. 1980. *Genealogical Demography.* New York: Academic Press.

Echeverri-Gent, E. 1992. Forgotten workers: British West Indians and the early days of the banana industry in Costa Rica and Honduras. *Journal of Latin American Studies.* **24**: 275–308.

Elizondo, J., Sáenz, G.F., Paez, C.A., and Arroyo, G. 1979. Rare hemoglobi-nopathies in Costa Rica. *Revista de Biologia Tropical.* **27**: 51–5.

Eltis, D. 1984. Mortality and voyage length in the middle passage: new evidence from the nineteenth century. *Journal of Economic History.* **44**: 301–8.

Elvin, S.J., Williamson, E.D., Scott, J.C., *et al.* 2004. Ambiguous role of CCR5 in *Y. pestis* infection. *Nature.* **430**(6998): 417.

Emmer, P. 1998. *The Dutch in the Atlantic Economy, 1580–1880: Trade, Slavery and Emancipation.* Variorum Collected Studies Series CS 614. Norfolk: Ashgate Variorum.

Endtz, H.P., van West, H., Godschalk, P.C.R., *et al.* 2003. Risk factors associated with Campylobacter jejuni infections in Curacao, Netherlands Antilles. *Journal of Clinical Microbiology.* **41**: 5588–92.

Erasmus, R.T., Blanco, E.B., Okesina, A.B., *et al.* 2001. Prevalence of diabetes mellitus and impaired glucose tolerance in factory workers from Transkei, South Africa. *South African Medical Journal.* **9**: 157–60.

Ewald, P.W. 1994. *Evolution of Infectious Disease.* New York: Oxford University Press.

Excoffier, L., Pellegrini, B., Sanchez-Mazas, A., Simon, C., and Langaney, A. 1987. Genetics and history of Sub-Saharan Africa. *Yearbook of Physical Anthropology.* **30**: 151–94.

Failde, I., Bakau, B., Costagliola, D., *et al.* 1996. Arterial hypertension in the adult population of Guadeloupe, and associated factors in subjects of African origin. *Reviste de Epidémiologie et Santé Publique.* **44**: 417–26.

Farmer, P. 1996. Social inequalities and emerging infectious diseases. *Emerging Infectious Diseases.* **2**: 259–69.

Farmer, P. and Castro, A. 2004. Pearls of the Antilles? Public health in Haiti and Cuba. In *Unhealthy Health Policy. A Critical Anthropological Examination*, eds. A. Castro and M. Singer. Walnut Creek, CA: Altamira Press, pp. 3–28.

Farooqi, I.S. and O'Rahilly, S. 2004. Monogenic human obesity syndromes. *Recent Progress in Hormone Research.* **59**: 409–24.

Faust, E.C. 1941. The distribution of malaria in North America, Mexico, Central America and the West Indies. In *A Symposium on Human Malaria with Special Reference to North America and the Caribbean Region*, ed. F. Moulton. Publication of the American Association for the Advancement of Science no. 15. American Association for the Advancement of Science, pp. 8–18.

Feldman, D.A. and Miller, J.W. 1998. *The AIDS Crisis. A Documentary History.* Westport, CT: Greenwood Press.

Ferdinand, S., Sola, C., Verdol, B., *et al.* 2003. Molecular characterization and drug resistance patterns of strains of Mycobacterium tuberculosis isolated from patients in an AIDS counseling center in Port-au-Prince, Haiti: a 1-year study. *Journal of Clinical Microbiology.* **41**: 694–702.

Fernandez-Cobo M.F., Jobes, D.V., Yanagihara, R., *et al.* 2001. Reconstructing population history using JC virus: Amerinds, Spanish, and Africans in the ancestry of modern Puerto Ricans. *Human Biology.* **73**: 385–402.

Fernandez-Esquivel, F. and Mendez-Ruiz, H.L. 1973. *El negro en la historia de la politica Costarricense.* Tesis de licenciatura, Universidad de Costa Rica.

Fisch, A., Pichard, E., Prazuck, T., *et al.* 1987. Prevalence and risk-factors of diabetes mellitus in the rural region of Mali (West-Africa): a practical approach. *Diabetologia.* **30**: 859–62.

Fleming, A.F., Akintunde, A., Attai, E.D.E., *et al.* 1985. Malaria and haemoglobin genotype in young northern Nigerian children. *Annals of Tropical Medicine and Parasitology.* **79**: 1–5.

Fletcher, A. and Maegraith, B. 1972. The metabolism of the malaria parasite and its host. In *Advances in Parasitology*, vol. 10, ed. B. Dawes. London: Academic Press, pp. 31–48.

Flint, J., Harding, R.M., Boyce, A.J., and Clegg, J.B. 1998. The population genetics of the haemoglobinopathies. *Baillieres Clinical Haematology.* **11**: 1–51.

Forrester, T., Cooper, R.S., and Weatherall, D. 1998. Emergence of Western Diseases in the tropical world: the experience with chronic cardiovascular diseases. *British Medical Bulletin.* **54**: 463–73.

Fort, M. 2004. Globalization and health. In *Sickness and Wealth. The Corporate Assault on Global Health*, eds. M. Fort, M.A. Mercer, and O. Gish. Cambridge, MA: South End Press, pp. 1–7.

Fort, M., Mercer, M.A., and Gish, O. (eds.). 2004. *Sickness and Wealth. The Corporate Assault on Global Health.* Cambridge, MA: South End Press.

Foster, C., Rotimi, C., Fraser, H., *et al.* 1993. Hypertension, diabetes and obesity in Barbados: findings from a recent population-based survey. *Ethnicity and Disease.* **3**: 404–12.

Foster J.E., Bennett, S.N., Carrington, C.V.F., Vaughan, H., and McMillan, W. O. 2004. Phylogeography and molecular evolution of dengue 2 in the Caribbean basin, 1981–2000. *Virology.* **324**: 48–59.

Franco, J.L. 1978. *The Slave Trade in the Caribbean and Latin America. The General History of Africa: Studies and Documents, 2.* Paris: UNESCO, pp. 88–100.

Franks, P.W., Knowler, W.C., Nair, S., Koska, J., *et al.* 2004. Interaction between an 11βHSD1 gene variant and birth era modifies the risk of hypertension in Pima Indians. *Hypertension.* **44**: 681–8.

Fraser, H.S. 2003. Obesity: diagnosis and prescription for action in the English-Speaking Caribbean. *Revista Panamericana de Salud Publica.* **13**: 336–40.

Friedman, G.C. 1982. The heights of slaves in Trinidad. *Social Science History.* **6**: 482–515.

Friedman, M.J. 1983. Expression of inherited resistance to malaria in culture. Malaria and the red cell. *Ciba Foundation Symposium.* **94**: 196–205.

Frisancho, A.R., Matos, J., and Flegel, P. 1983. Maternal nutritional status and adolescent pregnancy outcome. *American Journal of Clinical Nutrition.* **38**: 739–46.

Frisancho, A.R., Farrow, S., Friedenzohn, I., *et al.* 1999. Role of genetic and environmental factors in the increased blood pressures of Bolivian blacks. *American Journal of Human Biology.* **11**: 489–98.

Fulton, J.E. and Kohl, H.W. 1999. The epidemiology of obesity, physical activity, diet and type 2 diabetes mellitus. In *Lifestyle Medicine*, ed. J.M. Rippe. Malden, MA: Blackwell Science, pp. 867–83.

Gage, T.B. 2000. Demography. In *Human Biology: an Evolutionary and Biocultural Perspective*, eds. S. Stinson, B. Bogin, R. Huss-Ashmore, and D. O'Rourke. New York: Wiley-Liss, pp. 507–51.

Garcés, J.L. and Paniagua, F. 2003. *Interrupción de la transmisión de la filariasis bacrofti en al ciudad de Puerto Limón. Costa Rica.* Serie Documentos Técnicos No. 3. San José, Costa Rica: Ministerio de Salud.

Garn, S.M., Sullivan, T.V., and Ten Have, T.R. 1988. Interpreting blood pressure and "modernization" in Brazil. *American Anthropologist. New Series.* **90**: 164–5.

Garnham, P.C.C. 1988. Malaria parasites of man: life-cycles and morphology (excluding ultrastructure). In *Malaria. Principles and Practice of Malariology*, eds. W.H. Wernsdorfer and I. McGregor. New York: Churchill Livingstone, pp. 61–96.

Gaspar, D.B. 1993. Sugar cultivation and slave life in Antigua before 1800. In *Cultivation and Culture. Labor and the Shaping of Slave Life in the Americas*, eds. I. Berlin and P.D. Morgan. Charlottesville: University Press of Virginia, VA, pp. 101–23.

Gaunt, M.W., Sall, A.A., de Lamballerie, X., *et al.* 2001. Phylogenetic relationships of flaviviruses correlate with their epidemiology, disease association and biogeography. *Journal of General Virology.* **82**: 1867–76.

Gearing, J. 1992. Family planning in St. Vincent, West Indies: a population history perspective. *Social Science and Medicine.* **35**: 1273–82.

Geggus, D.P. 1985/6. Toussaint Loverture and the slaves of the Breda plantations. *Journal of Caribbean History.* **20**: 30–48.

1993. Sugar and coffee cultivation in Saint Domingue and the shaping of the slave labor force. In *Cultivation and Culture. Labor and the Shaping of Slave Life in the Americas*, ed. I. Berlin and P.D. Morgan. Charlottesville, VA: University Press of Virginia, pp. 73–98.

George, P.M., Ebanks, G.E., Nobbe, C.E., and Anwar, M. 1976. Fertility differences between the family of orientation and the family of procreation in Barbados. *International Journal of Sociology of the Family.* **6**: 57–69.

German, M. 2004. Transformation of progenitor cells to beta cells. *Forefront.* Summer/Fall: 3–6.

Giraud, M. 1999. Les migrations guadeloupéenne et martiniquaise en France métropolitaine. *Review.* **22**: 435–48.

Gish, O. 2004. The legacy of colonial medicine. In *Sickness and Wealth. The Corporate Assault on Global Health*, eds. M. Fort, M.A. Mercer, and O. Gish. Cambridge, MA: South End Press, pp. 19–26.

Glaser, K. 1999. Consensual unions in two Costa Rican communities: an analysis using focus group methodology. *Journal of Comparative Family Studies.* **30**: 57–79.

Goncalvez, A.P., Escalante, A.A., Pujol, F.H., *et al.* 2002. Diversity and evolution of the envelope gene of dengue virus type 1. *Virology.* **303**: 110–19.

Gonzales, N.L. 1984. Rethinking the consanguineal household and matrifocality. *Ethnology.* **23**: 1–12.

Goodenough, U. 1991. Deception by pathogens. *American Scientist.* **79**: 344–55.

Goodman, A.H., Martin, D.L., Armelagos, G.J., and Clark, G. 1984. Indications of stress from bone and teeth. In *Paleopathology at the Origins of Agriculture*, eds. M.N. Cohen and G.J. Armelagos. New York: Academic Press, pp. 13–49.

Granados, J. and Estrada, L. 1967. *Reseña historica de Limón*. San José, Costa Rica: Asamblea Legislativa.

Gray, R.H. 1999. The changing face of paediatrics in the English-speaking Caribbean. *West Indian Medical Journal.* **48**: 106–9.

Greene, L.S. and Danubio, M.E. 1997. *Adaptation to Malaria: the Interaction of Biology and Culture.* Amsterdam: Gordon and Breach Publishers.

Grim, C.E. and Robinson, M. 1996. Blood pressure variation in Blacks: genetic factors. *Seminars in Nephrology.* **16**: 83–93.

2003. Commentary: salt, slavery and survival. Hypertension in the African diaspora. *Epidemiology.* **14**: 120–2.

Groer, M. 2001. Hypertension. In *Advanced Pathophysiology: Application to Clinical Practice*, ed. M. Groer. Philadelphia: Lippincott, pp. 285–301.

Grosfoguel, R. 2001. "Cultural racism" and "borders of exclusion" in the capitalist world-economy: colonial Caribbean migrants in core zones. *Proto Sociology.* **15**: 274–96.

Gudmundson, L. 1977. *Mestizaje y la poblacion de procedencia Africana en la Costa Rica colonial.* Programa Centroamericano de Ciencias Sociales. Seminario Centroamericano de Historia Economica y Social. San José, Costa Rica: Ciudad Universitaria Rodrigo Facio.

Gulliford, M.C. 1996. Epidemiological transition in Trinidad and Tobago, West Indies 1953–1992. *International Journal of Epidemiology.* **25**: 357–65.

Gulliford, M.C. and Mahabir, D. 1999. A five year evaluation of intervention in diabetes care in Trinidad and Tobago. *Diabetic Medicine.* **16**: 939–45.

Gulliford, M.C., Mahabir, D., and Rocke, B. 2004. Socioeconomic inequality in blood pressure and its determinants: cross-sectional data from Trinidad and Tobago. *Journal of Human Hypertension.* **18**: 61–70.

Gusmão, L., Sanchez-Diz, P., Alves, C., *et al.* 2003. Results of the GEP-ISFG collaborative study on the Y chromosome STRs GATA A10, GATA C4, GATA H4, DYS437, DYS438, DYS439, DYS460 and DYS461: population data. *Forensic Science International.* **135**: 150–7.

Guzmán, M.G. and Kourí, G. 2002. Dengue: an update. *Lancet Infectious Diseases.* **2**: 33–42.

Hadinegoro, S.R., Purwanto, S.H., and Chatab, F. 1999. *Dengue Shock Syndrome: Clinical Manifestations, Management and Outcome.* Dengue Bulletin, vol. 23, December 1999. http://www.whosea.org/en/Section10/Section332/Section521_2461.htm

Hadley, T.J., Klotz, F.W., and Miller, L.H. 1986. Invasion of erythrocytes by malaria parasites: a cellular and molecular overview. *Annual Review of Microbiology.* **40**: 451–77.

Halberstein, R.A. 1980. Population regulation in an island community. *Human Biology.* **52**: 479–98.

1999. Blood pressure in the Caribbean. *Human Biology.* **71**: 659–84.

Halberstein, R.A. and Davies, J.E. 1984. Biosocial aspects of high blood pressure in people of the Bahamas. *Human Biology.* **56**: 317–28.

Halberstein, R.A., Davies, J.E., and Mack., A.K. 1981. Hemoglobin variations on a small Bahamian island. *American Journal of Physical Anthropology.* **55**: 217–21.

Haldane, J.B.S. 1949. Disease and evolution. *La Ricerca Scientifica. Supplemento.* **19**: 3–11.

Hales C., and Barker D. 1992. Type-2 (non-insulin-dependent) diabetes mellitus: the thrifty phenotype hypothesis. *Diabetologia.* **35**: 595–601.

2001. The thrifty phenotype hypothesis. *British Medical Bulletin.* **60**: 5–20.

Hales C., Desai, M., and Ozanne, S. 1997. The thrifty phenotype hypothesis: how does it look after 5 years? *Diabetic Medicine.* **14**: 189–95.

Hall, D.G. 1996. People in slavery. The 1985 Elsa Goveia memorial lecture. In *Inside Slavery. Process and Legacy in the Caribbean Experience*, ed. H.McD. Beckles. Jamaica: Canoe Press, University of West Indies, pp. 12–30.

Hall, J.E. 2003. The kidney, hypertension and obesity. Novartis lecture. *Hypertension.* **41** (part 2): 625–33.

Hall, N.A. and Higman, B.W. 1992. *Slave Society in the Danish West Indies. St. Thomas, St. John and St. Croix.* Mona, Cave Hill and St. Augustine: University of the West Indies Press.

Handler, J.S. 2002. Plantation slave settlements in Barbados, 1650s to 1834. In *In the Shadow of the Plantation. Caribbean History and Legacy. In Honour of Professor Emeritus Woodville K. Marshall*, ed. A.O. Thompson. Kingston: Ian Randle Publishers, pp. 123–61.

Handler, J.S. and Corruccini, R.S. 1983. Plantation slave life in Barbados: a physical anthropological analysis. *Journal of Interdisciplinary History.* **14**: 65–90.

1986. Weaning among West Indian slaves: historical and bioanthropological evidence from Barbados. *William and Mary Quarterly*. **43**: 111–17.

Handler, J.S., Corruccini, R.S., and Mutaw, R.J. 1982. Tooth mutilation in the Caribbean: evidence from a slave burial population in Barbados. *Journal of Human Evolution*. **11**: 297–313.

Handler J.S., Aufderheide, A.C., Corruccini, R.S., Brandon, E.M., and Wittmers, L.E. 1988. Lead contact and poisoning in Barbados slaves: historical, chemical and biological evidence. In *The African Exchange. Towards a Biological History of Black People*, ed. K.F. Kiple. Durham, NC: Duke University Press, pp. 140–66.

Handwerker, P. (ed.). 1986. *Culture and Reproduction. An Anthropological Critique of Demographic Transition Theory*. Boulder, CO: Westview Press.

Handwerker, P. 1992. West Indian gender relations, family planning programs and fertility decline. *Social Science and Medicine*. **35**: 1245–57.

Harewood, J. 1976. *Caribbean Demography Workbook*. Institute of Social and Economic Research. St. Augustine, Trinidad: University of the West Indies.

1984. *Mating and Fertility: Results from Three WFS Surveys in Guyana, Jamaica and Trinidad and Tobago*. WFS Scientific Reports no. 67. Voorburg, The Netherlands: International Statistical Institute.

Harpelle, R.N. 1993. The social and political integration of West Indians in Costa Rica: 1930–50. *Journal of Latin American Studies*. **25**: 103–20.

2000. Bananas and business: West Indians and United Fruit in Costa Rica. *Race and Class*. **42**: 57–72.

Harrison, G.A. and Boyce, A.J. 1972. *The Structure of Human Populations*. Oxford: Clarendon Press.

Hart, R. 2001. Diabetes. In *Advanced Pathophysiology: Application to Clinical Practice*, ed. M.W. Groer. Philadelphia: Lippincott, pp. 204–29.

Hartl, D. 1988. *A Primer of Population Genetics*, 2nd edn. Sunderland, MA: Sinauer Associates.

Headley, A., and Sandino, N. 1983. *Algunas characterísticas de la familia negra en la ciudad de Limón basada en una comparación con la familia blanca*. Tesis de licenciatura, Universidad de Costa Rica.

Hebbel, R.P. 2003. Sickle hemoglobin instability: a mechanism for malarial protection. *Redox Report*. **8**: 238–40.

Henriques, F. 1953. *Family and Colour in Jamaica*. London: Eyere & Spottiswoode.

Heraud, J.M., Hommel, D., and Hulin, A. 1999. First case of yellow fever in French Guiana since 1902. *Emerging Infectious Diseases*. **5**: 429–32.

Herring, D.A. and Swedlund, A.C. (eds.). 2003. *Human Biologists in the Archives: Demography, Health, Nutrition and Genetics in Historical Populations*. Cambridge: Cambridge University Press.

Herzfeld, A. 1995. Language and identity: Limonense Creole and the black minority of Costa Rica. *Explorations in Ethnic Studies*. **18**: 77–95.

2002. *Mekaytelyuw. La lengua criolla*. San José, Costa Rica: Editorial de la Universidad de Costa Rica.

Higgs, D.R., Pressley L., Serjeant, G.R., Clegg, J.B., and Weatherall, D.J. 1981. The genetics and molecular basis of alpha thalassaemia in association with Hb S in Jamaican Negroes. *British Journal of Haematology*. **47**: 43–56.

Higman, B.W. 1975. The slave family and household in the British West Indies, 1800–1834. *Journal of Interdisciplinary History*. **6**: 261–87.

1984. Slave populations of the British Caribbean 1807–1834. Baltimore, MD: Johns Hopkins University Press.

Hill, A.V.S. 1992. Malaria resistance genes: a natural selection. *Transactions of the Royal Society of Tropical Medicine and Hygiene*. **86**: 225–6.

1996. Some attempts at measuring natural selection by malaria. In *Molecular Biology and Human Diversity*, eds. A.J. Boyce and C.G.N. Mascie-Taylor. Society for the Study of Human biology, Symposium 38. Cambridge: Cambridge University Press, pp. 81–92.

2001. Immunogenetics and genomics. *Lancet*. **357**: 2037–41.

Himmelgreen, D.A., Pérez-Escamilla, R., Segura-Millan, S., *et al*. 2000. Food insecurity among low-income Hispanics in Hartford, Connecticut: Implications for public health policy. *Human Organization*. **59**: 334–42.

Himmelgreen, D.A., Pérez-Escamilla, R., Martinez, D., *et al*. 2004. The longer you stay, the bigger you get: Length of time and language use in the U.S. are associated with obesity in Puerto Rican women. *American Journal of Physical Anthropology*. **125**: 90–6.

Ho, C.G.T. 1999. Caribbean transnationalism as a gendered process. *Latin American Perspectives*. **26**: 34–54.

Hobcraft, J. 1985. Family-building patterns. In *Reproductive Change in Developing Countries. Insights from the World Fertility Survey*, eds. J. Cleland and J. Hobcraft. New York: Oxford University Press, pp. 64–86.

Hoff, C., Thorneycroft, I., Wilson, F., and Williams-Murphy, M. 2001. Protection afforded by sickle-cell trait (Hb AS): what happens when malarial selection pressures are alleviated? *Human Biology*. **73**: 583–6.

Holder, Y. and Lewis, M.J. 1997. *Health Conditions in the Caribbean*. Washington, D.C.: Pan American Health Organization, Pan American Sanitary Bureau.

Holtz, T. and Kachur, S.P. 2004. The reglobalization of malaria. In *Sickness and Wealth. The Corporate Assault on Global Health*, eds. M. Fort, M.A. Mercer, and O. Gish. Cambridge, MA: South End Press, pp. 131–43.

Hoosen, S., Seedat, Y.K., Bhigjee, A.I., and Neerahoo, R.M. 1985. A study of urinary sodium and potassium excretion rates among urban and rural Zulus and Indians. *Journal of Hypertension*. **3**: 351–8.

Hutchinson, S.E., Powell, C.A., Walker, S.P., Chang, S.M., and Grantham-McGregor, S.M. 1997. Nutrition, anaemia, geohelminth infection and school achievement in rural Jamaican primary school children. *European Journal of Clinical Nutrition*. **51**: 729–35.

Hutchinson-Miller, C. 2002. *In Memory of My Ancestors: Contributions of Afro-Jamaican Female Migrants in Port Limón, Costa Rica. 1872–1890*. Centre for Gender and Development Studies, Working Paper Series (Cave Hill Campus). Mona, Barbados: University of the West Indies.

Hyam, R. 1990. *Empire and Sexuality. The British Experience.* Studies in Imperialism. New York: Manchester University Press.

Iseman, M.D. 1995. Evolution of drug-resistant tuberculosis: a tale of two species. In *Infectious Diseases in an Age of Change. The Impact of Human Ecology and Behavior on Disease Transmission,* ed. B. Roizman. Washington, D.C.: National Academy of Sciences, pp. 135–40.

Itzigsohn, J. 1995. Migrant remittances, labor markets, and household strategies: a comparative analysis of low-income household strategies in the Caribbean basin. *Social Forces.* **74**: 633–55.

Jackson, F.L.C. 1991. An evolutionary perspective on salt, hypertension, and human genetic variability. *Hypertension.* **17** (suppl. I): I129–32.

1993a. Evolutionary and political economic influences on biological diversity in African Americans. *Journal of Black Studies.* **23**: 539–60.

1993b. The bioanthropological context of disease. *American Journal of Kidney Diseases.* **21** (suppl. 1): 10–14.

2000. Human adaptations to infectious disease. In *Human Biology: an Evolutionary and Biocultural Perspective,* eds. S. Stinson, B. Bogin, R. Huss-Ashmore, and D. O'Rourke. New York: Wiley-Liss, pp. 273–93.

Jacobi, K.P., Cook, D.C., Corruccini, R.S., and Handler, J.S. 1992. Congenitalsyphilis in the past-slaves at Newton plantation, Barbados, West-Indies. *American Journal of Physical Anthropology.* **89**: 145–58.

JAPDEVA. 1999. *Limón hacia el siglo XXI. Potencialidades y oportunidades para el desarrollo humano. Documento I. Conceptualización y diagnóstico.* Plan de Desarrollo Regional Provincia de Limón. San José, Costa Rica: Imprenta Nacional.

Jaramillo-Correa, J.P., Keyeux, G., Ruiz-Garcia, M., Rodas, C., and Bernal, J. 2001. Population genetic analysis of the genes APOE, APOB (3'VNTR) and ACE in some black and Amerindian communities from Colombia. 2001. *Human Heredity.* **52**: 14–33.

Jimenez-Arce, G. 2000. *Variacion del cromosoma Y en la poblacion afrocostarricense de Limón, Costa Rica.* Tesis de Licenciatura en biologia, Universidad de Costa Rica.

Johnson B.C. and Remington, R.D. 1961. A sampling study of blood pressure levels in White and Negro residents of Nassau, Bahamas. *Journal of Chronic Diseases.* **13**: 39–51.

Johnston, F.E. and Little, M.A. 2000. History of human biology in the United States of America. In *Human Biology: an Evolutionary and Biocultural Perspective,* eds. S. Stinson, B. Bogin, R. Huss-Ashmore, and D. O'Rourke. New York: Wiley-Liss, pp. 27–46.

Jones, C.P. 2001. Invited commentary: "Race," racism, and the practice of epidemiology. *American Journal of Epidemiology.* **154**: 299–304.

Käferstein, F. 2003. Foodborne diseases in developing countries: aetiology, epidemiology and strategies for prevention. *International Journal of Environmental Health Research.* **13**: S161–8.

Kaplan, J.B. and Bennett, T. 2003. Use of race and ethnicity in biomedical publication. *Journal of the American Medical Association.* **289**: 2709–16.

Kaplan, N. 2001. *Treatment of Hypertension in General Practice*. London: Martin Dunitz. www.netLibrary.com/urlapi.asp?action=summary&v=1& bookid=92472.

Kaufman, J.S. 1999. How inconsistencies in racial classification demystify the race construct in public health statistics. *Epidemiology*. **10**: 101–3.

Kaufman, J.S. and Cooper, R.S. 2001. Commentary: considerations for use of racial/ethnic classification in etiologic research. *American Journal of Epidemiology*. **154**: 291–8.

Kaufman, J.S. and Hall, S.A. 2003a. The slavery hypertension hypothesis: dissemination and appeal of a modern race theory. *Epidemiology*. **14**: 111–18.

2003b. The slavery hypertension hypothesis: the authors respond. *Epidemiology*. **14**: 124–6.

Kéclard, L., Ollendor, V., Berchel, C., Loret, H., and Mérault, G. 1996. $\beta^S$ haplotypes, $\alpha$-globin gene status, and hematological data of sickle cell disease patients in Guadelupe (F.W.I.) *Hemoglobin*. **20**: 63–74.

Kéclard, L., Romana, M., Lavocat, E., *et al.* 1997. Sickle cell disorder, $\beta$-globin gene cluster haplotypes and $\alpha$-thalassemia in neonates and adults from Guadeloupe. *American Journal of Hematology*. **55**: 24–7.

Kenney, E. and Madrigal, L. 2004. Obesity in East-Indian and African derived groups in Costa Rica. *American Journal of Physical Anthropology*. Suppl. 38: 124.

Kertzer, D.I. and Fricke, T. 1997a. Toward an anthropological demography. In *Anthropological Demography. Towards a New Synthesis*, eds. D.I. Kertzer and T. Fricke. Chicago: University of Chicago Press, pp. 1–35.

Kertzer, D.I. and Fricke, T. (eds.). 1997b. *Anthropological Demography. Towards a New Synthesis*. Chicago: University of Chicago Press.

Khaw, K. and Rose, G. 1982. Population study of blood pressure and associated factors in St. Lucia, West Indies. *International Journal of Epidemiology*. **11**: 372–7.

Khudabux, M.R. 1999. Effects of life conditions on the health of a Negro slave community in Suriname. In *African Sites Archaeology in the Caribbean*, ed. J.B. Haviser. Princeton: Markus Wiener Publishers; Kingston: Ian Randle Publishers, pp. 291–313.

King, H. and Rewers, M. 1993. Global estimates for prevalence of diabetes mellitus and impaired glucose tolerance in adults. *Diabetes Care*. **16**: 157–77.

King, H. and Roglic, G. 1999. Diabetes and the "thrifty genotype": commentary. *World Health Organization*. **77**: 692–3.

Kiple, K.F. 1985. Cholera and race in the Caribbean. *Journal of Latin America Studies*. **17**: 157–77.

1988. A survey of recent literature on the biological past of the black. In *The African Exchange. Toward a Biology History of Black people*, ed. K.F. Kiple. Durham, NC: Duke University Press, pp. 74–8.

2001. Response to Sheldon Watts, "yellow fever immunities in West Africa and the Americas in the age of slavery and beyond: a reappraisal". *Journal of Social History*. **34**: 969–74.

Kiple, K.F. and Ornelas, K.C. 1996. After the encounter. Disease and demographics in the Lesser Antilles. In *The Lesser Antilles in the Age of European Expansion*, eds. R.L. Paquette and S.L. Engerman. Gainesville, FL: University Press of Florida, pp. 50–67.

Klein, H.S. 1978. *The Middle Passage. Comparative Studies in the Atlantic Slave Trade*. Princeton, NJ: Princeton University Press.

1986. *African Slavery in Latin America and the Caribbean*. New York: Oxford University Press.

Klemba, M., Gluzman, I., and Goldberg, D.E. 2004. A *Plasmodium falciparum* dipeptidyl aminopeptidase I participates in vacuolar hemoglobin degradation. *Journal of Biological Chemistry*. **279**: 43000–7.

Knight, F.W. 1991. Slavery and lagging capitalism in the Spanish and Portuguese American empires, 1492–1713. In *Slavery and the Rise of the Atlantic System*, ed. B.L. Solow. Cambridge: Cambridge University Press, pp. 62–74.

1997. *General History of the Caribbean. Volume III. The Slave Societies of the Caribbean*. London: UNESCO Publishing.

Koch, C. 1975. *Ethnicity and Livelihoods: a Social Geography of Costa Rica's Atlantic Zone*. Ph.D. dissertation, University of Kansas.

1977. Jamaican blacks and their descendants in Costa Rica. *Social and Economic Studies*. **26**: 339–61.

Krieger, N. 2000. Epidemiology, racism, and health: the case of low birth weight. *Epidemiology*. **11**: 237–9.

Krumeich, A., Weijts, W., Reddy, P., and Meijer-Weitz, A. 2001. The benefits of anthropological approaches for health promotion research and practice. *Health Education Research. Theory and Practice*. **16**: 121–30.

Kum, H. and Ruiz, H. 1939. A malaria survey of the republic of Costa Rica, Central America. *American Journal of Tropical Medicine*. **19**: 425–46.

Kurane, I. and Takasaki, T. 2001. Dengue fever and dengue haemorrhagic fever: challenges of controlling an enemy still at large. *Reviews in Medical Virology*. **11**: 301–11.

Kuzawa, C. 1998. Adipose tissue in human infancy and childhood: an evolutionary perspective. *Yearbook of Physical Anthropology*. **41**: 177–209.

Lalueza-Fox, C., Calderon, F.L., Calafell, F., Morera, B., and Bertranpetit, J. 2001. MtDNA from extinct Tainos and the peopling of the Caribbean. *Annals of Human Genetics*. **65** (part 2): 137–51.

Lalueza-Fox, C., Gilbert, M.T.P., Martinez-Fuentes, A.J., Calafell, F., and Bertranpetit, J. 2003. Mitochondrial DNA from pre-Columbian Ciboneys from Cuba and the prehistoric colonization of the Caribbean. *American Journal of Physical Anthropology*. **121**: 97–108.

Langford, H.G., Watson, R.L., and Douglas, B.H. 1968. Factors affecting blood pressure in population groups. *Transactions of the Association of American Physicians*. **81**: 135–46.

Lauzardo, M. and Ashkin, D, 2000. Physiology at the dawn of the new century: a review of tuberculosis and the prospects for its elimination. *Chest*. **117**: 1455–73.

Lawless, R. 1991. Haitians, AIDS, anthropology and the popular media. *Florida Journal of Anthropology*. Special Publication. **16**(7): 1–7.

Leal, E.D.S., Holmes, E.C., and Zanotto, P.M.D.A. 2004. Distinct patterns of natural selection in the reverse transcriptase gene of HIV-1 in the presence and absence of antiretroviral therapy. *Virology*. **325**: 181–91.

Lee, K., Buse, K., and Futukian, S. (eds.). 2002. *Health Policy in a Globalizing World*. Cambridge: Cambridge University Press..

Lee, K., Futukian, S., and Buse, K. 2002. An introduction to global health policy. In *Health Policy in a Globalizing World*, eds. K. Lee, K. Buse, and S. Futukian, Cambridge: Cambridge University Press, pp. 3–17.

Lee, M.G., Barrow, K.O., and Edwards, C.N. 2001. Helicobacter pylori infection in the Caribbean: update in management. *West Indian Medical Journal*. **50**: 8–10.

Lefever, H.G. 1992. *Turtle Bogue: Afro-Caribbean Life and Culture in a Costa Rican Village*. Pennsylvania: Susquehanna University Press.

Le Franc, E.R.-M. 1990. *Health Status and Health Services Utilization in the English-Speaking Caribbean*, vol. II, a project financed and supported by WHO/PAHO/Caricom secretariat and executed by the Institute of Social and Economic Research. Mona: University of the West Indies.

Legrand, E., Goh, K.S., Sola, C., and Rastogi, N. 2000. Description of a novel *Mycobacterium simiae* allelic variant isolated from Caribbean AIDS patients by PCR-restriction enzyme analysis and sequencing of Hsp65 gene. *Molecular and Cellular Probes*. **14**: 355–63.

Lepiniec, L., Dalgarno, L., and Huong, V.T.Q. 1994. Geographic-distribution and evolution of yellow-fever viruses based on direct sequencing of genomic cDNA fragments. *Journal of General Virology*. **75**: 417–23.

Levine, M.M. and Levine O.S. 1995. Changes in human ecology and behavior in relation to the emergence of diarrheal diseases, including cholera. In *Infectious Diseases in an Age of Change. The Impact of Human Ecology and Behavior on Disease Transmission*, ed. R. Roizman. Washington, D.C.: National Academy Press, pp. 31–42.

Lev-Ran, A. 1999. Thrifty genotype: how applicable is it to obesity and type 2 diabetes? *Diabetes Reviews*. **7**: 1–22.

Lewis, M.J. 1991. Yellow fever activity in Trinidad: an historical review, 1620–1978. In *Studies on the Natural History of Yellow Fever in Trinidad*, ed. E.S. Tikasingh Monograph Series 1. Port of Spain: CAREC, pp. 6–13.

Lewis, M.J., Gayle, C., Piggott, W., and Saint-Victor, R. 1997. Acquired immunodeficiency syndrome and human immunodeficiency virus infections in the Caribbean, 1982–1994. In *Health Conditions in the Caribbean*. Scientific publication no. 561. Pan American World Health Organization. Pan American Sanitary Bureau, Regional Office of the World Health Organization, pp. 265–87.

Libert, F., Cochaux, P., Beckman, G., *et al.* 1998. The Delta ccr5 mutation conferring protection against HIV-1 in Caucasian populations has a single and recent origin in Northeastern Europe. *Human Molecular Genetics*. **7**: 399–406.

Lieberman, L.S. 2003. Dietary, evolutionary, and modernizing influences on the prevalence of Type-2 diabetes. *Annual Review of Nutrition*. **23**: 345–77.

Lieberson, S. and Waters, M.C. 1989. The location of ethnic and racial groups in the United States. In *Demography as an Interdiscipline*, ed. J.M. Stycos. New Brunswick, NJ: Transaction Publishers, pp. 162–92.

Lifton, R.P. 1996. Molecular genetics of human blood pressure variation. *Science.* **272**: 676–80.

1997. Molecular genetics of human blood pressure variation. *FASEB Journal.* **11** (Suppl. S): 916.

Lightbourne, R.E. 1984. *Fertility Preferences in Guyana, Jamaica and Trinidad and Tobago, from World Fertility Survey, 1975–77: a Multiple Indicator Approach.* WFS Scientific Report no. 68. Voorburg, The Netherlands: International Statistical Institute.

Lin, S.S. and Kelsey, J.L. 2000. Use of race and ethnicity in epidemiologic research: concepts, methodological issues, and suggestions for research. *Epidemiologic Reviews.* **22**: 187–202.

Lindgren, C.M. and Hirschhorn, J.N. 2001. The genetics of type 2 diabetes. *The Endocrinologist.* **11**: 178–87.

Lindo, J.F., Validum, L., Ager, A.L., *et al.* 2002. Intestinal parasites among young children in the interior of Guyana. *West Indian Medical Journal.* **51**: 25–7.

Lisker, R. 1983. Distribution of abnormal hemoglobins in Latin America. In *Distribution and Evolution of Hemoglobin and Globin Loci*, ed. J.E. Bowman. Proceedings of the Fourth Annual Comprehensive Sickle Cell Center Symposium on the Distribution and Evolution of Hemoglobin and Globin Loci, University of Chicago, Chicago, IL, USA, October 10–12, pp. 261–80.

Livingstone, F.B. 1957. Sickling and malaria. *British Medical Journal.* **1**: 762–3.

1958. Anthropological implications of sickle cell gene distribution in West Africa. *American Anthropologist.* **60**: 533–62.

1971. Malaria and human polymorphisms. *Annual Review of Genetics.* **5**: 33–64.

1976. Hemoglobin history in East Africa. *Human Biology.* **48**: 487–500.

1989a. Simulation of the diffusion of the β-globin variants in the Old World. *Human Biology.* **61**: 297–309.

1989b. Who gave whom hemoglobin S: the use of restriction site haplotype variation for the interpretation of the evolution of the $\beta^S$–globin gene. *American Journal of Human Biology.* **1**: 289–302.

Lobo-Wiehoff, T. and Meléndez-Obando, M. 1997. *Negros y blancos. Todo mezclado.* San José, Costa Rica: Editorial de la Universidad de Costa Rica.

Long, J. 1991. The genetic structure of admixed populations. *Genetics.* **127**: 417–26.

Luján, E. 1962–3. La abolicion de la esclavitud en Costa Rica. *Anales de la Academia de Geografia e Historia de Costa Rica.* 68–74.

Luke, A., Cooper, R., Prewitt, T., Adeyemo, A., and Forrester, T. 2001. Nutritional consequences of the African diaspora. *Annual Review of Nutrition.* **21**: 47–71.

Lynch J. 2001. Socioeconomic factors in the behavioral and psychosocial epidemiology of cardiovascular disease. In *Integrating Behavioral and Social Sciences with Public Health*, eds. N. Schneiderman, M.A. Speers, J.M. Silva, H. Tomes, and J.H. Gentry. Washington, D.C.: American Psychological Association, pp. 51–71.

Madrigal, L. 1988. *Hemoglobin Genotype and Fertility in a Malarial Environment: Limón, Costa Rica*. Ph.D. dissertation, Department of Anthropology, University of Kansas.
  1989. Hemoglobin genotype, fertility and the malaria hypothesis. *Human Biology*. **61**: 311–25.
  1991. The reliability of recalled estimates of menarcheal age in a sample of older women. *American Journal of Human Biology*. **3**:105–10.
  1994. Mortality seasonality in Escazú, Costa Rica: 1851–1921. *Human Biology*. **66**: 433–52.
  1999/2000. *Statistics for Anthropology*. Cambridge: Cambridge University Press.

Madrigal, L., Sáenz, G., and Chavez, M. 1990. Deficiencia de la dehidrogenasa de la glucosa-6-fosfato: su frequencia en individuos Hb AS y Hb AA de la poblacion negra de Limón (letter). *Sangre*. **35**: 413–4.

Madrigal, L., Ware, B., Miller, R., Sáenz, G., Chavez, M., and Dykes, D. 2001a. Ethnicity, gene flow and population subdivision in Limón, Costa Rica. *American Journal of Physical Anthropology*. **114**: 99–108.

Madrigal, L., Sáenz, G., Chavez, N., and Dykes, D. 2001b. The frequency of twinning in two Costa Rican ethnic groups: an update. *American Journal of Human Biology*. **13**: 220–6.

Madrigal, L., Otárola, F., Bell, M., and Ruiz, E. 2004. The Culís of Costa Rica: An initial health assessment of an East-Indian-derived group in Costa Rica. *American Journal of Physical Anthropology*. Suppl. **38**: 140.

Mairuhu, A.T.A., Wagenaar, J., Brandjes, D.P.M., and van Gorp, E.C.M. 2004. Dengue: an arthropod-borne disease of global importance. *European Journal of Clinical Microbiology & Infectious Diseases*. **23**: 425–33.

Malaria Action Programme (WHO). 1987. World malaria situation: 1985. *World Health Statistics Quarterly*. **40**: 142–64.

Manderson, L. 1998. Applying medical anthropology in the control of infectious disease. *Tropical Medicine and International Health*. **3**: 1020–7.

Marieb, E. 2004. *Human Anatomy & Physiology*, 6th edn. Redwood City, CA: Benjamin Cummings.

Markovic, I. and Clouse, K.A. 2004. Recent advances in understanding the molecular mechanisms of HIV-1 entry and fusion: revisiting current targets and considering new options for therapeutic intervention. *Current HIV Research*. **2**: 223–34.

Martínez-Cruzado, J.C., Toro-Labrador, G., Ho-Fung, V., *et al.* 2001. Mitochondrial DNA analysis reveals substantial native American ancestry in Puerto Rico. *Human Biology*. **73**: 491–511.

Martinez-Labarga, C., Rickards, O., Scacchi, R., *et al.* 1999. Genetic population structure of two African-Ecuadorian communities of Esmeraldas. *American Journal of Physical Anthropology*. **109**: 159–74.

Mascie-Taylor, C.G.N. 1996. The relationship between disease and subfecundity. In *Variability in Human Fertility*, eds. L. Rosetta and C.G.N. Mascie-Taylor. Cambridge Studies in Biological Anthropology. Cambridge: Cambridge University Press, pp. 106–22.

Matthews, D.B. 1953. *Crisis of the West Indian Family. A Sample Study.* Westport, CT: Greenwood Press.

Mbanya, J.C.N., Cruickshank, J.K., Forrester, T., *et al.* 1999. Standardized comparison of glucose intolerance in West African-origin populations of rural and urban Cameroon, Jamaica, and Caribbean migrants to Britain. *Diabetes Care.* **22**: 434–40.

McDermott, R. 1998. Ethics, epidemiology and the thrifty gene: biological determinism as a health hazard. *Social Science and Medicine.* **47**: 1189–95.

McGowan, W. 2002. The origins of slave rebellions in the Middle Passage. *In the Shadow of the Plantation. Caribbean History and Legacy. In Honour of Professor Emeritus Woodville K. Marshall*, ed. A. O. Thompson. Kingston: Ian Randle Publishers, pp. 74–99.

McGranahan, G., Lewin, S., Fransen, T., *et al.* 1999. Environmental change and human health in countries of Africa, the Caribbean and the Pacific. *Global Change and Human Health.* **1**: 7.

McGregor, I. 1983. Current concepts concerning Man's resistance to infection with malaria. *Bulletin De la Societe de Pathologie Exotique.* **76**: 433–45.

McIlwaine, C. 1997. Vulnerable or poor? A study of ethnic and gender disadvantage among Afro-Caribbeans in Limón, Costa Rica. *European Journal of Development Research.* **9**: 35–61.

McLarty, D.G., Kitange, H.M., Mtinangi, B.L., *et al.* 1989. Prevalence of diabetes and impaired glucose tolerance in rural Tanzania. *Lancet.* April: 871–5.

McMurray, C. and Smith, R. 2001. *Diseases of Globalization. Socioeconomic Transitions and Health.* London: Earthscan Publications.

McQueen, P.G. and McKenzie, F.E. 2004. Age-structured red blood cell susceptibility and the dynamics of malaria infections. *Proceedings of the National Academy of Sciences of the United States of America.* **101**: 9161–6.

Mecsas, J., Franklin, G., Kuziel, W.A., *et al.* 2004. CCR5 mutation and plague protection. *Nature.* **427**: 606.

Melendez, C. 1981. Aspectos sobre la inmigracion Jamaicana. In *El Negro en Costa Rica*, 8th edn, eds. C. Melendez and Q. Duncan. San José, Costa Rica: Editorial Costa Rica, pp. 59–93.

Menken, J. 1989. Proximate determinants of fertility and mortality: a review of recent findings. In *Demography as an Interdiscipline*, ed. J.M. Stycos. New Brunswick, NJ: Transaction Publishers, pp. 79–99.

Mennen, L.I., Jackson, M., Sharma, S., *et al.* 2001. Habitual diet in four populations of African origin: a descriptive paper on nutrient intakes in rural and urban Cameroon, Jamaica and Caribbean migrants in Britain. *Public Health Nutrition.* **4**: 765–72.

Mennerick, L. 1964. *A Study of Puerto Limón, Costa Rica.* San José, Cost Rica: Associated Colleges of the Midwest Central American Field Program.

Merbs, C.F. 1992. A new world of infectious disease. *Yearbook of Physical Anthropology.* **35**: 3–42.

Miall, W.E., Kass, E.H., Ling, J., and Stuart, K.L. 1962. Factors influencing arterial pressure in the general population in Jamaica. *British Medical Journal.* **5303**: 497–506.

Micklin, M. 1994. Population policies in the Caribbean: present status and emerging issues. *Social and Economic Studies.* **43**: 1–32.

Miller, J.C. 1981. Mortality in the Atlantic slave trade: statistical evidence on causality. *Journal of Interdisciplinary History.* **11**: 385–423.

Miller, L.H. 1995. Impact of malaria on genetic polymorphism and genetic diseases in Africans and African Americans. In *Infectious Diseases in an Age of Change. The Impact of Human Ecology and Behavior on Disease Transmission*, ed. B. Roizman. Washington, D.C.: National Academy of Sciences, pp. 99–111.

Mobasher, M.M. and Sadri, M. 2004. *Migration, Globalization and Ethnic Relations. An Interdisciplinary Approach.* Upper Saddle River, NJ: Pearson/ Prentice Hall.

Mohammed, P. and Perkins, A. 1999. *Caribbean Women at the Crossroads. The Paradox of Motherhood among Women of Barbados, St. Lucia and Dominica*, research project report, Center for Gender and Development Studies, University of the West Indies. Kingston: Canoe Press.

Moitt, B. 2001. *Women and Slavery in the French Antilles, 1635–1848.* Bloomington, IN: Indiana University Press.

Momsen, J.D. 1986. Migration and rural development in the Caribbean. *Tijdschrift voor Economische en Sociale Geografie.* **77**: 50–8.

Monath, T.P. 1994. Yellow-fever and dengue: the interactions of virus, vector and host in the reemergence of epidemic disease. *Seminars in Virology.* **5**: 133–45.

1995. Dengue: the risk to developed and developing countries. In *Infectious Diseases in an Age of Change. The Impact of Human Ecology and Behavior on Disease Transmission*, ed. R. Roizman. Washington, D.C.: National Academy Press, pp. 43–58.

Monplaisir, N., Merault, G., Poyart, C., *et al.* 1986. Hemoglobin-S Antilles: a variant with lower solubility than hemoglobin-s and producing sickle-cell disease in heterozygotes. *Proceedings of the National Academy of Sciences of the United States of America.* **83**: 9363–7.

Monsalve, M.V. and Hagelberg, E. 1997. Mitochondrial DNA polymorphisms in Carib people of Belize. *Proceedings of the Royal Society of London Series B - Biological Sciences.* **264**: 1217–24.

Montestruc, E., Berdonneau, R., Benoist, J., and Collet, A. 1959. Hemoglobines anormales et groupes sanguins A,B, O, chez les Martiniquais. *Bulletin de la Société de Pathologie Exotique.* **52**: 156–8.

Morrison, L. 2001. The global epidemiology of HIV/AIDS. *British Medical Bulletin.* **58**: 7–18.

Morrissey, M. 1989. *Slave Women in the New World. Gender Stratification in the Caribbean.* Lawrence, KA: University Press of Kansas.

Moser, M., Morgan, R., Hale, M., *et al.* 1959. Epidemiology of hypertension with particular reference to the Bahamas. *American Journal of Cardiology.* **47**: 727–33.

Muñíz-Fernández, A., Puig-Cano, A., Cabrera-Zamora, M., Fernández-Aguila, J., and Martínez-Antuña, G. 2000. Marcadores genéticos en pacientes con anemia drepanocítica de la provincia de Cienfuegos: haplotipos del bloque β y α-talasemia. *Revista Cubana de Hematologia e Immunologia y Hemoterapia.* **16**: 142–4.

Nagel, R.L. 1984. The origin of the hemoglobin S gene: clinical, genetic and anthropological consequences. *Einstein Quarterly Journal of Biology and Medicine.* **2**: 53–62.

Nagel, R.L. and Labie, D. 1985. The consequences and implications of the multicentric origin of the Hb S gene. In *Experimental Approaches for the Study of Hemoglobin Switching*, eds. G. Stamatoyannopoulos and A.W. Nienhuis. New York: Alan R. Liss, pp. 93–103.

Nagel, R.L., Fabry, M.E., Pagnier, J., *et al.* 1985. Hematologically and genetically distinct forms of sickle cell anemia in Africa. *New England Journal of Medicine.* **312**: 880–4.

Navarro, F. and Landau, N.R. 2004. Recent insights into HIV-1 Vif. *Current Opinion in Immunology.* **16**: 477–82.

Neel, J.V. 1962. Diabetes mellitus: a "thrifty genotype rendered detrimental by "progress"? *American Journal of Human Genetics.* **14**: 353–62.

Neel, J.V., Weder, A.B., and Julius, S. 1998. Type II diabetes, essential hypertension, and obesity as "syndromes of impaired genetic homeostasis": the "thrifty genotype" hypothesis enters the 21st century. *Perspectives in Biology and Medicine.* **42**: 44–74.

Nesse, R.M. and Williams, G.C. 1996. *Why We Get Sick. The New Science of Darwinian Medicine.* New York: Vintage Books.

Newsome, C., Shiell, A., Fall, C., *et al.* 2003. Is birth weight related to later glucose and insulin metabolism? A systematic review. *Diabetic Medicine.* **20**: 339–48.

Nickel, R.G., Willadsen, S.A., Freidhoff, L.R., *et al.* 1999. Determination of Duffy genotypes in three populations of African descent using PCR and sequence-specific oligonucleotides. *Human Immunology.* **60**: 738–42.

Nicolas, M., Perez, J.M., Strobel, M., and Carme, B. 2003. Malaria in Guadeloupe (French West Indies). 1991–2000. *West Indian Medical Journal.* **52**: 199–202.

Nguyen, L., Li, M., Chaowanachan, T., *et al.* 2004. CCR5 promoter human haplogroups associated with HIV-1 disease progression in Thai injection drug users. *AIDS.* **18**: 1327–33.

Nobbe, C.E., Ebanks, G.E., and George, P.M. 1976. A re-exploration of the relationship between types of sex unions and fertility: the Barbadian case. *Journal of Comparative Family Studies.* **7**: 295–308.

Norman, L.R. 2003. Predictors of consistent condom use – a hierarchical analysis of adults from Kenya, Tanzania and Trinidad. *International Journal of STD and AIDS.* **14**: 584–90.

Ockenhouse, C.F., Schulman, S., and Shear, H.L. 1984. Oxidative killing of malaria parasites by mononuclear phagocytes. In *Malaria and the Red Cell*, eds. J.W. Eaton and G.J. Brewer. New York: Alan R. Liss, pp. 93–108.

Oeschsli, F.W. and Kirk, D. 1975. Modernization and the demographic transition in Latin America and the Caribbean. *Economic Development and Cultural Change.* **23**: 391–419.

Okesina, A.B., Oparinde, D.P., Akindoyin, K.A., and Erasmus, R.T. 1999. Prevalence of some risk factors of coronary heart disease in a rural Nigerian population. *East African Medical Journal.* **76**: 212–16.

Olien, M. 1968. Levels of urban relationships in a complex society: a Costa Rican case. In *Urban Anthropology: Research Perspectives and Strategies*, ed. E.M. Eddy. Proceedings of the Southern Anthropological Society, no. 2. Athens, GA: Southern Anthropological Society, pp. 83–92.

    1980. Black and part-black populations in colonial Costa Rica: ethnohistorical resources and problems. *Ethnohistory*. **27**: 13–29.

Olwig, K.F. 1981. Women, 'matrifocality' and systems of exchange: an ethnohistorical study of the Afro-American family on St. John, Danish West Indies. *Ethnohistory*. **28**: 59–78.

O'Neal, E. 2001. *From the Field to the Legislature. A History of Women in the Virgin Islands*. Contributions in Women's Studies, no. 187. Westport: Greenwood Press.

Oppenheimer, G.M. 2001. Paradigm lost: race, ethnicity, and the search for new population taxonomy. 2001. *American Journal of Public Health*. **91**: 1049–55.

Ordúñez-García, P.O., Espinosa-Brito, A.D., Cooper, R.S., Kaufman, J.S., and Nieto, F.J. 1998. Hypertension in Cuba: evidence of a narrow black-white difference. *Journal of Human Hypertension*. **12**: 111–16.

O'Rourke, D.H. 2000. Genetics, geography and human variation. In *Human Biology: an Evolutionary and Biocultual Perspective*, eds. S. Stinson, B. Bogin, R. Huss-Ashmore, and D. O'Rourke. New York: Wiley-Liss, pp. 87–133.

Ortmayer, N. 1997. Church, marriage and legitimacy in the British West Indies (nineteenth and twentieth centuries). *History of the Family*. **2**: 141–70.

Otterbein, K.F. 1965. Caribbean family organization: a comparative analysis. *American Anthropologist*. **67**: 66–79.

Owoaje, E.E., Rotimi, C.N., Kaufman, J.S., Tracy, J., and Cooper, R.S. 1997. Prevalence of adult diabetes in Ibadan, Nigeria. *East African Medical Journal*. **74**: 299–302.

Pagnier, J., Mears, J.G., Dunda-Belkhodia, O., *et al.* 1984. Evidence for the multicentric origin of the sickle cell hemoglobin gene in Africa. *Proceedings of the National Academy of Sciences* of the United States of America. **81**: 1771–3.

Palatnik, M., da Silva, W.A., Estalote A.C., *et al.* 2002. Ethnicity and type 2 diabetes in Rio de Janeiro, Brazil, with a review of the prevalence of the disease in Amerindians. *Human Biology*. **74**: 533–44.

Pan American Health Organization (PAHO). 1994. *Health, Social Equity and Changing Production Patterns in Latin American and the Caribbean*. Pan American Sanitary Bureau, Regional Office of the World Health Organization. 25th session. Cartagena, Colombia: PAHO.

    1996. Malaria in the Americas. *Epidemiological Bulletin*. **17**: 1–8.

    2000. *Lymphatic Filariasis Elimination in the Americas: Report*. First Regional Program Manager's Meeting. Dominican Republic: PAHO.

    2002. *Lymphatic Filariasis Elimination in the Americas*. Regional Program Manager's Meeting. Port-au-Prince, Haiti: PAHO.

Paniagua, F., Garcés, J.L., Granados, C., *et al.* 1983. Prevalence of Bancroftian filariasis in the city of Puerto Limón and the province of Limón, Costa Rica. *American Journal of Tropical Medicine and Hygiene*. **32**: 1294–7.

Pante-de-Sousa, G., Mousinho-Ribeiro, D.C., Melo dos Santos, E.J., and Guerreiro, J.F. 1999. β-Globin haplotypes analysis in Afro-Brazilians from the Amazon region: evidence for a significant gene flow from Atlantic West Africa. *Annals of Human Biology.* **26**: 365–73.

Pape, J.W. 1999. AIDS in Haiti. 1980–96. In *The Caribbean AIDS Epidemic,* eds. G. Howe and A. Cobley. Kingston: University of the West Indies Press, pp. 226–42.

Parker, J.N. and Parker, P.M. 2002. *The 2002 Official Patient's Sourcebook on Yellow Fever.* San Diego, CA: ICON Health Publications.

Parra, E.J., Marcini, A., Akey, L., *et al.* 1998. Estimating African American admixture proportions by use of population-specific alleles. *American Journal of Human Genetics.* **63**: 1839–51.

Pasvol, G. 1996. Malaria and resistance genes: they work in wondrous ways. *Lancet.* **348**: 1532–4.

2001a. Targeting voracious appetite of malaria-infected red-blood cell. *Lancet.* **357**: 408–10.

2001b. Cell–cell interaction in the pathogenesis of severe falciparum malaria. *Clinical Medicine.* **1**: 495–500.

2003. How many pathways for invasion of the red blood cell by the malaria parasite? *Trends in Parasitology.* **19**: 430–2.

Pasvol, G. and Wilson, R.J.M. 1982. The interaction of malaria parasites with red blood cells. *British Medical Bulletin.* **38**: 133–40.

1989. Red-cell deformability and invasion by malaria parasites. *Parasitology Today.* **5**: 218–21.

Pasvol, G., Weatherall, D.J., and Wilson, R.J.M. 1978. Cellular mechanism for the protective effect of haemoglobin S against P. falciparum malaria. *Nature.* **274**: 701–3.

Pellegrino, A. 2000. *Trends in International Migration in Latin America and the Caribbean.* UNESCO. Oxford: Blackwell Publishing.

Pereira, L., Macaulay, V., Torroni, A., *et al.* 2001. Prehistoric and historic traces in the mtDNA of Mozambique: insights into the Bantu expansions and the slave trade. *Annals of Human Genetics.* **65**: 439–58.

Perrin, L.H., Mackey, L.J., and Miescher, P.A. 1982. The hematology of malaria in man. *Seminars in Hematology.* **19**: 70–82.

Perzigian, A.J., Tench, P.A., and Braun, D.J. 1984. Prehistoric health in the Ohio River valley. In *Paleopathology at the Origins of Agriculture,* eds. M.N. Cohen and G.J. Armelagos. New York: Academic Press, pp. 347–66.

Pescatello, A.M. (ed.). 1975. *The African in Latin America.* New York: University Press of America.

Petchesky, R.P. 2003. *Global Prescriptions: Gendering Health and Human Rights.* United Nations Research Institute for Social Development. New York: Zed Books.

Phillips, D. 1996. The internationalization of labour. The migration of nurses from Trinidad and Tobago (a case study). *International Sociology.* **11**: 109–27.

Playfair, J.H.L. 1982. Immunity to malaria. *British Medical Bulletin.* **38**: 153–9.

Plummer, G. 1985. Haitian migrants and backyard imperialism. *Race and Class.* **26**: 35–43.

Pobee, J.O.M., Larbi, E.B., Belcher, D.W., Wurapa, F.K., and Dodu, S.R.A. 1977. Blood-pressure distribution in a rural Ghanaian population. *Transactions of the Royal Society of Tropical Medicine and Hygiene.* **71**: 66–72.

Poinsignon, Y., Arfi, C., Sarfati, C., Farge-Bancel, D., and Raccurt, C.P. 1999. Case report. French West Indies: a tourist destination at risk for Plasmodium falciparum transmission? *Tropical Medicine & International Health.* **4**: 255–6.

Porter, J., Lee, K., and Ogden, J. 2002. The globalization of DOTS: tuberculosis as a global emergency. In *Health Policy in a Globalizing World,* eds. K. Lee, K. Buse, and S. Fustukian. Cambridge: Cambridge University Press, pp. 181–94.

Poston, W.S.C., Pavlik, V.N., Hyman, D.J., *et al.* 2001. Genetic bottlenecks, perceived racism, and hypertension risk among African Americans and first-generation African immigrants. *Journal of Human Hypertension.* **15**: 341–51.

Pozos, T.C. and Ramakrishan, L. 2004. New models for the study of *mycobacterium*–host interactions. *Current Opinion in Immunology.* **16**: 499–505.

Prabhakar, P. 2000. Emerging drug resistant mycobacterium tuberculosis in the Caribbean. *West Indian Medical Journal.* **49**: 86–7.

Prineas, R.J. and Gillum, R. 1985. U.S. Epidemiology of hypertension in Blacks. In *Hypertension in Blacks: Epidemiology, Pathophysiology and Treatment,* eds. W.D. Hall, E. Saunders, and N. Shulman. Chicago, IL: Year Book Medical Publishers, pp. 17–36.

Purcell, T.W. 1987. Structural transformation and social inequality in a plural society: the case of Limón, Costa Rica. *West Indian Law Journal.* **11**: 119–42.

1993. *Banana Fallout. Class, Color and Culture among West Indians in Costa Rica.* Los Angeles: Center for Afro-American Studies Publications, University of California.

Purcell, T.W. and Sawyers, K. 1993. Democracy and ethnic conflict: blacks in Costa Rica. *Ethnic and Racial Studies.* **16**: 298–322.

Putnam, L. 2002. *The Company They Kept. Migrants and the Politics of Gender in Caribbean Costa Rica, 1870–1960.* Chapel Hill: University of North Carolina Press.

Quinlan, R.J. 2001. Effect of household structure on female reproductive strategies in a Caribbean village. *Human Nature.* **12**: 169–89.

Quinn, T.C. 1995. Population migration and the spread of types 1 and 2 human immunodeficiency viruses. In *Infectious Diseases in an Age of Change. The Impact of Human Ecology and Behavior on Disease Transmission,* ed. B. Roizman. Washington, D.C.: National Academy of Sciences, pp. 77–97.

Ramírez-Mayorga, V. and Cuenca-Berger, P. 2002. Daño del ADN en trabajadoras banaeras expuestas a plaguicias en Limón, Costa Rica. *Revista de Biología Tropical.* **50**: 507–18.

Ramsay, M. and Jenkins, T. 1987. Globin gene-associated restriction-fragment-length polymorphism in Southern African peoples. *American Journal of Human Genetics.* **41**: 1132–44.

Raoult, D., Aboudharam, G., Crubezy, E., *et al.* 2000. Molecular identification by "suicide PCR" of Yersinia pestis as the agent of Medieval Black Death. *Proceedings of the National Academy of Sciences of the United States of America.* **97**: 12800–3.

Rawley, J.A. 1981. *The Transatlantic Slave Trade. A History.* Toronto: W W. Norton and Company.

Rawlins, S.C. 1993. The malaria situation in the Caribbean region. *West Indian Medical Journal.* **42**: 134–6.

1999. Emerging and re-emerging vector-borne diseases in the Caribbean region. *West Indian Medical Journal.* **48**: 252–3.

2000. The continuing challenge of malaria in the Caribbean. *West Indian Medical Journal.* **49**: 254–6.

Renne, E.P. 1994. *An Anthropological Approach to Fertility Change.* Working Papers in Demography. Canberra: Research School of Social Sciences, The Australian National University.

Rice, M. 1991–2. Sociocultural factors affecting reproductive health in Latin America and the Caribbean. *International Quarterly of Community Health Education.* **12**: 69–80.

Richardson, D. 1987. The slave trade, sugar and British economic growth, 1748–1776. In *British Capitalism and Caribbean Slavery. The Legacy of Eric Williams*, eds. B.L. Solow and S.L. Engerman. Cambridge: Cambridge University Press, pp. 103–33.

Richardson, R.K. 1979. Advances in tuberculosis control. In *Four Decades of Advances in Health in the Commonwealth Caribbean.* Scientific Publication no. 383. Washington, D.C.: PAHO-WHO, pp. 55–64.

Ridzon, R. 2004. HIV infection in TB patients: money in the bank. *International Journal of Tuberculosis and Lung Diseases.* **8**: 923.

Riley, N.E. and McCarthy, J. 2003. *Demography in the Age of the Postmodern.* Cambridge: Cambridge University Press.

Rivara, F.P. and Finberg, L. 2001. Use of the terms race and ethnicity. *Archives of Pediatrics & Adolescent Medicine.* **155**: 119.

Rivera, A. 1967. *Datos numericos y estadisticos minimos sobre la incidencia de hemoglobinas anormales en Costa Rica.* Tesis de licenciatura, Universidad de Costa Rica.

Rives, N.W. and Serow, W.J. 1984. *Introduction to Applied Demography: Data Sources and Estimation Techniques.* Beverly Hills, CA: Sage Publications.

Rizzo, T. and Odle, T.G. 2003. Hypertension. In *Gale Encyclopedia of Medicine*, 2nd edn, ed. J.L. Longe. Farmington Hills, MI: Gale Group.

Roberts, G.W. 1975. *Fertility and Mating in Four West Indian Populations. Trinidad, Barbados, St. Vincent, Jamaica.* Institute of Social and Economic Research. Jamaica: University of the West Indies.

Roberts, G.W. and Sinclair, S.A. 1978. *Women in Jamaica. Patterns of Reproduction and Family.* New York: KTO Press.

Robinson, D., Day, J., and Bailey, A. 1980. Blood pressure in urban and tribal Africa. *Lancet.* **2**: 424.

Rodas, C., Gelvez, N., and Keyeux, G. 2003. Mitochondrial DNA studies show asymmetrical Amerindian admixture in Afro-Colombian and Mestizo populations. *Human Biology*. **75**: 13–30.

Rodríguez-Romero, W.E., Sáenz-Renauld, G.F., and Chaves-Villalobos, M.A. 1998. S hemoglobin haplotypes: their epidemiologic, anthropologic, and clinical significance. *Revista Panamericana de Salud Publica*. **3**: 1–8.

Romana, M., Kéclard, L., Guillemin, G., *et al.* 1996. Molecular characterization of β-thalassemia mutations in Guadeloupe. *American Journal of Hematology*. **53**: 228–33.

Romana, M., Kéclard, L., Froger, A., *et al.* 2000. Diverse genetic mechanisms operate to generate atypical $\beta^S$ haplotypes in the population of Guadeloupe. *Hemoglobin*. **24**: 77–87.

Rondero, M. 2004. *Las enfermedades cardiovasculares in Costa Rica.* San José, Costa Rica: Programa de Prevención y Control de Enfermedades No-Tranmisibles de la OPS-OMS Representación en Costa Rica.

Root, M. 2001. The problem of race in medicine. *Philosophy of the Social Sciences*. **31**: 20–39.

Rosero-Bixby, L. 1985. The case of Costa Rica. In *Health Policy, Social Policy and Mortality Prospects*, eds. J. Vallin and A. Lopez. Liège: Ordina Editions, pp. 341–69.

Rosetta, L. 1996. Non-pathological source of variability in fertility: between/within subjects and between populations. In *Variability in Human Fertility*, ed. L. Rosetta and C.G.N. Mascie-Taylor. Cambridge Studies in Biological Anthropology. Cambridge: Cambridge University Press, pp. 91–105.

Rosetta, L. and Mascie-Taylor, C.G.N. (eds.). 1996. *Variability in Human Fertility*. Cambridge Studies in Biological Anthropology. Cambridge: Cambridge University Press.

Roth, E.A. 2004. *Culture, Biology and Anthropological Demography*. Cambridge: Cambridge University Press.

Roth, E.F., Friedman, M., Ueda, Y., *et al.* 1978. Sickling rates of human AS red cells infected in vitro with *Plasmodium falciparum* malaria. *Science*. **202**: 650–2.

Roth, E.F., Raventos-Suarez, C., Rinaldi, A., and Nagel, R.L. 1983a. Glucose-6-phosphate dehydrogenase deficiency inhibits in vitro growth of *Plasmodium falciparum*. *Proceedings of the National Academy of Sciences of the United States of America*. **80**: 298–9.

Roth, E.F., Suarez, C.R., Rinaldi, A., and Nagel, R.L. 1983b. The effect of x-chromosome inactivation on the inhibition of plasmodium falciparum malaria growth by glucose-6-phosphate-dehydrogenase def red-cells. *Blood*. **62**: 866–8.

Roussel, H., Theodore, M., and Rastogi, N. 1996. Evolution de la tuberculose en Guadeloupe entre 1982 et 1994. *Bulletin Epidemiologique Hebdomadaire*. **2**: 5–6.

Roychoudhury, A. and Nei, M. 1988. *Human Polymorphic Genes. World Distribution*. New York: Oxford University Press.

Rucknagel, D.L. and Neel, J.V. 1961. The hemoglobinopathies. In *Progress in Medical Genetics*, vol. 1, ed. A.G. Steinberg. New York: Grune and Stratton, pp. 158–260.

Sáenz, G.F. 1985. Estado actual del estudio de las hemoglobinopatías en Costa Rica. *Sangre*. **30**: 168–80.

Sáenz, G.F., Arroyo, G., Jiménez, J., *et al.* 1971. Investigación de hemoglobinas anormales en población de raza negra costarricense. *Revista de Biologia Tropical*. **19**: 251–6.

Sáenz, G.F., Alvarado, M. d. A., and Arroyo, G. 1974a. F (delta-beta) talasemia en Costa Rica. *Acta Médica Costarricense*. **17**: 63–76.

Sáenz, G.F., Arroyo, G., Alvarado, M. d. A., *et al.* 1974b. Hemoglobinas anormales en una población estudiantil universitaria. *Revista de Biologia Tropical*. **21**: 417–24.

Sáenz, G.F., Sánchez, G., and Monge, B. 1976. Síndrome drepanocíticos en Costa Rica. IV. Hemoglobina S-beta-delta talasemia (S-F-talasemia). *Acta Médica Costarricense*. **19**: 3–9.

Sáenz, G.F., Elizondo, J., Arroyo, G., Jiménez, J., and Montero, G. 1977. Talasemia A₂ en raza negra Costarricense. A propósito de un caso. *Acta Médica Costarricense*. **4**: 373–7.

Sáenz, G.F., Elizondo, J., Arroyo, G., *et al.* 1981a. Diagnostico de hemoglobinopatias y de trastornos afines. Enfoque poblacional del problema. *Boletin de las Oficinas Sanitarias Panamericanas*. **90**: 127–43.

1981b. Hallazgo de la hemoglobina Gphiladelphia$^{\alpha68(E17)ASN-SIS}$ en Costa Rica. Consideraciones bioquímico-genéticas. *Sangre*. **26**: 224–8.

Sáenz, G.F., Chávez, M., Grant, S., *et al.* 1984. Hemoglobinas anormales, alfa talasemia y deficiencia de la G6PD eritrocítica en recién nacidos de raza negra. *Sangre*. **29**: 861–7.

Salas, A., Richards, M., Lareu, M.V., *et al.* 2004a. The African Diaspora: mitochondrial DNA and the Atlantic slave trade. *American Journal of Human Genetics*. **74**: 454–65.

Salas, A., Torroni, A., Richards, M., *et al.* 2004b. The phylogeography of mitochondrial DNA haplogroup L3g in Africa and the Atlantic slave trade – reply. *American Journal of Human Genetics*. **75**: 524–6.

Sallares, R. 2002. *Malaria and Rome. A History of Malaria in Ancient Italy*. Oxford: Oxford University Press.

Sanchez, C.C. 1970. *Algunos aspectos demográficos de la ciudad de Limón y sus implicaciones sobre la fertilidad*. Tesis de licenciatura, Universidad de Costa Rica.

Sans, M. 2000. Admixture studies in Latin America: from the 20th to the 21st century. *Human Biology*. **72**: 155–77.

Sattenspiel, L. 2000a. The epidemiology of human disease. Human adaptations to infectious disease. In *Human biology: an Evolutionary and Biocultural Perspective*, eds. S. Stinson, B. Bogin, R. Huss-Ashmore, and D. O'Rourke. New York: Wiley-Liss, pp. 225–71.

2000b. Tropical environments, human activities, and the transmission of infectious diseases. *Yearbook of Physical Anthropology*. **43**: 3–31.

Schneckloth, R.E., Corcoran, A.C., Moore, F.E., and Stuart, K.L. 1962. Arterial pressure and hypertensive disease in a West Indian negro population report of a survey in St. Kitts, West Indies. *American Heart Journal*. **63**: 607–28.

Scott, R.S. 1985. Explaining abolition: contradiction, adaptation and challenge in Cuban slave society, 1860–1886. In *Between Slavery and Free Labor: the Spanish-Speaking Caribbean in the Nineteenth Century*, eds. M. Moreno-Fraginals, F. Moya-Pons, and S.L. Engerman. Baltimore, MD: Johns Hopkins University Press, pp. 25–53.

Scott, S. and Duncan, C.J. 2001. *Biology of Plagues. Evidence from Historical Populations*. Cambridge: Cambridge University Press..

Seedat, Y.K., Seedat, M.A., and Hackland, D.B.T. 1982. Biosocial factors and hypertension in urban and rural Zulus. *South African Medical Journal*. **61**: 999–1002.

Seedat, Y.K., Mayet, F.G.H., Latiff, G.H., and Joubert, G. 1993. Study of risk-factors leading to coronary heart-disease in urban Zulus. *Journal of Human Hypertension*. **7**: 529–32.

Seidell, J.C. 2001. The epidemiology of obesity. In *International Textbook of Obesity*, ed. P. Björntorp. Chichester: John Wiley and Sons, pp. 23–9.

Serjeant, G.R. 1992. *Sickle Cell Disease*, 2nd edn. Oxford: Oxford Medical Publications.

Serjeant, G.R. and Serjeant, B.E. 1972. A comparison of erythrocyte characteristics in sickle cell syndromes in Jamaica. *British Journal of Haematology*. **23**: 205–13.

Serjeant, G.R., Richards, R., Harbor, P.R.H., and Milner, P.F. 1968. Relatively benign sickle-cell anaemia in 60 patients aged over 30 in the West Indies. *British Medical Journal*. July **13**: 86–91.

Serjeant, G.R., Ennis, J.T., and Middlemiss, H. 1973a. Haemoglobin SC disease in Jamaica. *British Journal of Radiology*. **46**: 935–42.

1973b. Sickle cell β thalassaemia in Jamaica. *British Journal of Radiology*. **46**: 951–9.

Serow, W.J. and Cowart, M.E. 1998. Demographic transition and population aging with Caribbean nation states. *Journal of Cross-Cultural Gerontology*. **13**: 201–13.

Shaper, A.G. 1997. Annotation: hypertension in populations of African origin. *American Journal of Public Health*. **87**: 155–6.

Shepherd, V.A. 2002. "Petticoat rebellion?" the Black woman's body and voice in the struggles for freedom in colonial Jamaica. In *In the Shadow of the Plantation. Caribbean History and Legacy. In Honour of Professor Emeritus Woodville K. Marshall*, ed. A.O. Thompson, Kingston: Ian Randle Publishers, pp. 17–38.

Sheridan, R.B. 1996. Why the condition of the slaves was "less intolerable in Barbados than in the other sugar colonies". The 1987 Elsa Goveia memorial lecture. In *Inside Slavery. Process and Legacy in the Caribbean Experience*, ed. H.McD. Beckles. The University of West Indies. Jamaica: Canoe Press, pp. 31–50.

Shryock, H.S., Siegel, J.S., and Stockwell, E.G. 1976. *The Methods and Materials of Demography*. New York: Academic Press.

Siegel, J.S. and Swanson, D.A. (eds.). 2004. *The Methods and Materials of Demography*, 2nd edn. San Diego, CA: Elsevier Academic Press.

Simmons, A.B. and Guengant, J.P. 1992. Caribbean exodus and the world system. In *International Migration Systems. A Global Approach*, eds. M.N. Kritz, L.L. Lim, and H. Zlotnik. New York: Clarendon Press, pp. 94–114.

Simmons, D. 1983. Blood pressure, ethnic group and salt intake in Belize. *Journal of Epidemiology and Community Health.* **37**: 38–42.

Singh, S. and Casterline, J. 1985. The socio-economic determinants of fertility. In *Reproductive Change in Developing Countries. Insights from the World Fertility Survey*, eds. J. Cleland, J. Hobcraft, B. Dinesen, G. Maurice, and M.G. Kendall. New York: Oxford University Press, pp. 199–222.

Smith, R.T. 1988. *Kinship and Class in the West Indies. A Genealogical Study of Jamaica and Guyana.* Cambridge: Cambridge University Press.

1996. *The Matrifocal Family. Power, Pluralism and Politics.* New York: Routledge.

Snieder, H. Harshfield, G.A., and Treiber, F.A. 2003. Heritability of blood pressure and hemodynamics in African and European-American youth. *Hypertension.* **41**: 1196–201.

Sobal, J. 2001. Social and cultural influences on obesity. In *International Textbook of Obesity*, ed. P. Björntorp. Chichester: John Wiley and Sons, pp. 305–22.

Sobesky, M., Dabis, F., and Le Beux, P. 2000. HIV/AIDS epidemic in French Guiana: 1979–1997. *Journal of Acquired Immune Deficiency Syndromes.* **24**: 178–81.

Sobngwi, E., Mauvais-Jarvis, F., Vexiau, P., Mbanya, J.C., and Gautier, J.F. 2001. Diabetes in Africans–Part 1: epidemiology and clinical specificities. *Diabetes & Metabolism.* **27**: 628–34.

Sobngwi, E., Mbanya, J.C.N., Unwin, N.C., *et al.* 2002. Physical activity and its relationship with obesity, hypertension and diabetes in urban and rural Cameroon. *International Journal of Obesity.* **26**: 1009–16.

Sola, C., Horgen, L., Goh, K.S., and Rastogi, N. 1997. Molecular fingerprinting of *Mycobacterium tuberculosis* on a Caribbean island with IS6110 and DRr probes. *Journal of Clinical Microbiology.* **35**: 843–46.

Sola, C., Devallois, A., Horgen, L., *et al.* 1999. Tuberculosis in the Caribbean: using spacer oligonucleotide typing to understand strain origin and transmission. *Emerging Infectious Diseases.* **5**: 404–14.

Solow, B.L. 1998. The Dutch and the making of the second Atlantic system. In *The Dutch in the Atlantic Economy, 1580–1880. Trade, Slavery and Emancipation*, ed. P.C. Emmer. Variorum Collected Studies Series CS614. Norfolk: Ashgate Variorum, pp. 11–32.

Sosa, J., Ramirez-Arcos, S., Ruben, M., *et al.* 2003. High percentages of resistance to tetracycline and penicillin and reduced susceptibility to azithromycin characterize the majority of strain types of *Neisseria gonorrhoea* isolates in Cuba, 1995–1998. *Sexually Transmitted Diseases.* **30**: 443–8.

Sreevatsan, S., Pan, X., Stockbauer, K.E., *et al.* 1997. Restricted structural gene polymorphism in the *Mycobacterium tuberculosis* complex indicates evolutionarily recent global dissemination. *Proceedings of the National Academy of Sciences of the United States of America.* **94**: 9869–74.

Stark, D.M. 1999. Surviving slavery: marriage strategies and family formation patterns among the eighteenth-century Puerto Rican slave population. In *Crossing Boundaries. Comparative History of Black People in Diaspora*, eds. D.C. Hine and J. McLeod. Bloomington, IN: Indiana University Press, pp. 246–81.

Stephens, J.C., Reich, D.E., Goldstein, D.B., *et al.* 1998. Dating the origin of the CCR5-Delta 32 AIDS-resistance allele by the coalescence of haplotypes. *American Journal of Human Genetics.* **62**: 1507–15.

Stewart, Rigoberto. 1999. *Limón real. Región autónoma y libre.* San José, Costa Rica: Litografía e imprenta LIL, S.A.

Stewart, Robert. 1999. Slandered people – views on "negro character" in the mainstream Christian churches in post-emancipation Jamaica. In *Crossing Boundaries. Comparative History of Black People in Diaspora*, eds. D.C. Hine and J. McLeod. Bloomington, IN: Indiana University Press, pp. 179–201.

Stewart, W. 1964. *Keith y Costa Rica.* San José, Costa Rica: Editorial Costa Rica.

Stinchcombe, A.L. 1994. Freedom and oppression of slaves in the 18th century Caribbean. *American Sociological Review.* **59**: 911–29.

1995. *Sugar Island Slavery in the Age of Enlightenment. The Political Economy of the Caribbean World.* Princeton, NJ: Princeton University Press.

Stouse, P.A.D. 1970. Instability of tropical agriculture: the Atlantic lowlands of Costa Rica. *Economic Geography.* **46**: 78–97.

Strobel, M. and Lamdury, I. 2001. Fievre dengue: mise au point. *Revue de medecine interne.* **22**: 638–47.

Struik, S.S., and Riley, E.M. 2004. Does malaria suffer from lack of memory? *Immunological Reviews.* **201**: 268–90.

Strull, G.E. and Dym, H. 1995. Tuberculosis: diagnosis and treatment of resurgent disease. *Journal of Oral and Maxillofacial Surgery.* **53**: 1334–40.

Stuart, S. 1999. The reproductive health challenge. Women and AIDS in the Caribbean. In *The Caribbean AIDS Epidemic*, eds. G. Howe and A. Cobley. Kingston: University of the West Indies Press, pp. 122–38.

Stycos, J.M. (ed.). 1989. *Demography as an Interdiscipline.* New Brunswick, NJ: Transaction Publishers.

Stycos, J.M. and Back, K.W. 1964. *The Control of Human Fertility in Jamaica.* Ithica, NY: Cornell University Press.

Swedlund, A.C. 1978. Historical demography as population ecology. *Annual Review of Anthropology.* **7**: 137–73.

Swedlund, A.C. and Armelagos, G.J. 1976. *Demographic Anthropology.* Dubuque, IA: WCB Brown Company Publishers.

Taylor, E.W. and Siddiqui, W.A. 1982. Recent advances in malarial immunity. *Annual Review of Medicine.* **33**: 69–96.

Teelucksingh, S. 2003. What do we do about the problem of overweight and obesity in the Americas? *Revista Panamericana de Salud Publica.* **13**: 275–6.

Teuscher, T., Rosman, J.B., Baillod, P., and Teuscher, A. 1987. Absence of diabetes in a rural West African population with a high carbohydrate/cassava diet. *Lancet.* April **4**: 765–8.

Theodore-Gandi, B. 1991. Summary report of emergency meeting on cholera preparedness in the Caribbean (May 16–17, 1991). *West Indies Medical Journal.* **40**: 149–51.

Thomas, H. 1997. *The Slave Trade. A Story of the Atlantic Slave Trade: 1440–1870.* New York: Simon and Schuster.

Thompson, A.O. 2002. Enslaved children in Berbice, with special reference to the government slaves, 1803–31. In *In the Shadow of the Plantation. Caribbean History and Legacy. In Honour of Professor Emeritus Woodville K. Marshall,* ed. A.O. Thompson. Kingston: Ian Randle Publishers, pp. 163–94.

Thonnon, J., Spiegel, A., Diallo, M., *et al.* 1998. Yellow fever outbreak in Kaffrine, Senegal 1996: epidemiological and entomological findings. *Tropical Medicine & International Health.* **3**: 872–8.

Towghi, F. 2004. Shifting policies toward traditional midwives: implications for reproductive health care in Pakistan. In *Unhealthy Health Policy. A Critical Anthropological Examination,* eds. A. Castro and M. Singer. Lanham, MD: Altamira Press, pp. 79–95.

Trabuchet, G., Elion, J., Baudot, G., *et al.* 1991. Origin and spread of beta-globin gene-mutations in India, Africa, and Mediterranean: analysis of the 5′ flanking and intragenic sequences of beta-S and beta-C genes. *Human Biology.* **63**: 241–52.

Trachtenberg, E.A., Keyeux, G., Bernal, J., Noble, J.A., and Erlich, H.A. 1996. Results of Expedicion Humana. 2. Analysis of HLA class II alleles in three African American populations from Colombia using the PCR/SSOP: Identification of a novel DQB1*02 (*0203) allele. *Tissue Antigens.* **48**: 192–8.

Trejos, M.E. 2004. Development in banana producing regions: transnational wealth, local poverty. www.foroemaus.org/english/history/02_06.html.

Tropical Disease Program. 1986. Malaria control in the Americas: a critical analysis. *PAHO Bulletin.* **20**: 304–20.

Turner, A., Gough, K.R., and Leeming, J.P. 1999. Molecular epidemiology of tetM genes in *Neisseria gonorrhoeae. Sexually Transmitted Infections.* **75**: 60–6.

van den Berghe, P. 1979. *Human Family Systems. An Evolutionary View.* Prospect Heights, IL: Waveland Press.

van den Boogaart, E. 1998. The Dutch participation in the Atlantic slave trade, 1596–1650. In *The Dutch in the Atlantic Economy, 1580–1880. Trade, Slavery and Emancipation,* ed. P. Emmer. Variorum Collected Studies Series CS614. Norfolk: Ashgate Variorum, pp. 33–64.

van Tilburg, J., van Haeften, T.W., Pearson, P., and Wijmenga, C. 2001. Defining the genetic contribution of type 2 diabetes mellitus. *Journal of Medical Genetics.* **38**: 569–78.

Viales-Hurtado, R.J. 1998. *Después del enclave.* San José, Costa Rica: Editorial de la Unversidad de Costa Rica, Colección Nueva Historia.

Vívenes de Lugo, M., Rodriguez-Larralde, A., and Castro de Guerra, D. 2003. Beta-globin gene cluster haplotypes as evidence of African gene flow to the northeastern coast of Venezuela. *American Journal of Human Biology.* **15**: 29–37.

Wainscoat, J.S., Hill, A.V.S., Boyce, A.L., *et al.* 1986. Evolutionary relationships of human populations from an analysis of nuclear DNA polymorphisms. *Nature.* **319**: 491–3.

Walrond, E.R. 1999. Regional policies in relation to the HIV/AIDS epidemic in the commonwealth Caribbean. In *The Caribbean AIDS Epidemic*, eds. G. Howe and A. Cobley. Kingston: University of the West Indies Press, pp. 57–70.

Wang, H., Jennings, A.D., and Ryman, K.D. 1997. Genetic variation among strains of wild-type yellow fever virus from Senegal. *Journal of General Virology.* **78**: 1349–52.

Wasserheit, J.N. 1995. Effect of human ecology and behavior on sexually transmitted diseases, including HIV infection. In *Infectious Diseases in an Age of Change. The Impact of Human Ecology and Behavior on Disease Transmission*, ed. B. Roizman. Washington, D.C.: National Academy of Sciences, pp. 141–56.

Watkins, S.C. 1989. The fertility transition: Europe and the third world compared. In *Demography as an Interdiscipline*, ed. J.M. Stycos. New Brunswick, NJ: Transaction Publishers, pp. 27–55.

Watson, R.B. and Hewitt, R. 1941. Topographical and related factors in the epidemiology of malaria in North America, Central America and the West Indies. In *A Symposium on Human Malaria with Special Reference to North America and the Caribbean Region*, ed. F. Moulton. Publication of the American Association for the Advancement of Science, no. 15. American Association for the Advancement of Science, pp. 8–18.

Watts, S. 2001. Yellow fever immunities in West Africa and the Americas in the age of slavery and beyond: a reappraisal. *Journal of Social History.* **34**: 955–67.

Weinberger, M. 1996. Salt sensitivity of blood pressure in humans. *Hypertension.* **27**: 481–90.

Weinstok-Wolfowicz, H., Paniagua, F., Garcés, J.L., *et al.* 1977. Bancroftian filariasis in Puerto Limón, Costa Rica. *American Journal of Tropical Medicine and Hygiene.* **26**: 1148–52.

    1979. *Estudio epidemiologico de las infecciones por wuchereria bancrofti en Puerto Limón, Costa Rica, 1976 (informe preliminar)*. San José, Costa Rica: Federación Latinoamericana de Parasitólogos y Asociación Costarricense de Microbiología y Parasitología, Conferencias Magistrales, Mesas Redondas y de Trabajo, p. 109.

Weiss, K.M. 1993. *Genetic Variation and Human Disease. Principles and Evolutionary Approaches*. Cambridge Studies in Biological Anthropology 11. Cambridge: Cambridge University Press.

    2003. Commentary: not guilty by reason of doubt? *Epidemiology.* **14**: 122–4.

Weiss, K.M., Ferrell, R.E., and Hanis, C. L. 1984. A new world syndrome of metabolic diseases with a genetic and evolutionary basis. *Yearbook of Physical Anthropology.* **72**: 153–78.

Weiss, M.L. 2000. An introduction to genetics. In *Human Biology: an Evolutionary and Biocultual Perspective*, eds. S. Stinson, B. Bogin, R. Huss-Ashmore, and D. O'Rourke. New York: Wiley-Liss, pp. 47–85.

Wendorf, M. and Goldfine, I. 1991. Archaeology of NIDDM: excavation of the thrifty genotype. *Diabetes.* **40**: 161–5.

Werker, D., Blount, S., and White, F.M.M. 1994. The control of tuberculosis in the Caribbean. *West Indian Medical Journal.* **43**: 48–51.

West, K. 1978. *Epidemiology of Diabetes and its Vascular Lesions.* New York: Elsevier.

Westoff, C.F. and Bankole, A. 2000. Trends in the demand for family limitation in developing countries. *International Family Planning Perspectives.* **26**: 56–62, 97.

Wheeler, V.W. and Radcliffe, K.W. 1994. HIV infection in the Caribbean. *International Journal of STD and AIDS.* **5**: 79–89.

Whiteford, L.M. 1997. The ethnoecology of dengue fever. *Medical Anthropology Quarterly.* **11**: 202–23.

Wierenga, K.J.J., Hambleton, I.R., and Lewis, N.A. 2001. Survival estimates for patients with homozygous sickle-cell disease in Jamaica: a clinic-based population study. *Lancet.* **357**: 680–3.

Wilkinson, R.L. 1995. Yellow fever: ecology, epidemiology, and role in the collapse of the classic lowland Maya civilization. *Medical Anthropology.* **16**: 269–94.

Wilks, R., Rotimi, C., Bennett, F., *et al.* 1999. Diabetes in the Caribbean: results of a population survey from Spanish Town, Jamaica. *Diabetic Medicine.* **16**: 875–83.

Williams, D.R.R. 1993. Epidemiologic and geographic factors in diabetes. *Eye.* **7**(2): 202–4.

Williams, N.P., Hanchard, B., and Wilks, R. 1989. Amebiasis in Jamaica: a forgotten cause of hepato-intestinal disease. *West Indian Medical Journal.* **38**: 159–63.

Williams, R.C. 1989. Restriction fragment length polymorphism (RFLP). *Yearbook of Physical Anthropology.* **32**: 159–84.

Wilson, T.W. 1987. Africa, Afro-Americans, and hypertension: a hypothesis. In *The African Exchange. Towards a Biological History of Black People,* ed. K.F. Kiple. Durham, NC: Duke University Press, pp. 257–68.

Wilson, T.W. and Grim, C. 1991. Biohistory of slavery and blood pressure differences in Blacks today. A hypothesis. *Hypertension.* **17** (suppl. I): I122–8.

Wong, M.S., Simeon, D.T., Powell, C.A., and Grantham-MCG., S.M. 1994. Geohelminth infections in school-aged children in Jamaica. *West Indian Medical Journal.* **43**: 121–2.

Wood, J.W. 1994. *Dynamics of Human Reproduction: Biology, Biometry, Demography.* New York: Aldine de Gruyter.

Wood, J.W. and DeWitte-Aviña, S. 2003. Was the Black Death Yersinial plague? *Lancet Infectious Diseases.* **3**: 327–8.

2004. Was the Black Death Yersinial plague? *Lancet Infectious Diseases.* **4**: 485.

World Bank, The. 2001. *HIV/AIDS in the Caribbean. Issues and Options.* A World Bank Country Study. Washington, D.C.: The World Bank.

World Health Organization (WHO). 2001. *Global Prevalence and Incidence of Selected Curable Sexually Transmitted Infections. Overview and estimates.* Geneva: WHO.

Yelvington, K. 2004. African Diaspora in the Americas. In *Encyclopedia of Diasporas: Immigrant and Refugee Cultures Around the World*, vol. 1, eds. C.R. Ember, M. Ember and I. Skoggard Hingham, MA: Kluwer, pp. 24–35.

Yinger, J., Sherbinin, A., Ochoa, L., Morris, L., and Hirsch, J. 1992. *Adolescent Sexual Activity and Childbearing in Latin America and the Caribbean: Risks and Consequences*. A collaborative production of the Population Reference Bureau, the Demographic and Health Surveys Project of Macro International and the Division of Reproductive Health of the Centers for Disease Control. Atlanta, GA.

Zago, M.A., Figueiredo, M.S., and Ogo, S.H. 1992. Bantu beta-s cluster haplotype predominates among Brazilian blacks. *American Journal of Physical Anthropology*. **88**: 295–8.

Zimmet, P. 1999. Diabetes epidemiology as a tool to trigger diabetes research and care. *Diabetologia*. **42**: 499–518.

Zimmet, P. and Thomas, C.R. 2003. Genotype, obesity and cardiovascular disease – has technical and social advancement outstripped evolution? *Journal of Internal Medicine*. **254**: 114–25.

Zimmet, P., Alberti, K., and Shaw. J. 2001. Global and societal implications of the diabetes epidemic. *Nature*. **414**: 782–7.

Zubrow, E.B.W. 1976. Demographic anthropology: an introductory analysis. In *Demographic Anthropology*, ed. E.B.W. Zubrow. A School of American Research Book. Albuquerque, NM: University of New Mexico Press, pp. 1–25.

## Useful websites

http://diabetes.niddk.nih.gov/dm/pubs/africanamerican/#2
http://palmm.fcla.edu/map/
www.biosci.ohio-state.edu/~parasite/ascaris.html
www.carec.org/data/tb/tb_cases_chart_80_20.html
www.cdc.gov/diabetes/statistics/prev/national/f5dt2000.htm
www.cdc.gov/hiv/bscience.htm
www.cdc.gov/nchs/products/pubs/pubd/hus/03hustop.htm
www.cdc.gov/ncidod/dbmd/diseaseinfo/cholera_g.htm
www.cdc.gov/ncidod/index.htm
www.cdc.gov/mmwr/preview/mmwrhtml/00001341.htm
www.cvdinfobase.ca/
www.diabetes.org/home.jsp
www.endocrineweb.com/diabetes/index.html
www.lalecheleague.org/
www.nationmaster.com/graph-T
www.nematodes.org/nematodeESTs/Necator/Necator.html
www.netdoctor.co.uk/travel/diseases/yellowfever.htm

www.netsalud.sa.cr/ms/index.htm

www.niaid.nih.gov/factsheets/hivinf.htm;

www.nlm.nih.gov/medlineplus/aids.html

www.orthoteers.co.uk/Nrujp~ij33lm/Orthtb.htm

www.ots.ac.cr/rdmcnfs/datasets/exsrch.phtml?words=Limón&ds=global

www.paho.org/default.htm

www.paho.org/english/sha/prflcor.htm

www.rbm.who.int/amd2003/amr2003/summary.htm

www.tulane.edu/~dmsander/garryfavweb.html

www.unicef.org/infobycountry/costarica_statistics.html

www.virusmyth.net/aids/

www.who.int/en/

www.who.int/ctd/dengue/disease.htm

www.who.int/nut/db_bmi.htm.

www.who.int/reproductive-health/publications/MSM_97_16/MSM_
97_16>chapter4

www.who.int/whr/2004/annex/country/cri/en

www.worldhealthcare.net

# Index